DATE DUE

Public Executions

**Recent Titles in
Crime, Media, and Popular Culture**

Public Executions

The Death Penalty and the Media

Christopher S. Kudlac

Crime, Media, and Popular Culture
Frankie Y. Bailey and Steven Chermak, Series Editors

Westport, Connecticut
London

Library of Congress Cataloging-in-Publication Data

Kudlac, Christopher S.
   Public executions : the death penalty and the media / Christopher S. Kudlac.
      p. cm. — (Crime, media, and popular culture, ISSN 1549–196X)
   Includes bibliographical references and index.
   ISBN 978-0-275-99307-8 (alk. paper)
1. Capital punishment—United States. 2. Capital punishment—United States—Public opinion.
3. Executions and executioners—Press coverage—United States. 4. Death row inmates—Press
coverage—United States. 5. Mass media and public opinion—United States. I. Title.
HV8699.U6K83 2007
364.660973—dc22   2007016221

British Library Cataloguing in Publication Data is available.

Library of Congress Catalog Card Number: 2007016221
ISBN-13: 978–0–275–99307–8
ISBN-10: 0–275–99307–8

First published in 2007

Praeger Publishers, 88 Post Road West, Westport, CT 06881
An imprint of Greenwood Publishing Group, Inc.
www.praeger.com

Printed in the United States of America

The paper used in this book complies with the
Permanent Paper Standard issued by the National
Information Standards Organization (Z39.48-1984).

10 9 8 7 6 5 4 3 2 1

Table of Contents

Acknowledgments

I would like to thank my entire family for all the support they have given me over the years. I would like to especially thank my wife who read draft after draft of the book and was a big reason why it was completed. Also, I can not say enough about the sacrifices that my parents made to provide me the educational opportunities to be in this position. I would like to express my gratitude to Lynn Chancer who was invaluable in helping this work evolve over the years. Additionally, Jeanne Flavin and Mary Bosworth were very important in early drafts of the book. Steve Chermak was an integral part of the final work, his insights were extremely important and, my editor at Greenwood, Suzane Staszak-Silva was extremely supportive throughout the process.

Series Foreword

When Timothy McVeigh was executed in 2001, it provided a dramatic end-point to one of the most sensationalized criminal cases in the history of the United States. This mass casualty attack satisfied the news media's preference for serious criminal events, and the intense media coverage led many to claim that this was the crime of the century. The event also opened a window of opportunity to examine policy issues related to terrorism. Politicians held congressional hearings, introduced and supported new legislation, and funded initiatives to respond to a social problem that became a top priority. McVeigh's arrest, conviction, and death sentence also provided an important opportunity to revisit America's fascination with the death penalty. Media personnel from all over the world visited the federal penitentiary located in Terre Haute, Indiana, to document and report on his execution. It was also significant that the event then became intertwined with the larger public debate about capital punishment. Proponents used McVeigh as an ideal example of a need for the ultimate punishment: such evil can only be countered with death. Opponents, however, were equally robust with their arguments highlighting concerns about missing law enforcement documents that were uncovered in the eleventh hour and warning that such punishments only brutalize and not deter other offenders.

Christopher Kudlac, in this most recent addition to Praeger's *Crime, Media, and Popular Culture* series, engages an incredibly important but understudied topic: the media's coverage of the death penalty. Media coverage of McVeigh's execution is one of the cases that Kudlac uses to demonstrate the seminal place of celebrated cases in the death penalty debate. Other cases discussed include Ted Bundy, John Wayne Gacy, Richard Ramirez, Aileen Wuornos, Karla Faye Tucker, and Mumia Abu-Jamal. These cases are organized thematically into three clusters: serial killers (Bundy, Gacy, Ramirez, and Wuornos), protest cases (Tucker and Abu-Jamal), and terrorism (McVeigh). Importantly, he discusses how the nature of these cases intersects with public interest and opinion about the death penalty. In short, the cases became media events not only because of salient characteristics of the incident, but because they offered an opportunity for the public to struggle with important issues of significance in its evaluation of the death penalty debate. Perhaps the most surprising conclusion from his analysis is that most death penalty cases receive little to no national news attention: a defendant's arrest, trial, conviction, sentence, appeals, and execution are completely ignored. The result is that the public comes to think about and understand the death penalty only through the most sensational cases.

Kudlac's book, like the other books in the series, provides an innovative and thoughtful account of an important crime and mass media issue. In this series, scholars engaged in research on such issues examine the complex nature of our relationship with media. Peter Berger and Thomas Luckman coined the phrase the "social construction of reality" to describe the process by which we acquire knowledge about our environment. They and others have argued that reality is a mediated experience. We acquire what Emile Durkheim described as "social facts" through a pronged process of personal experience, interaction with others, academic education, and, yes, the mass media. With regard to crime and the criminal justice system, many people acquire much of their information from the news and from entertainment media. Issues tied to the role of the media are important to examine because what we consume affects us.

What we do know is that we experience this mediated reality as individuals. We are not all affected in the same way by our interactions with mass media. Each of us engages in interactions with mass media/popular culture that are shaped by factors such as our social environment, interests, needs, and opportunities for exposure. We do not come to the experience of mass media/popular culture as blank slates waiting to be written upon or voids waiting to be filled. It is the pervasiveness of mass media/popular culture and the varied backgrounds (including differences in age, gender, race/ethnicity, religion, etc.) that we bring to our interactions with media that make this a particularly intriguing area of research.

Moreover, the role of mass media in creating the much discussed "global village" of the twenty-first century that is also fertile ground for research.

We exist not only in our communities, our cities, and states, but in a world that spreads beyond national boundaries. Technology has made us a part of an ongoing global discourse about issues not only of criminal justice but of social justice. Technology has placed us there "as it happens" to events around the world. It was technology that allowed Americans around the country to experience the collapse of the World Trade Center on September 11, 2001. In the aftermath of this "crime against humanity," we have been witnesses to and participants in an ongoing discussion about the nature of terrorism and the appropriate response to such violence. Similarly, the present book provides readers the opportunity to consider their role in the engaging and lively debate about the role of capital punishment in a civilized society.

Frankie Y. Bailey and Steven Chermak,
Series Editors

Introduction

The death penalty is one of the country's most controversial issues. The fairness of its application is debated in coffeehouses, classrooms, political arenas, and the media. Capital punishment is certainly one of the most hotly contested criminal justice issues that receive significant media attention. What is interesting, however, is that despite this representation in the media, most death penalty cases receive surprisingly little national media attention. In fact, of the 1,000 people executed in the United States since 1977 and the 3,500 inmates currently awaiting execution, only a handful of cases can be recalled by the news-consuming public. Only a very few cases are memorable because only a handful are dramatically represented in the media.

This book is a study of why death row cases came to be publicized intensively by newspapers from the 1970s through the present. Simultaneously, this work focuses on changes in public opinion about the death penalty and how newspaper coverage and evolving mass sentiment relate to one another. Overall, the book suggests that media coverage can be one useful way of assessing popular feelings about the death penalty at a given time. I look in detail at the seven inmates that have received the most newspaper attention, analyzing local and national newspaper articles for each case along with interviews with reporters and editors who covered the cases. Additionally, I examine the recent issues involving DNA evidence and the Supreme Court rulings regarding juveniles and the mentally retarded.

This book examines seven of the most highly publicized death penalty cases during the last 30 years. I present a case study of each one, including a firsthand account of public reactions and media interest. I analyzed media coverage of these cases with three questions in mind. First, focusing on public opinion, do the types of death row cases that become highly profiled during a particular timeframe correspond with the direction of Americans' views about capital punishment in that given period? Second, focusing on the media, why and how does it come to pass that some death row cases are selected to become high-profile over other similar types of cases? Lastly, focusing on both the public and the media, how can the interactive relationship between public opinion and press coverage of capital punishment cases be best understood—and what are the implications of this relationship for journalists, the public, and criminal justice policymakers?

Based on my analysis, I discovered that the cases that received the most media attention between 1977 and 2005 fall thematically and chronologically into distinct clusters: serial killers, protest cases, and terrorism. More specifically, the serial killers cluster included the Ted Bundy, John Wayne Gacy, Richard Ramirez, and Aileen Wuornos cases; the protest cluster included the Karla Faye Tucker and Mumia Abu-Jamal cases; terrorism cases are represented by Timothy McVeigh.

Serial killing broke into American popular culture starting in the late 1970s and early 1980s. Media coverage of serial killing proliferated from 1977 onward, with intense reporting on several cases that attracted immense public interest. These helped shape perceptions of the emerging problem. The serial killers fit into a strict punitive ideal, as society demands their execution, and in many cases, celebrates its carrying out. These cases also corresponded to the growth of punitive attitudes toward crime that occurred between 1977 and 1994 as public opinion toward capital punishment became increasingly favorable. Indeed, serial killers were the only death row cases that became highly profiled throughout this period.

However, public opinion and mainstream newspaper coverage of capital punishment both began to change around the mid-1990s. Stories about serial killers roaming the country and murdering random victims were no longer dominating the media. At the same time, attitudes in favor of capital punishment were starting to weaken. This can be seen in what appears to have been an analogous shift in the death row inmates whose cases received high-profile coverage during this period. Between 1994 and 2001, protest cases emerged as the most highly publicized cases. The Karla Faye Tucker and Mumia Abu-Jamal cases generated debates and, quite literally, protests about the practice of capital punishment. In so doing, the cases challenged what seemed to be a consensus about "getting tough on crime" as they triggered debates about race, class, and gender discrimination in American society. Consequently, these two figures cast a different image on the death penalty than their Bundy, Gacy, Ramirez, and Wuornos predecessors. Unlike the serial killers, whose coverage coincided with overwhelming support for capital punishment, the coverage of protest cases centered on the appropriateness of capital punishment. For Tucker, the issue was whether or not a white, female, born-again Christian should be executed. For Abu-Jamal, public debate centered on his alleged innocence and on whether his trial was fair or racially biased. What is interesting is that, while both cases began before this time period, with Tucker's crime taking place in 1983 and Abu-Jamal's in 1981, neither received national attention until much later. The cases received consistent local coverage, but did not become high profile until 1994, when support for capital punishment began to fall substantially.

The next case discussed in this book is the Timothy McVeigh case. His was the most highly publicized death penalty case of all during the last several decades; to the extent one could see an analogue to the O.J. Simpson high profile crime case among "death penalty" cases, this would be McVeigh's crime, trial, and execution. His case represented something altogether different than the other cases. By 1994, growing opposition to the death penalty was becoming visible across the country. The Oklahoma City bombing and subsequent arrest of Timothy McVeigh in 1995 arguably affected this trend by reinvigorating many people's support for capital punishment. In addition, the new threat of terrorism was used to justify the continued practice of the death penalty. Public support of the state capital system began to decline in 1994. Yet, in the same year, the federal death penalty expanded and the United States continued to support capital punishment in the international arena.

McVeigh was convicted of blowing up the Alfred P. Murrah Federal Building in Oklahoma City, killing 168 people. His case would spark debate about the death penalty across the country. Timothy McVeigh was different than the parties discussed in previous cases. He did not fit the same mold as the earlier serial killers, nor did he elicit the same sympathy as Tucker and Abu-Jamal. Rather, McVeigh's case was one of stark contrasts. He was the perpetrator of the worst domestic terrorist attack in history at the time. Overwhelming support existed for his execution, yet no rejoicing took place at its completion. Thus, the McVeigh case symbolically brings together two opposing strands surrounding the death penalty as illustrated through previous cases: he is a mass murderer, yet his case also raised controversial issues about the administration of capital punishment. Thus, in this book, I will argue that the new focus on terrorism in the United States, to which McVeigh contributed, helped to keep the federal death penalty alive and public opinion about capital punishment in an ambivalent state.

The book then turns to more recent developments in capital punishment; focusing first on the important role DNA evidence is playing in the death penalty debate. Specifically, I will discuss the case of Earl Washington, who was freed from Virginia's death row after 17 years when DNA tests showed he did not commit the murder, and Anthony Porter, who was freed from Illinois' death row after a Northwestern journalism professor and his students were able to prove his innocence. Porter's case had a huge impact on Illinois Governor Ryan's decision in 2000 to institute a moratorium on executions after the release of 13 death row inmates. This event had monumental ramifications for capital punishment across the country. Additionally, this chapter will look at recent Supreme Court cases regarding the practice of capital punishment, focusing specifically on the 2002 Supreme Court ruling in *Atkins v. Virginia* in which the justices ruled that executing mentally retarded criminals violates the Constitution's ban on cruel and unusual punishment. I will also examine the 2005 Supreme Court case *Roper v. Simmons*, in which the court ruled that the Constitution forbids the execution of killers who were under 18 when they committed their crimes, ending a practice used in 19 states. These events demonstrate the public's continuing uneasiness with capital punishment.

1

Capital Punishment, the Media, and Changing Sensibilities

The judge denies the inmate's last appeal, sealing his fate. The prisoner is transferred to a cell close to the execution chamber. Guards are put on 24-hour suicide watch. The inmate's possessions are boxed up. Family members and a religious advisor visit for the last time. The last meal is served. The inmate receives a change of clothes. Prison officials read the death warrant. The inmate is escorted to the death chamber and strapped to the gurney. The needles are injected into the inmate's arm. The curtain is lifted, revealing the witnesses in the viewing area. The prisoner is asked for any last words. Then, at the same time, three chemicals are injected: an anesthetic, another to paralyze the respiratory muscles, and a third to stop the heart. The inmate is pronounced dead. The curtain is closed. This exact scenario has played out over 1,000 times in 33 states since 1977 across the United States. However, what goes on with the public and media leading up the execution outside the prison walls can be drastically different. Ninety-nine percent of executions take place unnoticed by the public, garnering little, if any, media attention. But then a Ted Bundy or Karla Faye Tucker comes along and breaks this mold wide open. Intense media coverage and public debate accompany these high profile cases.

In the eighteenth century, executions used to take place in public, attract large crowds, and arouse public interest. Beginning in the early nineteenth century, capital punishment in the United States has increasingly become invisible, removed from public view, and now takes place behind closed prison doors. Contemporary journalists in the United States actually dedicate very little attention to the men and women on death row, and to those later executed.[1] Interestingly, capital punishment has been a topic of much discussion in the early years of the twenty-first century through debates over DNA evidence, the moratorium in Illinois, and the Supreme Court's ruling prohibiting the execution of the mentally retarded and juveniles. This focus on the capital system is unusual for the media, given its tendency to concentrate on individuals rather than policy issues.

This book is a study of why certain death row cases came to be publicized intensively by newspapers from the 1970s through the present. Simultaneously, I focus on changes in public opinion about the death penalty and how newspaper coverage and evolving mass sentiment relate to one another. Overall, I suggest and try to show that media coverage can be one useful way of assessing popular feelings at a given time. This can be seen by looking at crimes which are rarely reported unless news workers see them as related to past or emerging trends in criminality or law enforcement.[2] This does not mean that media coverage and public opinion are exactly the same; rather, each exists in a complex relationship to the other.

Public sentiment can be influenced by political climate as well as the media, for instance, by changing laws and through politicians' speeches that may be less persuasive to journalists than to diverse public audiences. This does not mean that the media does not have extraordinary influence. The point of this book is to chart how media coverage of death row cases and public opinion have evolved in tandem, each strongly influencing but not eliminating the relative autonomy of the other. For example, during the 1980s and early 1990s public support for capital punishment was at an all time high. During this same time period, the cases that dominated the newspaper headlines were serial killers (Ted Bundy, John Wayne Gacy, Richard Ramirez, and Aileen Wuornos), who represented a need for greater punishment and executions. Then, as public opinion started to change around 1994, the types of cases the media covered changed as well. No longer were serial killers attracting newspaper attention; rather, cases that raised questions about the fairness of capital punishment (Karla Faye Tucker and Mumia Abu-Jamal) dominated the media.

In this chapter, I begin by discussing media influences on perceptions of crime and public attitudes toward the death penalty as measured through public opinion.

CRIME, THE MEDIA, AND PUBLIC OPINION

The mass media has a powerful effect on people with issues like crime and the death penalty, issues in which people have little direct experience.[3] Individuals gain their knowledge of crime in numerous ways, including from direct experience, friends and family, and from social institutions like schools, churches, and government agencies. But mass media has a particularly strong role to play regarding social events with which people do not have much direct contact—for example, wars occurring far away, natural disasters and, certainly, crime.[4] This applies especially to death row cases, which, as will later be shown in greater detail, have historically become more and more "privatized" and removed from public view. Thus, one can contend that with regard to crime and death penalty cases in particular, the public is particularly reliant on media coverage. Since the abolition of public executions, the media has been the primary source through which the public learns about executions.[5]

In their book *Cultural Criminology*, Ferrell and Sanders outline the importance of the media's relationship to crime in emphasizing how media reporting constructs rather than "reflects" reality. It is no longer possible to hold that journalists "objectively" observe what happens in the world and then simply report their observations to the public:

Instead, the most viable model is one in which media presentations, real-life events, personal perceptions, public policies, and individual actions spiral about each other in complex, mutually affecting, and ever-changing structure of inter-relationships.[6]

It is likely that, in addition to having a hugely influential role in shaping public opinion, changes in public opinion may be one factor that affects how the media constructs the social world itself. What, then, do public opinion polls indicate about widely held attitudes toward crime and capital punishment specifically?

Public opinion polls provide one important index for assessing society's attitudes about crime and capital punishment. Polls show that public support for the death penalty has fluctuated greatly over the past 60 years. Gallup poll results found that 65 percent of people favored capital punishment for murder in 1938. Support rose to 68 percent in 1953. By the mid-1950s, social reforms that had taken a backseat to WWII and the Great Depression over the past two decades began to revive, among them anti-death penalty sentiments. In 1957, support for the death penalty dropped to just 47 percent.[7]

Figure 1.1 Support for Capital Punishment 1974–2004

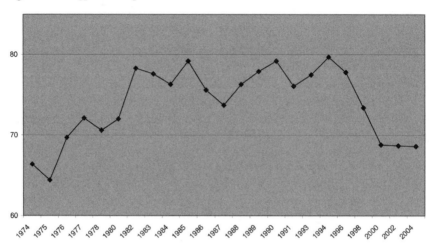

By 1966, social protests of the time had heightened people's moral sensitivity to killing in general.[8] In that year, support for capital punishment reached its lowest level ever at 42 percent. After the reinstatement of the death penalty and an increased fear of crime in society, support of capital punishment rose throughout the 1970s with over 60 percent favoring capital punishment.[9] Public support of capital punishment continued to increase throughout the 1980s and early 1990s (See Table 1).

Then, public opinion regarding the death penalty would follow a drastic change of course. According to the General Social Survey, public support for capital punishment was 79.7 percent in 1994, its highest peak since reinstatement. After this peak, the number of people in favor of capital punishment would decline continuously over the next six years from 77.8 percent in 1996 to 73.4 percent in 1998 and 68.8 percent in 2000. Support has remained stable with 68.7 percent in 2002 and 68.6 percent in 2004. While two-thirds of the country was still in favor of capital punishment in 2000, it was the lowest level in 20 years. This figure drops further, to about 55 percent, when the polls offer life imprisonment without parole as an alternative.[10] Another national poll showed that, when reminded about cases in which death row inmates had been released on the basis of DNA evidence, 64 percent of Americans favored a temporary halt to executions while steps are taken to ensure that the system works fairly. A large part of the public's changing feeling regarding capital punishment was due in part to accounts of DNA testing results establishing that ordinary, innocent people were sometimes convicted of murder, among other offenses, perhaps not regularly but not rarely either. According to a 2002 Harris survey, 94 percent of Americans believe that innocent people are sometimes convicted of murder.[11]

Michael Tonry, in his work *Thinking about Crime*, details how the public's changing sensibilities regarding punishment have helped shaped crime policies. He outlines how high profile crime events can induce a "moral panic," where public outrage and concern about a particular issue is increased. The moral panic opens a "window of opportunity" for policy makers who, according to Tonry, typically overreact to the public outcry. For example, the kidnapping and murder of Polly Klass in California led policy makers to enact the Three Strikes Law, which hands down a life sentence for a third felony conviction regardless of the severity of the crime. The type of policy adopted by lawmakers will reflect the prevailing sensibilities at the time.[12] This will be seen in Chapter 3, where concern about serial killers reached a state of moral panic among law enforcement and the public. Also, Chapter 6 will highlight how declining support for capital punishment and DNA exonerations opened a "window of opportunity" that was followed by prohibitions on executing juveniles and the mentally retarded and statewide moratoriums on executions.

Looking at changes in public opinion is important to understanding capital punishment policy and its depiction in the media. A new relationship between politicians, the public, and penal experts has emerged in which politicians are more directive, penal experts are less influential, and public opinion becomes a key reference point for evaluating options. Criminal justice is now more vulnerable than ever to shifts of public mood and political reaction.[13] In our society, public opinion itself is increasingly shaped by the mass media. To understand the current political and social context of punishment, in general and in regard to the death penalty specifically, it is necessary to examine both in relation to the media.

NEWS SELECTION CRITERIA

Since the reinstatement of the death penalty in 1976, there have been high profile death row cases like Bundy, Gacy, Ramirez, McVeigh, Wuornos, Tucker, and Abu-Jamal. These cases are classified as "high profile" as they received more newspaper coverage than any other death row inmate. (See Appendix) Why did these stories stand out from the hundreds of other people who have been executed? What criteria do news organizations use to select their stories?

To understand why some cases attract a large amount of news coverage, it is necessary to understand the traditional criteria newspapers use to determine whether or not to cover a story. Studies of the media and story selection have focused on criteria used by journalists to determine the "newsworthiness" of a particular story. Herbert Gans, in his book *Deciding What's News,* asserts that considerations of story selection and content happen without much deliberation because of deadlines and time constraints. This, however, does not fully apply when dealing with death row cases, because the court dates and execution are planned well in advance and would give journalists enough time to schedule their stories. To determine whether a story is suitable to print, journalists use a number of suitability considerations, all of which are interrelated. Gans distinguishes between three categories, the first category being substantive considerations, which judge story content and the newsworthiness of what sources supply; they rely on the importance and interest of stories.[14] The second criteria rely on product considerations to evaluate the "goodness" of stories; medium considerations, format considerations, novelty, action, and balance are evaluated to decide on the stories' suitability. The third consideration deals with competitive interests that test stories for their ability to help the continuing rivalry among news sources.[15] Others discuss similar criteria for a story to be considered newsworthy: stories must tie into a current event or preoccupation in the news (a peg), crime stories must point to some kind of moral, and news must be about something that is new or unusual.[16]

Cohen and Young, in their book *The Manufacture of News*, argue that two interrelated and simple concepts of unusualness and human interest are the most frequently used to explain the quality of the news that appears. They discern four factors that lead to "newsworthiness" among crime reports: (1) the seriousness of the offense, (2) "whimsical" (i.e. humorous, ironic, unusual) circumstances, (3) sentimental or dramatic circumstances associated with offender or victim, and (4) the involvement of a famous or high status person in any capacity.[17] News selection thus rests on inferred knowledge about the audience, assumptions about society, and a professional code or ideology. The news is not a set of unrelated items; news stories are coded and classified, referred to their relevant contexts, assigned to different (and differently graded) spaces in the media, and ranked in terms of presentation, status, and meaning.[18]

The various suitability considerations illustrate that story selection involves more than story content. Journalists make value judgments about society that result from values built into the news industry. They decide what is normal, novel, and newsworthy. When journalists decide that something is new or novel, they must also make assumptions about what is old and routine and therefore no longer newsworthy; when they report what is wrong or abnormal, they must also decide what is normal. The type of death row stories that are covered affect people's perception about who is the typical death row inmate and who is deemed novel or more newsworthy.

In *Crime News and the Public*, Doris Graber argues that the sociological model of story selection is most accurate in her research on newspapers' coverage of crime. She describes this model:

> News is a product of socially determined notions of who or what is important. These notions, in turn, lead to organizational structures that routinize news collection by establishing regular "beats." News from these beats is allotted space and airtime according to fairly regular patterns. Consequently, there is a steady stream of news of varying degrees of importance from these beats.[19]

This points to the fact that there is considerable similarity between the type of news presented by different newspapers and television sources and substantial stability in the frequency with which these news topics are covered. The news media share their notion about newsworthiness of particular institutions, events, and people, and develop an organizational structure that provides regular coverage for those pre-selected institutions, events, and people.[20] What accounts for this consistency in the lack of diversity of news media is a reliance on shared journalistic routines, on the same news sources, and on interaction between fundamental news values and society's core values.[21] These shared routines suggest that the different newspapers should display similar amounts and type of coverage of the death row cases.

The traditional criteria are problematic for a number of reasons. For one, they fail to discuss what types of crimes are considered serious and why. Additionally, they do not define what criminal circumstances are deemed humorous, who the public feels sentimental towards, and who the high status people are. These criteria cannot be useful unless we interject race, class, and gender dynamics into the scenario. These past studies of story selection are only useful to a point because of their broad nature. The theories contain talk of "novelty," "importance," and "seriousness" as the basis of story selection. The problem with such terms is that they do not specify what is novel, important, or serious, and by whose definition they are going. What executions are serious or novel? Who is deemed important, and why?

The most useful discussion of what makes some death row stories considered "newsworthy" while others are not comes from Steven Chibnall in *Law and Order News*, where he provides professional imperatives that lead to "at least five sets of informal rules of relevancy in the reporting of violence."

These guide the journalist's treatment of violence by asserting the relevance of:

1. visible and spectacular acts
2. sexual and political connotations
3. graphic presentation
4. individual pathology
5. deterrence and repression[22]

All death row cases, for the most part, are similar on criteria 1, 3, and 5. All executions are carried out in a similar manner, with no visible action or graphic presentation. Studies of deterrence and the death penalty are many and their conclusions are mixed; regardless, all of the cases would carry similar levels of deterrence and repression. This leaves the sexual and political connotations and individual pathology of the cases as the only areas that may differ. These two criteria will be examined in attempting to explain the amount of coverage dedicated to the high-profile death row cases. Sexual and political connotations will be discussed with reference to the protest cases (Karla Faye Tucker and Mumia Abu-Jamal) and individual pathology will be examined by looking at the interest in serial killers and mass murders (Ted Bundy, John Wayne Gacy, Richard Ramirez, Aileen Wuornos, and Timothy McVeigh). To look for answers to these questions, I will review studies of newsworthiness that look specifically at crime and the death penalty.

NEWSWORTHINESS, THE MEDIA AND THE DEATH PENALTY

Past studies have documented that stories about crime, law, and justice account for anywhere from a quarter to just under half of all stories in newspapers.[23] Yet with all the attention paid to crime by newspapers, there has been little research examining death row inmates and their executions. This is surprising, given that newspapers prefer covering solved rather than unsolved crimes because a known suspect adds to the story. Also, where sentences were reported, there was a very high tendency, again in all cases, to over-report the more serious punishments, particularly imprisonment.[24] Stories of inmates on death row and their executions fit this requirement and would seem to warrant extensive news coverage, but this is not the reality. Only a minority of cases attract detailed coverage. This discrepancy may have to do with the distinction within the media between crime incidents, which attract a lot of attention, and the punishment given to criminals, which does not attract as much interest.

If we look back, we find an important transition that took place in the coverage of executions by the media. A significant change in journalistic practices and printing technology had a great effect on people's views of capital punishment. Prior to the early nineteenth century, newspapers did not furnish lengthy accounts of public executions. A separate genre of gallows literature, broadsides, last words, and confessions and ministers' sermons provided the reading public with details, but newspapers mentioned the hanging only in a terse sentence or two. This changed in the 1820s and 1830s, facilitated by technological inventions; a new type of newspaper emerged that cost one cent rather than six. The penny press was pitched to the expanding market of daily buyers and hawked the "news" (in itself a new concept) to all segments of the community rather than an elite minority interested chiefly in commercial information. When public executions were abolished and the general population was blocked from witnessing executions firsthand, the press stood in and provided the detailed accounts of the scene.[25] Their reports tended to be more factually based, rather than the religiously toned descriptions of early accounts. Newspapers are still able to fulfill the role as our eyes to the execution.

In the United States, corrections is mentioned so infrequently in the news that content analysis studies discussing corrections are rare.[26] Studies show that only 2.2 percent of crime stories used corrections as their main thrust[27] and that only 4.2 percent of the sentences in crime cases reported in the press deal with the death penalty. Also, nearly half of the general discussions of criminal justice policy (4 percent of total stories) deal with penalties and the correctional system. These studies point to the fact that death row inmates and their executions make up a small percentage of crime news stories.

Jeff Ferrell disagrees that the death penalty is neglected in the news. In his article "Criminalising Popular Culture", he argues that the death penalty gets substantial news coverage because individual cases are frequently updated as they go through the system. In addition, articles dedicated to the death penalty in general are very popular, with frequent discussion of the racial composition of death row, the execution of juveniles and mentally retarded offenders, the deterrent or brutalization effect of an execution, and the moral implications around this issue. These aspects of the death penalty are constantly analyzed by reporters in support of both sides of this controversial issue.[28] His study indicates that executions are the subject of .5 percent of crime stories. This is due in part to the relative infrequency of executions compared to discovery of crime, arrest, and arraignments, for example. Yet, his assumption that individual death penalty cases receive substantial news coverage as they move through the system is not backed up by any supporting data.

Others have found that executions have become so routine that the news media no longer covers or even mentions all of them.[29] The lack of media attention is surprising, given that murderers are still a source of outrage and interest in contemporary society. The evening news and the number of crime-based television shows and movies, all of which contain a disproportionate amount of murder,[30] suggest that murder is still a source of interest. It is surprising, therefore, that more attention is not focused on death row inmates and executions by the media, which typically involve the most violent and prolific murderers. Additionally, the death penalty represents the pinnacle of the criminal justice system, the most extreme form of punishment. Taken together with the public fascination with crime and murder in general, the death penalty would seem to be one of the more interesting aspects. While murder and murderers still attract an overwhelming amount of interest in society, executions themselves are no longer automatically deemed interesting or newsworthy. Now, what appears to be public indifference to the annual number of executions might instead reflect the relatively little attention given to them by the media.[31] This raises an interesting question: does the media instill interest in the public, or does the media simply reflect the public's interest? For instance, did the media decide to pay attention to Ted Bundy on their own, or did they reflect society's desire for more coverage? This is a complex question that will be investigated throughout this work.

Studies of crime and the media, and particularly the social effects of violence in the media, are well documented; including studies that show media coverage of executions increases murder.[32] Yet cases concerning newsworthiness and the death penalty are a neglected area of research. Only a few researchers have touched upon some issues related to the media and the death penalty. Lipschultz and Hilt studied the local news coverage of the first three executions in Nebraska since reinstatement; they looked at differences between the local television news coverage of the executions. Their research focused on issues of journalist source selection and the use of symbols (signs, candlelight vigils, the prison, the electric chair, etc.) to portray justice and the framing of the stories. They argue that executions fit the model for local newsworthiness by focusing on the actions of government and the issue of crime.[33] The coverage of the cases was fairly consistent between television stations in part due to the routinization of sources and the need to keep up with the other stations' coverage for competitive interests. This consonance of reporting is important because it restricts perception and opinions offered to the public, narrowing the formation of pubic opinion.[34] The local coverage thus plays a powerful role in constructing the public view of the executions and public attitudes toward it. In Kaminer's study of the death penalty, she notes that cases that are publicized often generate considerable public support.

> Today, the public has little chance to revel in executions; most are barely even publicized: 38 people were executed in 1993, mainly in obscurity. Most Americans probably can't name them or their victims, whom they probably didn't read about in their local papers. Occasionally a high-profile case, usually including a strong claim of innocence, is highlighted by the national press, but in the average, uncelebrated case, an execution rates, at most, a paragraph or two buried deep in *The New York Times.*[35]

She notes two executions discussed in the middle of the newspaper. In the 1970s and early 1980s, executions were front-page news because they were still novel. Kaminer claims that some cases receive media coverage either because of the novelty of executions after their reinstatement or because of the defendant's claim of innocence. She doesn't address other factors contributing to large amounts of media coverage like race, class, and gender issues, or interest in serial killers.

Other studies of death row cases and the media focus on a variety of reasons for interest in particular cases. In his history of England's abolition of public executions, Cooper describes the high profile executions in the eighteenth century that drew large amounts of press coverage and huge crowds as large as 100,000. He argues that the reasons for large amounts of media attention are due to a criminal's well-publicized career, his position in society, or rumors that the criminal would be snatched from death. Haines studied "flawed executions," executions in which public sensibilities are offended by a breakdown in the routine procedures. These flaws can be technical (i.e. "botched executions"), involve the behavior of the prison staff, the behavior of the prisoner, or doubts concerning a prisoner's guilt or sentence.[36] Using newspaper coverage, he found that the press pays more attention to wrongful convictions than the other three types of flawed executions. He notes that newspapers are less inclined to cover executions outside of their local areas as the number of executions has increased. The *New York Times* reported on all executions after reinstatement until 1983, and then began to cover only those more newsworthy cases. Haines is concerned with the effect the media's coverage of these flawed executions has on death penalty groups and public opinion concerning capital punishment. Flawed executions have served as a source of outrage among the public, which has the potential to attract public support to the cause of abolition. This points to the fact that people may be fine with the death penalty when they are not aware of it or when everything runs smoothly, but any interruption in that process exposes the public's uneasiness with capital punishment. This is most poignant with wrongful executions, which can have the greatest impact on capital punishment in the United States. This has been demonstrated by the moratorium on executions in Illinois after the release of a number of innocent men from death row.

Past authors have identified a variety of reasons for large amounts of media attention given to specific cases: novelty of executions after reinstatement, claims of innocence by defendants, flaws in the execution, and position of power in society. These criteria are problematic; the novelty of executions after reinstatement wore off quickly and is not really helpful in explaining the amount of coverage currently dedicated to death row cases. It does point to the fact that some cases may draw a lot of attention because of the novelty within a state, if that state has not executed someone recently or ever. For example, when and if someone is executed in New York, that case will receive a substantial amount of coverage because no one has been executed there since 1963. A claim of innocence by the inmate is always a source for potential media attention, but many people have claims of innocence and do not receive a large amount of media attention. The idea that flaws in the execution are responsible for high-profile cases does not explain the amount of coverage leading up to an execution. The last criteria that has been found is position in society, which is extremely vague and does not point to any particular characteristics. If you take it to mean inmates who are wealthy or people of high status, there are few if any people who fit these characteristics who have been executed or are on death row.

RE-THINKING NEWSWORTHINESS

What makes a death penalty case become a media sensation? First, timing matters, because certain categories of cases (serial killers, protest, or terrorism) emerge as newsworthy at particular time periods. The idea of newsworthiness is not static; it changes based on the temper of the time. Journalists' decisions will be shown to parallel changes in public sentiments. Michael Tonry examines how changing sensibilities help shape crime policy. My interest is similar in looking at how changing sensibilities regarding capital punishment affect media coverage. Public opinion changes over time and the death row cases selected to become high profile reflect these changes. While Tonry outlines how penal sensibilities cycle from more tolerant to harsher throughout history, I am interested in how these cyclical changes are reflected in the types of death penalty cases covered by the media.

Certain types of death penalty cases have emerged as high profile corresponding with prevailing public sentiments. Within in each category, not all cases become high profile. For example, not every serial killer during the 1980s received substantial newspaper attention. While Bundy became a household name, Gerald Stano remained in obscurity. What makes one serial killer stand out from the rest? The academic literature on story selection rationale and newsworthiness leaves out sociological factors of context that influence the media. They fail to take into account how gender, race, and class biases, which go unacknowledged in traditional ideas of newsworthiness, also play a role. It is necessary to look at the characteristics of not only the offender but also victims in order to determine newsworthiness.

Thus, media coverage of certain cases at certain moments may emerge because of a confluence of factors: a) "traditional" media criteria, b) acknowledged gender, race, and class factors, and c) public sentiment, which changes over time. Thus, the media coverage is one gauge of public sentiment because it changes along with it (being itself part of society). The mainstream media and public sentiment interact in a reciprocal way, with the media influencing public perception and attitudes. Just as importantly, I will show that public sentiment influences the media and is reflected in the types of cases that are deemed newsworthy. This interplay between public sentiment and the mainstream media will be analyzed in the following chapters.

2

A Short History of the Death Penalty and Death Penalty Cases

With respect to the death penalty, there has been an evolution in sensibilities over the past 300 years, regarding views about appropriate and inappropriate methods of execution, which have triggered changes in policy, such as death by lethal injection rather than by public hangings. While this book looks at recent public opinion and changes in the death penalty, history demonstrates that debates, policy changes, and high profile cases are nothing new to the issue.

Since its introduction into the United States, the death penalty has changed considerably in how it is administered, how the media covers it, and people's opinions of it. There has been a steady civilizing process in the administration of the death penalty. The changes have occurred gradually over time, with decreases in the number of crimes subject to death, moves away from more "gruesome" methods of execution, and a rise and decline in public support. In order to understand the contemporary practice, media depiction, and public opinion regarding capital punishment in the United States, it is necessary to understand its origin, history, and evolution.

EARLY DEVELOPMENTS OF THE DEATH PENALTY

The first death penalty laws date as far back as the eighteenth century B.C. in the Code of King Hammurabi of Babylon that established the death penalty for 25 different crimes. The death penalty was also part of the fourteenth century B.C.'s Hittite Code and the seventh century B.C.'s Draconian Code in Greece, in which one penalty, death, was assigned to all crimes.[37] Death sentences were carried out by such means as crucifixion, drowning, beating to death, burning alive, and impalement. By the 1700s in England, 222 crimes were punishable by death.[38] However, because of the severity of the death penalty, many juries would not convict defendants if the offense were not serious, making executions at the time quite rare.[39] This led to reform of England's death penalty early in the eighteenth century when the death penalty was eliminated for over 100 of the 222 crimes punishable by death. Public hangings were abolished in 1868, and eventually the death penalty was eliminated all together in 1964.[40]

In America, capital punishment has been a fixture since the arrival of European settlers. But capital punishment was never used as extensively in the American colonies as in England. The first known execution in the new colonies took place in 1608: Captain George Kendall of Virginia was executed for spying on behalf of Spain.[41] In 1622 the first legal execution of a criminal was Daniel Frank in Virginia for the crime of theft. The most famous use of the death penalty in early America was in Salem, Massachusetts, during the witch trials in 1692–1694. 20 people, including 14 women, were condemned as witches or collaborators and hanged.[42]

Early reforms of the death penalty occurred from 1776–1800. Thomas Jefferson and four others proposed a law, *A Bill for Proportioning Crimes and Punishments in Cases Heretofore Capital* (1779), recommending that the death penalty be used only for treason and murder. After a heated debate, the legislature defeated the bill by one vote.[43]

Organizations were formed in different colonies for the abolition of the death penalty and to relieve poor prison conditions. Dr. Benjamin Rush, considered the founder of the American abolition movement, published *An Enquiry How Far the Punishment of Death is Necessary in Pennsylvania* (1787); he strongly insisted that the death penalty be retained but admitted it was useless in preventing certain crimes. In response, in 1794, the Pennsylvania legislature abolished capital punishment for all crimes except murder "in the first degree." This was the first time murder had been broken down into "degrees" corresponding to the seriousness and premeditation involved with the offense. New York, Virginia, Kentucky, Vermont, Massachusetts, and New Hampshire followed suit in reducing the number of capital crimes. A few states, though, went in the opposite direction. Rhode Island restored the death penalty for rape and arson; Massachusetts, New Jersey, and Connecticut raised death penalty crimes from six to ten including sodomy, maiming, robbery, and forgery. Many southern states made more crimes capital, especially for slaves.[44] And, important for this study's purposes, changes in death penalty laws were accompanied by changes in the practice of executions.

THE END OF PUBLIC EXECUTIONS

Until the late nineteenth century, public executions were standard practice. They often had the trappings of a sporting event, family picnic, or carnival,[45] mimicking the level and intensity of violence characteristic of society in general. For offenders charged with the most serious capital crimes such as treason or the murder of a member of nobility, a simple speedy execution was not enough. Rather, the death was designed so that the crowd would not soon forget the offender or his/her crime. By comparison with modern standards, the methods of execution were horrific. Until 1790, women hanged for coining or murdering their husbands had their corpses publicly burned after hanging. As late as 1820, male traitors had their heads hacked off and held up to the crowd.[46] One particularly gruesome method used in medieval England and some other European countries was hanging, drawing, and quartering. Offenders were lifted up by the neck, but before they died, the executioner cut out their intestines; these were then burned in front of them, and four limbs were severed from the body or, in some cases, torn away by horses tied to each limb. According to witnesses, some victims of quartering remained alive through much of the ordeal.[47]

Many American states moved executions inside prison walls in the nineteenth century, largely in response to growing appeals for the abolition of capital punishment and because of fears of possible riots. Rhode Island (1833), Pennsylvania (1834), New York (1835), Massachusetts (1835), and New Jersey (1835) all abolished public hangings. By 1849, this meant that 15 states were holding private hangings. Many death penalty abolitionists, who thought public executions would eventually cause people to cry out against them, opposed this move. For example, in 1835, Maine enacted what was in effect a moratorium on capital punishment after over 10,000 people who watched a hanging had to be restrained by police after they became unruly and began fighting.[48] The last official public execution in the United States took place in Kentucky on August 14, 1936, when a 20-year-old black man was hanged before a crowd of over 20,000.[49] While the end of public executions is seen as a moment of progress in the civilization process, Vic Gatrell argues:

A civilizing process may redeploy, sanitize, and camouflage disciplinary and other violence without necessarily diminishing it. Inside prisons for a century yet, murderers continued to be strangled on ropes too short or ropes too long, dying more dreadfully in private than in public, in chilly proceedings with crowd support withdrawn.[50]

Yet, executions in general were falling out of favor. In 1846, Michigan became the first state to abolish the death penalty except in the case of treason against the state. In 1852, Rhode Island abolished the death penalty led by Unitarians, Universalists, and Quakers. In the same year, Massachusetts limited its death penalty to first-degree murder.[51] Religious groups played a key role in abolition across the country. Indeed, a close connection remains between religion and capital punishment throughout U.S. history. Some activists on the issue used religious ideals as the basis of their support for the practice while others applied their religious beliefs to the cause of abolishing capital punishment.

During the last half of the nineteenth century the death penalty abolition movement began to slow. At the same time, states began to pass laws against mandatory death sentences. Laws in eighteen states shifted away from mandatory to discretionary capital punishment by 1895, not to save lives, but to try to increase convictions and executions of murderers. Still, abolitionists gained a few victories. Maine ushered in reforms with the passing of the Maine Law in 1835. The Maine Law held that all felons sentenced to death had to remain in prison at hard labor and could not be executed until one year had elapsed, and then only on the governor's order. No governor ordered an execution under the Maine Law for 27 years, and Maine finally abolished the death penalty in 1887 after a botched hanging. Iowa abolished the death penalty for six years. Kansas passed a "Maine Law" in 1872, which operated as de facto abolition.[52]

Another development during this period was the move away from hangings as the dominant method of execution. In 1888, New York approved the dismantling of its gallows and built the nation's first electric chair. The first person electrocuted was William Kemmler in 1890, and although there were some problems, other states soon followed the lead.[53] Electrocution as a method of execution came onto the scene in an unlikely manner. Edison Company with its DC electrical systems began attacking Westinghouse Company and its AC electrical systems as they were pressing for nationwide electrification with alternating current. To show how dangerous AC could be, Edison Company began public demonstrations by electrocuting animals. People reasoned that if electricity could kill animals, it could also kill people.[54]

Reforms continued through 1897 when the U.S. Congress passed a bill reducing the number of federal death crimes. Then, in 1907, Kansas took the "Maine Law" a step further and abolished all death penalties. Between 1911 and 1917, eight more states abolished capital punishment (Minnesota, North Dakota, South Dakota, Oregon, Arizona, Missouri, Tennessee, and Washington). Votes in other states came close to ending the death penalty. However, overall the death penalty abolition movement was slowing down. Washington, Arizona, and Oregon, in 1919 and 1920, reinstated the death penalty.[55]

A different execution method began in 1924 when the first execution by cyanide gas took place in Nevada. Tong war gang murderer Gee Jon became its first victim. The state wanted to pump cyanide gas into his cell at night while he was asleep as a more humanitarian way of carrying out the penalty, but technical difficulties prohibited this and a special "gas chamber" was hastily built.[56] Other concerns developed when less "civilized" methods of execution failed. In 1930, Mrs. Eva Dugan became the first female to be executed by the state of Arizona. The execution was botched when the hangman misjudged the drop and Mrs. Dugan's head was ripped from her body. Incidents like these and changing sensibilities led to a move away from hangings as more states converted to electric chairs and gas chambers. However, the gas chamber also began to lose its appeal because of its association with Nazi Germany's genocidal campaign that began shortly after the first gas chambers were put into place.[57]

During the 1930s, Americans were suffering through the Great Depression, and many criminologists argued that the death penalty was a necessary social measure.[58] This resulted in the highest number of executions than in any other previous decade in American history (1,676 executions).[59] At this time, abolitionist organizations sprang up all across the country, but they had little effect; in fact, between 1917 and 1957, no state abolished the death penalty. During the 1940s, there were a number of emotional protests against the execution of certain convicted felons but little opposition against the death penalty itself.[60] But the 1950s saw many European countries abolish or severely limit capital punishment, and the number of executions and support diminished in the United States.

Between 1960 and 1976, the capital punishment debate became as heated as at any time in U.S. history. Social unrest through these decades increased people's attention to the issue of capital punishment. The civil rights movement, the Vietnam war, and the draft all contributed to the simultaneous waning of support for capital punishment by heightening people's moral sensitivity to killing in general.[61] Moreover, debate about capital punishment shifted away from moral, religious, and utilitarian grounds toward legal philosophy, and the location of the debate moved into the courtroom.[62]

In 1972, after a five-year period without any executions, the Supreme Court ruled in *Furman v. Georgia* that the death penalty violated the prohibition against "cruel and unusual punishment" in the Eighth Amendment. In the five to four decision, the justices objected to the lack of standards, the broad discretion permitted trial judges, and the often-discriminatory manner in which death sentences were handed down. As a result, more than 600 death row inmates in 32 states had their sentences commuted to life imprisonment.[63] This turnabout was short-lived—the numbers on death row quickly began to build up again as states enacted revised legislation designed to satisfy the Supreme Court's objections. The country was turning back toward more punitive sentiments. By late 1972, Nixon's director of prisons declared that rehabilitation had been tried and failed, and that the Federal Bureau of Prisons was getting out of the rehabilitation business. Parole was abolished in the federal prison system, with many states following suit, most often by severely restricting parole or by mandating sentences of life imprisonment without parole. The nation's crime rate was continuing to climb, and more importantly, a punitive mentality was taking shape after years of more rehabilitative ideals and practices. Public support for capital punishment also began to rise.

REINSTATEMENT OF THE DEATH PENALTY

By early 1975, 30 states had again passed death penalty laws, and nearly 200 prisoners were on death row. In *Gregg v. Georgia* (1976), the Supreme Court upheld Georgia's newly passed death penalty and said that the death penalty was not always cruel and unusual punishment. Death row executions began again. In 1976, after 35 states and the federal government had reinstated capital punishment, the Supreme Court ruled that in view of new statutes designed to reduce the arbitrary imposition of the death penalty, it was no longer cruel and unusual punishment. The first person executed after the reinstatement of the death penalty was Gary Gilmore in Utah. Gilmore was executed on January 17, 1977, by firing squad, which he chose as his method of execution. The Gilmore case became a national spectacle attracting worldwide attention; reporters, activists on both sides, and spectators all flocked to Utah State Prison. Two years later, in Florida on May 25, 1979, John Spenkelink was the second man executed by the electric chair; followed by Jesse Bishop in Nevada on October 22, 1979, executed in the gas chamber. All of these cases received large amounts of attention because of the novelty of executions after reinstatement. Over the next 15 years, the number of executions rose consistently, with varying amounts of media attention dedicated to each.

After considerable debate and publicity for the first few executions after reinstatement, interest in the death penalty began to fall off. Throughout the 1980s, the number of executions continued to rise as the death penalty reemerged as a mainstay of the criminal justice system. Then the early 1990s movement toward getting "tough on criminals" saw many states expand their death penalty statutes to include more offenses and additional categories of victims. With the expansion of the death penalty during this period, the methods of execution also changed. Lethal injection is now used in 32 states and is regarded as a more humane and less painful method of execution than electrocution and lethal gas. Oklahoma passed the first death by lethal injection law in 1977, based on economics as much as humanitarian reasons. The old electric chair that had not been used in 11 years would have required expensive repairs. Estimates of over $200,000 were given to build a gas chamber, while lethal injection would cost no more than 10 to 15 dollars "per event."[64]

As the United States' penal system embraced capital punishment more and more fervently during the 1990s, the rest of the Western world had largely chosen to avoid the death penalty. The United Nations Human Rights Commission passed the *Resolution Supporting Worldwide Moratorium On Executions* in April 1999. The resolution calls on countries that have not abolished the death penalty to restrict their use of the death penalty, including not imposing it on juvenile offenders and limiting the number of offenses for which it can be imposed. Ten countries, including the United States, China, Pakistan, Rwanda, and Sudan voted against the resolution. Presently, more than half of the countries in the international community have abolished the death penalty completely, de facto, or for ordinary crimes. However, over 90 countries retain the death penalty, including China, Iran, and the United States, all of which rank among the highest for international executions.

There was also a demand for mandatory sentences and laws like "three strikes," which mandated life sentences for those convicted of three felonies. But after more than a decade of tougher penalties for criminals and increasing public support for the death penalty, a swing toward less punitive sentiments began across the country. In California, where the first "three strikes law" took effect in 1994, growing doubt about its effectiveness started to fuel criticism of these practices. These changing feelings came along as the country was beginning the most dramatic decrease in crime in the nation's history.

An article detailing the history of capital punishment noted that, in 1966, crime was down, the economy was up, and public support for the death penalty fell to a record low 42 percent.[65] This situation was being mirrored during the mid-1990s. Crime was down, the economy was doing well, and support for the death penalty began to fall, both among the public and with government officials. However, the number of executions across the country continued to rise throughout the 1990s; this was due in large part to the number of inmates that had been sentenced to death during the 1980s and the streamlining of the appeals process. While cracks were beginning to show in capital punishment, the execution machinery would take more time to slow down, as it began to do in 2000.

A turning point in the capital punishment debate nationally occurred when Illinois' Governor Ryan issued a moratorium on executions in January of 2000. This followed the release of 13 inmates from death row after Northwestern college students found new evidence that proved their innocence. After the Illinois decision, Nebraska, Maryland, Oregon, and New Hampshire decided to review their capital systems as well. The death penalty debate started to take center stage across the nation in 2000. *Newsweek* ran a cover story on the growing problems involved with the capital system. The story discussed then Texas governor George W. Bush's first stay of execution in five years, noting "the doubts that concerned Bush were the ones spreading across the country about the fairness of a system with life-and-death stakes."[66] The record number of executions in 1999 forced people to confront the reality of the system more than ever before. Also, a renewed opposition came from the Pope and religious and political leaders across the country. National conferences and full-page ads in the *New York Times* called for a national moratorium, and another botched electrocution in Florida led that state to adopt lethal injection. Both state and federal governments began to look at the death penalty with an increasingly more critical eye.

These changing feelings about the death penalty also started to affect its administration. In June 2002, public concern about the fair administration of the death penalty helped prompt the court's change of heart in *Atkins v. Virginia*, one of two decisions within a week limiting the death penalty. In *Atkins v. Virginia*, the court ruled by a six to three margin that executing mentally retarded inmates is unconstitutionally cruel, violating contemporary standards of decency. In the other case, *Ring v. Arizona*, the court ruled that only juries, not judges, could sentence someone to death. Then in January 2003, Governor Ryan commuted the sentences of all 156 inmates on Illinois' death row. Ryan's actions were covered worldwide as the death penalty debate continued to gain momentum. Then most recently in 2005, the Supreme Court prohibited executions of juvenile in offenders in *Roper v. Simmons*.

From the earliest colonial days, a total of 14,766 executions were documented in America and its territories.[67] This figure is certainly low, since many county records have been lost and many were not officially sanctioned. The frequency of lynching, obviously related to the death penalty and discussed in greater detail later, was also hard to accurately assess. During the two centuries that federal courts have existed, it is estimated that approximately 350 federal executions have occurred.[68]

From the public hanging to the private needle, the death penalty has adapted to the times, reflecting society's technology and sensibilities. Ideas about killing and dying are at the center of the death penalty and have evolved considerably over the ages. These ideas impart a different form and significance to the death penalty. The different sensibilities and stages of history are reflected directly in the race, class, and gender issues that follow.

RACE, CLASS, AND GENDER AND THE DEATH PENALTY

The death penalty has had a long history of racial controversy. Slavery, criminal justice, lynching, and capital punishment are historically intertwined in the United States. Under slavery, blacks were punished by means of "domestic discipline," which was the law on plantations; rarely were they the object of the criminal justice system or mob violence, because of their economic value to their masters. It was only after their freedom that they became the primary target of the criminal justice system, local mobs, and vigilante groups.[69] After the slaves were freed, lynching became widespread in the South based on ideas of racial superiority and threatened masculinity.[70] The vast majority of lynching victims were charged with alleged sexual misconduct with white women. More broadly, lynchings were used as a tool by white southern males to attempt to maintain their dominant position in society. As the culture became more inclusive, illegal lynchings gave way to legal executions. This connection with slavery is largely responsible for the overwhelming concentration of executions that take place in the South[71] and the continued racial discrimination found in the practice of capital punishment.

More recently in 1972, the death penalty process was ruled unconstitutional because of *Furman v. Georgia*, which gave evidence of racial bias in sentencing. More than half of the people legally executed in America since 1930 have been black, though blacks committed far less than half the crimes.[72] The ban on capital punishment did not last long as states drew up new legislation that tried to alleviate the discriminatory problems of the previous system. In 1973, Florida's *State v. Dixon* stated, "no longer will one man die and another live on the basis of race, or a woman live and a man die on the basis of sex." Yet issues of racial bias in the system did not die with new legislation. In 1987, *McClesky v. Kemp* introduced the results of a study of more than 2,000 Georgia homicide cases indicating that the victim's race was the most significant factor in determining whether someone convicted of murder would receive the death penalty. Despite these findings, the U.S. Supreme Court upheld the Georgia death penalty. Of those executed since 1976 (as of April 14, 2006), 58 percent have been white, 34 percent black, 6 percent Hispanic, and 2 percent Native American and Asian. Death row inmates total 3,525, with 46 percent of them white, 42 percent black, 10 percent Hispanic, and 2 percent other. Eighty percent of the victims of death row cases are white, 14 percent are black, 4 percent Hispanic, and 2 percent Asian, while only 50 percent of murders nationally involve white victims.

But biases of gender as well as race have affected the use of capital punishment. Changing views of gender and of women's role in society informed the ways in which criminal women were perceived and treated at every juncture of penal policy and practice. Penal responses to women have also changed over history, but what hasn't changed is the idea that "penal provisions must be differentiated on the basis of sex."[73] Surprisingly, the history of the United States shows that the execution of women has always been accepted. The first recorded execution of a woman in the United States is that of Jane Champion, in James City, Virginia, in 1632. She was hanged for an unknown crime.[74]

Many of the women who were victims of capital punishment in early America were black slave women; white women during this time were mostly executed for witchcraft. Since 1900, 185 women have been executed across the United States. Kathleen O'Shea, in her study of women and capital punishment across the United States, notes:

> The truth is that because executions are held behind locked doors in dark places, and before extremely small audiences, the vast majority of people who favor the death penalty are never touched by it personally. The likelihood of any of us knowing a woman on death row in our lifetime is actually quite rare. Unlike fires, accidents, cancer, or heart attacks, the death penalty does not usually happen to women in our family. Yet women are increasingly sentenced to death.[75]

Since the death penalty was reinstated, 152 death sentences have been imposed upon female offenders, constituting 2 percent of all death sentences since reinstatement.[76] Of these 152 women, 100 were white, 41 black, 10 Latino, and 4 Native American. As of April 14, 2006, only 48 remained under sentences of death in 17 states (29 white, 14 black, 5 Latino, and 1 Native American). This makes up 1.4 percent of the total death row population of about 3,725 persons and less than 0.1 percent of the approximately 50,000 women in prisons in the United States. Since 1976, 11 women have been executed (as of November 3, 2003): Velma Barfield (North Carolina, November 2, 1984); Karla Faye Tucker (Texas, February 3, 1998); Judy Buenoano (Florida, March 30, 1998); Betty Lou Beets (Texas, February 24, 2000); Christina Riggs (Arkansas, May 2, 2000); Wanda Jean Allen (Oklahoma, January 11, 2001); Marilyn Plantz (Oklahoma, May 1, 2001); Lois Nadean Smith (Oklahoma, December 4, 2001); Lynda Lyon Block (Alabama, May 10, 2002); Aileen Wuornos (Florida, October 9, 2002); and Frances Newton (Texas, September 14, 2005). Women, of course, do not kill as often as men, and when they do, their crimes tend to be explained by domestic conflict. They account for about 1 in 10 (10 percent) murder arrests and 1 in 50 (2 percent) death sentences imposed at the trial level.[77]

While race and gender are more visible sources of bias within the death penalty, class also plays an important role. The death penalty, historically, has been applied discriminately towards those of lower socioeconomic status. Vic Gatrell found this to be true in his study of England in the eighteenth and nineteenth centuries. He wrote that

apart from the execution of a few wealthy forgers or murderers, most of the hanged were poor and marginalized people—"the very lowest and worst people . . . the scum both of the city and country" as Elizabeth Fry amicably described her Newgate charges in 1818.[78]

At present, the poor and lower class continue to be affected discriminately by the death penalty. Robert Johnson argued in his book *Death Work* that "there are no rich men or women on death row, and no rich person has ever been executed in America."[79] For one, the wealthy are able to hire good lawyers who help their clients avoid death sentences. In the *Furman v. Georgia* (1972) decision, Justice William O. Douglas wrote that the death penalty was unconstitutionally discriminatory because of its disproportionate impact on minorities and individuals of lower socioeconomic means.

Race, class, and gender varieties of discrimination that appear in the history of the death penalty will be examined throughout this book, with special emphasis on the media's treatment of these issues. These social biases may have influenced whether and how particular cases were accorded media treatment. Also, the race, class, and gender characteristics of death row inmates affect which inmates are viewed as typical and which are seen as novel.

HIGH PROFILE CASES OF THE PAST

After researching the history and media coverage of the death penalty, I found that only a few cases in the twentieth century have captured the public's attention. I examined each of these cases in order to understand what these stories suggest about which cases became highly profiled, and why this is the case. For one thing, it was found that the surrounding historical and political events played a role; again, context mattered. The first modern capital punishment case that received a large amount of media attention was that of Nathaniel Leopold, 19, and Richard Loeb, 18. The two youths had everything in the world going for them. This all changed in 1924 when they decided to try to pull off the perfect murder. They were born into two of Chicago's wealthiest families. Both were extremely bright. Nathaniel's IQ was over 200, and he was a law student at the University of Chicago. Richard's IQ was 160, and he was the youngest graduate ever of the University of Michigan. After they became friends, they began to commit lesser crimes, including robbery, vandalism, arson, and stealing from Leopold's fraternity house at the University of Chicago, but this was not enough for Loeb. He dreamed of committing a bigger crime. A murder, he convinced his friend, would be their greatest intellectual challenge. Leopold was obsessed with crime and Nietzschean philosophy. He was especially interested in Nietzsche's criticism of moral codes, and believed that legal obligations did not apply to those who approached "the superman." Leopold's idea of the superman was his friend and admitted lover, Richard Loeb.[80]

They devised a plan to choose a victim from the nearby Harvard School. After not finding their original choice, they selected Jacob Franks. They lured him into the car, struck him over the head with a chisel, and then strangled him to death. They drove out to Wolf Lake outside of Chicago, just across the border in Indiana, where they tried to hide the body in a culvert under the railroad tracks. After dumping the body, they returned to the city and cleaned out the car. They had hoped to collect ransom money from the Franks family, but the body was discovered before the money could be collected.

The only piece of evidence found at the crime scene was a pair of horn-rimmed glasses. Luckily for the police, the glasses were extremely rare. A local optometrist was able to determine that only three pairs of these glasses had been sold in the Chicago area. When the police followed up on the list, one of the people was out of town, one had the glasses in their possession when the police arrived, and the other was Nathaniel Leopold. Leopold initially told the police that the glasses must be in his coat pocket; after going back to the house with the police he was unable to find them. He admitted that the glasses must be his. He told the police that he often went out to Wolf Lake bird watching. Leopold was a noted ornithologist, having published a number of articles on bird watching. But he was unable to explain how the glasses fell out of his jacket. The police also began to question Richard Loeb, after Leopold told police that he was with him the day of the murder. On May 31, 1924, they both confessed to the crime, each blaming the other one for the murder. [81]

The announcement that two sons of Chicago's wealthiest families were accused of murder made for media hysteria. The Chicago newspapers were obsessed with every detail of the lives of all involved in the crime. National attention also focused daily on the events of the investigation and trial. The attention continued to increase as they hired Clarence Darrow to defend them. Darrow was the most famous defense attorney of the time and a staunch death penalty opponent. After initially deciding to plead not guilty, Darrow convinced them to plead guilty and argue for their life in front of the judge. Under Illinois law at the time, if a defendant entered a guilty plea, the judge alone would determine the sentence. Darrow thought this was the best chance at saving the boys' lives.

The trial received national coverage, with intense scrutiny on the possible motivation of the defendants. Some attention was given to the intense relationship between Leopold and Loeb, with it sometimes being described as master and slave. The highlight of the trial was Darrow's 12-hour summation. In it, Darrow relied heavily on arguments against capital punishment with specific attention to executing juveniles. While Leopold and Loeb would not be considered juveniles today, at the time they were looked at as children. Darrow would put forth arguments that would influence the Supreme Court years later (discussed in Chapter 6):

Your Honor, if in this court a boy of eighteen and a boy of nineteen should be hanged on a plea of guilty, in violation of every precedent of the past, in violation of the policy of the law to take care of the young, in violation of all the progress that has been made and of the humanity that has been shown in the case of the young; in violation of the law that places boys in reformatories instead of prisons,—if your Honor in violation of all that and in the face of all the past should stand here in Chicago alone to hang a boy on a plea of guilty, then we are turning our faces backward toward the barbarism which once possessed the world. If your Honor can hang a boy eighteen, some other judge can hang him at seventeen, or sixteen, or fourteen. Some day, if there is any such thing as progress in the world, if there is any spirit of humanity that is working in the hearts of men, some day men would look back upon this as a barbarous age which deliberately set itself in the way of progress, humanity and sympathy, and committed an unforgivable act.[82]

Darrow's summation was printed in full in newspapers across the country. There were tears in the eyes of the audience when he was finished, including the judge. Judge Caverley's sentence was influenced greatly by the defendants' age:

It would have been the task of least resistance to impose the extreme penalty of the law. In choosing imprisonment instead of death, the court is moved chiefly by the consideration of the age of the defendants, boys of eighteen and nineteen years. It is not for the court to say that he will not, in any case, enforce capital punishment as an alternative, but the court believes it is within his province to decline to impose the sentence of death on persons who are not of full age. This determination appears to be in accordance with the progress of criminal law all over the world and with the dictates of enlightened humanity. More than that, it seems to be in accordance with the precedents hitherto observed in this State. The records of Illinois show only two cases of minors who were put to death by legal process...to which number the court does not feel inclined to make an addition.[83]

Leopold and Loeb were sentenced to life in prison plus 99 years. In 1936, Loeb was slashed and killed with a razor in a fight with another inmate. Leopold became a model prisoner, founding the prison library and working as a nurse in the infirmary. He was eventually released from prison in 1958, after 34 years of confinement. He moved to Puerto Rico to escape the media spotlight surrounding the release of the movie *Compulsion*, based on the 1924 crime. He died in 1971.[84]

The next high profile case was that of Nicola Sacco and Bartolomeo Vanzetti on August 23, 1927.[85] Sacco and Vanzetti, Italian immigrants who were anarchists and spoke only broken English, were convicted of a payroll robbery in Massachusetts in 1920; a paymaster and his bodyguard were shot to death. At their joint trial, dozens of witnesses provided alibis about Sacco and Vanzetti's whereabouts at the time of the robbery and murders, but to no avail. Some of the key prosecution witnesses, who were at first unable to identify the defendants, were suddenly, at the trial, sure of their identifications.

The context of their crime played a large role in their conviction and execution. Montgomery, in his study of the case, argues that "Massachusetts in 1920s, hatred of aliens, a fear of radicalism, and a sadistic fury made it impossible for anyone from juror to Governor, from policeman to university president, to act sanely, decently, or humanely when a radical was accused of a crime."[86] In the seven years between their convictions and electrocutions, much additional evidence surfaced to cast doubt on their guilt. In 1925, Celestine Madeiros, condemned to death in another murder case, confessed to being a member of the gang that committed the robbery for which Sacco and Vanzetti were tried. By the time of their executions, the Sacco and Vanzetti case had not only stirred up a maelstrom of protests in the United States, but around the world. Even after their death, debate continued over their trial. Ballistics tests done in 1961 suggested that Sacco was guilty and Vanzetti was innocent. In August 1977, 50 years after the execution, Governor Michael Dukakis of Massachusetts signed a proclamation clearing the names of Sacco and Vanzetti.

After Saco and Vanzetti came what many people called the "Crime of the Century." Bruno Richard Hauptmann, a German immigrant, was convicted of the 1932 kidnapping and murder of Charles Lindbergh's baby. Lindbergh, the first pilot to fly solo across the Atlantic, was an international hero, and the press descended on New Jersey en masse. It has been said that more journalists covered the Lindbergh kidnapping than covered World War I. Lindbergh's fame served to personalize the trial and made it not the State v. Hauptmann, but in a larger context, American Hero v. German immigrant, good v. evil. This dynamic was only added to as Lindbergh's attorney referred to the defendant as the immigrant non-American. Hauptmann was electrocuted in 1936. Again, the issue of Hauptmann's guilt is a continuing matter of controversy, never to be settled to everyone's satisfaction. There have even been recent allegations that Lindbergh or a member of his family accidentally killed the child, and that the kidnapping was staged to cover up that fact.[87]

While most of the death penalty cases that have aroused the public interest have been those involving white people, an exception was the Scottsboro Boys: Roy Wright, age 13, Eugene Williams, 13, Andy Wright, 17, Haywood Patterson, 17, Olen Montgomery, 17, Willie Roberson, 17, Ozzie Powell, 16, Charles Weems, 21, and Clarence Norris, 21.[88] The nine black youths were accused of raping two white girls, Ruby Bates and Victoria Price, on a freight train passing through Alabama on March 25, 1931. During the trial, which began one week after the youths were indicted, more than 100 national guardsmen were stationed at the courthouse, and upwards of 10,000 outsiders crowded into the small town.

Eight of the youths were convicted. A mistrial was declared in the case of 13-year-old Roy Wright when the jury was unable to reach a unanimous verdict, with eleven for execution and one for life imprisonment. The other eight were sentenced to die. The verdicts resulted in demonstrations in Europe and the United States. Liberal organizations, including the ACLU, NAACP, and International Labor Defense, sprang to the boys' defense. Eleven months after the arrest of the defendants, Ruby Bates wrote a letter denying that she had been raped. In November 1932, the U.S. Supreme Court overturned all of the convictions in *Powell v. Alabama*, which found that the defendants had been denied adequate legal counsel. But on April 9, 1933, Haywood Patterson was retried, convicted, and sentenced to death again. On May 7, 1933, thousands of persons marched in Washington in protest of the various trials. On June 22, 1933, Judge Horton vacated Haywood Patterson's conviction, granting a new trial.

The cases were moved to the jurisdiction of a different judge, and in November and December 1933, Haywood Patterson and Clarence Norris were retried, convicted, and again sentenced to death. In 1935, the U.S. Supreme Court overturned the conviction again in *Norris v. Alabama*, because blacks had been systematically excluded from the jury. The case of the Scottsboro Boys is remarkable for the number of trials, convictions, reversals, and reconvictions involved. On July 24, 1937, all charges were dropped against Roy Wright, Eugene Williams, Olen Montgomery, and Willie Roberson. On July 5, 1938, the last death sentence, that of Clarence Norris, was commuted to life imprisonment by Alabama's governor. Eventually all of the Scottsboro Boys were paroled from prison, with the exception of Haywood Patterson, who escaped from prison in 1948. Patterson was later convicted of manslaughter in Michigan following a barroom fight, and died in prison a year later.

The fifth high profile case, which was a federal case, was that of Julius and Ethel Rosenberg, who were convicted of giving atomic secrets to Russia during World War II and sentenced to die for treason. The Rosenberg case occurred during the McCarthy era, when fear of communism was not only widespread, but also nearly hysteric in nature. The Rosenbergs maintained their innocence, and opposition to their execution was widespread. They were electrocuted on June 19, 1953. J. Schuetz in his book on the case states that at the time of the execution, "the country was under siege of public paranoia brought on by the McCarthy hearings. The predominant public feelings were that all communists should be purged from American society."[89] This case illustrates how high profile cases cannot be explained without an understanding of the social and political context in which they took place.

The final case that generated debate across the country was that of Caryl Chessman in California.[90] In 1948, an armed robber and rapist was victimizing couples found on desolated roads in the Los Angeles area. The robber would occasionally use a flashing red light on his car roof, similar to the red lights used by police at that time, to pull the couples over. Among the many criminals questioned about this crime was Chessman. He signed a confession, which he later recanted, contending the police had coerced him to confess. There was almost no question that he had been interrogated for 72 hours and had been beaten to some extent, but the prosecutor maintained the confession was nonetheless voluntary.

Chessman was indicted under California's Little Lindbergh law, which allowed the death penalty in a case of kidnapping where the victim was harmed. The prosecutor contended that Chessman committed kidnapping when he moved the victims from their car to his car, for the purpose of raping them. Chessman represented himself and was convicted and sentenced to death. While on death row, he studied law and fought his case up to the U.S. Supreme Court seven times, winning small victories along the way. He also became a writer, authoring four books.

The last years of Chessman's life saw the nation begin to turn away from conservatism with the beginning of the great civil-rights advances, which paralleled the prisoners' rights and patients' rights movements. As Chessman's execution approached, it was greeted with tremendous protest, not only in the United States, but also around the world. Billy Graham, Eleanor Roosevelt, Robert Frost, Pablo Cassals, Aldous Huxley, and many thousands of others wrote to the governor, pleading for mercy for Chessman. California subsequently repealed the Little Lindbergh law, and by the time of Chessman's execution, kidnapping no longer carried the death penalty. When Chessman was executed in San Quentin's gas chamber on May 2, 1960, the debate about capital punishment had reached a peak. The debate was fueled further when it was revealed, after Chessman's execution, that a federal judge had granted him a last-minute reprieve, but the judge's clerk had lost precious minutes dialing a wrong number before getting through to the death chamber, and the cyanide pellets had been dropped only moments before word of the stay went through to San Quentin's warden.

These past cases point to the fact that the death penalty has not always been a private affair, and that very few death penalty cases receive large amounts of national attention. Each of these executions became the subject of national debate and stirred considerable emotion about punishment across the country. They reflected the times in which they took place and details about the political climate as well as society's view of individuals at the time. This book is interested in looking at the modern death penalty cases that have brought forth similar debate and emotions and what they have to reveal about our society's thoughts about punishment.

3

Serial Killers 1977–1994

Gerald Stano, who was in the cell next to Ted Bundy on Florida's death row, admitted to killing 41 young women, mostly hitchhikers and prostitutes, between 1969 and 1980. He was convicted of 10 murders, and like Bundy, sentenced to death three times between 1983 and 1986. But his trial and sentence received little newspaper attention outside of some local Florida coverage. Stano was executed March 23, 1998, also without much media attention. Why was Gerald Stano not a media sensation like Bundy, John Wayne Gacy, Richard Ramirez, or Aileen Wuornos? This chapter examines the Bundy, Gacy, Ramirez, and Wuornos cases for answers.

The media popularized the label "serial murderer" in the 1980s. The concept distinguishes between types of multiple homicides, depending on the time intervals that separate the individual attacks: murders committed in a brief period in one place are mass murders, while those carried out over a few days or a week are characterized as spree-killings. Serial murder implies that the killings are spread over months or years, with a cooling off period intervening. Media coverage of serial killing proliferated from 1977 through the early 1990s, with intense reporting on several cases that attracted immense public interest, which helped shape perceptions of the emerging problem. The notion of serial killing entered into popular culture, as evidenced by the amount of movies, books, and media coverage focusing on the issue. Legitimate concerns over crime were meshed with separate issues of missing and exploited children, organized pedophilia, and ill-defined concerns about the prevalence of homosexuality, to create an aura of "moral panic."[91]

The media's interest in serial killing took off once the number of killers and victims that were allegedly present in the country was reported by the F.B.I. on January 21, 1984. The press played upon the idea that this was a new and particularly American problem. The number of murders was seen as something unprecedented in American history. The serial murder problem was thought to have become "epidemic," a word attributed to the Justice Department's Robert O. Heck. The *New York Times* published a front-page story about the "rise in killers who roam the U.S. for victims." The *New York Times* article

asserts that history offers nothing to compare with the spate of such murders that has occurred in the United States since the beginning of the 1970s. Heck said that as many as four thousand Americans a year, at least half of them under the age of eighteen, are murdered in this way. He said he believes that at least 35 such killers are now roaming the country.[92]

Time and *Newsweek* followed up with articles dealing with the psychology of "mass killers" and "random killers." This was followed by the television documentary "Murder: No Apparent Motive" on HBO. There now emerged an influential stereotype of the serial killer, who was seen as a white male in his 30s or 40s, a sexually motivated murderer who preyed on either men or women, depending on his sexual orientation.[93] As we will see later, this stereotype of the serial killer would be an important factor in the coverage of high profile cases.

In the early 1980s, the extent of serial killing was being exaggerated across the country. The media and law enforcement authorities reported that there were four or five thousand victims, some 20 to 25% of the total homicide victims. This is compared with 1 or 2% of homicide victims decades earlier. The F.B.I., in a 1984 press conference, indicated that the number of victims was closer to 540 than the 4,000 detailed earlier.[94] Later challenges would further reduce the number of suspected victims.

Part of the increase in media coverage of serial killers can be explained by looking at changes in the reporting of news. Large metropolitan newspapers like the *New York Times* and *Los Angeles Times* did not expand their regional news coverage until after the 1950s. Regional and local newspapers increasingly became part of larger networks, which resulted in sensational stories being expanded outside of their local market and picked up by national newspapers. Also, a growing trend in sensationalistic news practices exploded during the 1980s. These trends made it possible for crimes and killers, who would have gone unnoticed earlier, to become national stories. This is especially true for serial killers, whose stories are ripe for sensationalism.

Additionally, the topic was highly visible in popular fiction, where true-crime books, novels, and films fueled the public's imagination. Both in fiction and in true crime, considerably more books were published in the three years from 1991 through 1993 than in the 1960s and 1970s combined. Multiple-murder was the theme of more American films in 1980 and 1981 than in the previous two decades together.[95] Even comedy movies such as *Serial Mom* and *So I Married an Axe Murderer* illustrate how the serial killer image had been integrated into the fabric of everyday life.[96]

This point is well articulated during an interview with David Von Drehle, a national staff writer for the *Washington Post*:

Serial killers were the zeitgeist of that time. You had family break ups, sexual liberation, the end of the home town, families not living all together, and the suburbanization of America. In the post war 60s and early 70s, people don't know their neighbor. Look at fiction, movies and journalism, you start to see the archetypal figure of a drifter, the lure of the open road, and the anti-hero, who is turned off by American values and rebels against them. You have Truman Capote making a hero out of Perry Smith and then Bundy comes along in the 70s and fits right into that. He looks like your next door neighbor; you wouldn't be nervous if saw him on your street but secretly he's driving his V.W. and raping and killing somebody at night. This information in the hands of good storytellers resonates with all different fears, and people are still talking about it 13 years later.

If you scratch hard, it was extremely awful in every respect. But somebody figured out that the serial killer was a zeitgeist figure for that period. It was not made up; there was an increase in murder rates, drug wars, and crack use, and an increase in stranger murder. All of these elements converged together, in reality, to form this zeitgeist and pop culture image.[97]

Serial killers became the "zeitgeist of the time." They were symbolic of the rising crime rates, the breakdown of the community, the need for tougher law enforcement policies, and individualistic crime explanations that were being promoted.

Many people were found guilty of capital charges and executed between 1977–1994, but four cases received more media attention than any other: Ted Bundy, John Wayne Gacy, Richard Ramirez, and Aileen Wuornos. To ascertain which death row cases received the most attention during this time period, I used the Lexis-Nexis database, a newspaper search engine that contains articles from 135 papers nationwide. All inmates who have been executed since the reinstatement of the death penalty in 1976, as well as those more well known inmates awaiting execution, were entered into the database. The number of articles that contained the inmate's name was used to isolate the cases that received the most coverage. Each inmate selected for more detailed analysis was investigated using content analysis of mainstream newspaper articles and in-depth interviews with both reporters who covered the cases and capital punishment activists. For each of the cases, I examined all *New York Times* and *Los Angeles Times* articles along with a major local daily paper. These stories were closely examined to demonstrate why these cases were the most newsworthy cases in the period examined, focusing specifically on the differences between the local and national coverage, the evolution of the coverage over time, connections that were made with larger political or social issues including serial killing, the death penalty, and public sentiments regarding punishment. (See Appendix for more details on research procedures)

THE CASE OF TED BUNDY

Ted Bundy had a promising future ahead of him as a youth in Tacoma, Washington. Extremely bright and articulate, he graduated from the University of Washington and was accepted to law school. He worked on campaigns for the Republican Party and volunteered at a suicide crisis center. However, his relationships with women grew more difficult. He learned that his "sister" was actually his mother and his "parents" were actually his grandparents. Bundy's mother was not married when she had Ted, and the lie was to protect her from the scrutiny of being an unwed mother.[98] Additionally, his girlfriend of five years broke up with him, leaving Ted devastated. After these events, his personality seemed to change. It was at this time that Bundy began a murder spree that would retain the public interest for more than a decade.

The affair first came to light in 1974 with a series of unsolved murders in Washington. Murders continued to occur in Utah and Colorado over the next two years, but it was not until Bundy's arrest in Colorado in January 1977 that his name was publicly attached to the incidents. Regional news media focused attention on Bundy and his alleged crimes with stories and interviews that were replayed numerous times over the next decade. His murders were well known across much of the Pacific Northwest as the "Ted" murders.

On August 16, 1975, Bundy was arrested in Utah for the kidnapping of Carol DaRonch, who he abducted from a parking lot after pretending to be a police officer. When DaRonch grew suspicious, she escaped from

Bundy's VW bug and notified the police.[99] Bundy was tried and found guilty of aggravated kidnapping and sentenced to 1 to 15 years in prison. While in prison, authorities collected evidence linking Bundy to a series of murders in Utah and Colorado. He was transferred to Colorado to await trial for the murder of Caryn Campbell. Bundy decided to defend himself, as he had been previously accepted to University of Utah Law School where he attended a few classes, and was granted permission to use the law library. On June 7, 1977, Bundy jumped out a second story window in the library and escaped. He eluded police in Aspen, Colorado, for a week before eventually being apprehended while trying to flee in a stolen car. Seven months later, Bundy escaped again, this time from his cell in Garfield County Jail. On December 30, 1977, he climbed out of his cell through a lighting fixture in the ceiling and crawled to another part of the jail, where he was able to lower himself from the ceiling and walk out of the jail. He was not detected missing for 15 hours, and by that time Bundy was long gone. He made his way across the country, stopping in Chicago before taking up residence under an assumed name in Florida.[100]

Although he was making a name for himself in the western part of the country for his murder trial in Colorado and his two escapes from prison, he did not reach the national papers until his second escape from a Colorado prison. [101] National attention continued after he was placed on the FBI's Ten Most Wanted list. "Mass Murder Suspect on F.B.I Fugitive List," read the headlines in the *New York Times* on February 11, 1978, which described Bundy as being "the most prolific mass murderer in American history, surpassing Juan V. Corona, who was convicted of killing 26 migrant farm workers in California." From here on, the newspaper coverage consistently focused on the number of victims, i.e. "36 sexual slayings."[102]

The national news did not take additional interest in the case until he was arrested for what has become known as the "Chi Omega Murders" and the death of a 12-year old girl, Kimberly Leach, in Florida in 1978. The "Chi Omega Murders" took place on the night of January 15, 1978, when Bundy entered the sorority house on the Florida State University campus, beating five women and raping and strangling two to death. One of the victims, Lisa Levy, was beaten on the head with a log, raped, and strangled. Bundy had also left bite marks on her buttocks and on one of her nipples. The bite marks would be an important piece of evidence in the trial.[103] Margaret Bowman, the other murder victim, had similar injuries, although she had not been sexually assaulted, and she showed no signs of bite marks. She had been strangled with a pair of panty hose and beaten on the head so severely that her skull was shattered and a portion of her brain was exposed. Almost a month later on February 9, Bundy took Kimberley Leach from her school grounds and murdered her; the body was found eight weeks later in a state park. Bundy was arrested on February 15 for driving a stolen car. After he was arrested, police were able to connect him to the three Florida murders. It is interesting to note that in the early coverage of Bundy, the media never refers to him as a serial killer. The notion and label had not yet entered the public arena; this would not happen until the mid-1980s.

The Trials

Bundy was now the confirmed suspect in 36 murders from 1974 to 1978 that stretched across five states. He was only charged with the three murders that took place in Florida. Between his arrest in Florida and the start of the trial for the Chi Omega murders, the Bundy story began to take shape in the papers. Mixed perceptions of Bundy still persisted at this point, demonstrated by the *Los Angeles Times* headline on May 3, 1978: "Experts Differ on Suspected Mass Killer: Some See Ted Bundy as Scapegoat in 40 Sex Slayings." A March 12, 1978 article in the *New York Times* articulates the debate on Bundy:

For several weeks now the police in this southern capital have held in armor-plated jail cells a man who either is a victim of unusual circumstances or—as the police in several states suspect—the killer of at least 36 women.[104]

The Bundy trial was covered in great detail by the press. The local Florida newspapers had daily stories concerning Bundy and the upcoming trial months before its beginning in June. The judge moved the trial from Tallahassee to Miami due to the amount of pretrial publicity.

Bundy stood trial for the "Chi Omega" murders first. The trial began on June 25, 1979, and was televised on the local public broadcasting station in Miami. Florida was one of the few states at this time to allow broadcasts of criminal trials. Two crucial pieces of evidence connected him to the crimes. First, one of the sorority sisters identified Bundy as the man she saw running from the house the night of the murders. Then, an orthodontist was able to match the bite marks found on the victim to Bundy's teeth. Unhappy with his attorneys, halfway through the trial he began acting as his own defense attorney. He did not call any witnesses in his defense. The jury deliberated for six and half hours before finding him guilty on July 23, 1978.[105] Then, after taking less than two hours to decide, they recommended a death sentence for the two murders on July 31, 1978. The *New York Times* had daily stories of the trial while the *Los Angeles Times* covered the major decisions in the trial but did not devote daily space to the story.

Bundy's second trial, which started on January 7, 1980, for the murder of 12 year-old Kimberly Leach, was covered locally as closely as the first trial, but nationally was not covered as extensively as the first. Bundy did not defend himself during the second trial, and he also pleaded guilty by reason of insanity. On February 7, the jury found Bundy guilty. Two days later, during the sentencing phase, while Bundy questioned Carol Boone, he asked her to marry him, to which she agreed.[106] Bundy was then sentenced to death for the third time.

Down Time

After Bundy's second trial and conviction, newspaper coverage of the case began to taper off, only to rise to new heights covering his execution in 1989. A few events received both local and national attention during this transitional time period. The news media would take interest each time his scheduled execution would approach, first in March 1986 for the Chi Omega murders and then again in July 1986 for the Kimberly Leach murder. Additionally, Bundy's name became synonymous with serial killing and evil. The Bundy case was the subject of several true-crime books, one of which, *The Deliberate Stranger* (1986), became a network miniseries, which suggests that publishers were responding to considerable public interest. In the miniseries, Mark Harmon, who had just been named *People's Sexiest Man Alive*, portrayed Bundy. People were becoming more fearful that a serial killer could be living next door or in their neighborhood. These killers were not easily identifiable and could be lurking anywhere; this idea was demonstrated by the title of Ann Rule's book on Bundy, *The Stranger Beside Me*.

In 1987, there was a considerable amount of media attention dedicated to Bundy when it was learned that he and John Hinckley, Jr. (who had attempted to assassinate President Ronald Reagan) had been corresponding and that Hinckley was planning on visiting Bundy during a planned release. Following this event, there was both national and local attention dedicated to a mental competency hearing for Bundy. Bundy was found competent in the hearing; the judge declared, "Ted Bundy is a diabolical genius and the most competent serial killer in the country at this time."

Also during this period, Bundy came to represent everything that was wrong with the death penalty system in Florida. His name was used to evoke the frustrations of people with the system as he won stay after stay on death row. As the judge declared during Bundy's competency hearing, "They either should abolish the death penalty itself or change the procedure."[107] Bundy became a political issue in the Florida Gubernatorial race, with the Democrats often criticizing the delays in the execution.

The Execution

As Bundy's execution approached, reporters wrote about every aspect of the case. Stories about the victims and their families and the appeals that were taking place were enough to provide daily coverage regarding the Bundy case for more than a week prior to the execution. Bundy helped the newspapers' desire for something to write about by confessing to a number of additional murders. He provided law enforcement officials information about bodies and insinuated that he knew about many more murders.

The execution itself was covered in great detail by local and national newspapers, with both providing step-by-step details about how the execution would take place and the last meal. Bundy declined to give a preference for his last meal; instead he received the traditional steak and eggs, orange juice, hash browns, and coffee.[108] The day of the execution, the *St. Petersburg Times* had six different articles about Bundy. The *Los Angeles Times* story covering the execution had the headline "Bundy is Electrocuted as Crowd of 500 Cheers."[109] When asked for any last words, Bundy stated: "Jim and Fred [his lawyers], I'd like you to give my love to my family and friends."[110] The sentiments surrounding Bundy's execution can be seen in the descriptions of the scene outside of the execution site:

Crowds of death penalty supporters outside the Florida State Prison cheered and applauded his death as a white hearse left the prison with Bundy's body. Many wore T-shirts and carried sparklers and banners with "Fry Bundy" slogans. Some carried effigies of Bundy strapped in a chair.[111]

Both the local and national news mentioned the lack of death penalty opponents outside of the prison. Comments from observers outside for the most part expressed pro-death penalty sentiments.

"I wish I could have been the one flipping the switch," said David Hoar, a policeman from St. Augustine, Fla..[112]

Former state Senator Wayne Hollingsworth of Lake City, a friend of the Leach family and a witness to the execution: "it was very, very humane. Probably too humane for the murders and atrocities he has committed."[113]

The reporters who were there said the scene was like nothing they have ever been part of before or since:

It was the most spectacular event I ever covered. The setting is rural Starke, Florida, which is a two and a half-hour drive from Tallahassee; it is that far from everywhere. By this time in Florida, it had become so routine, with most executions there were no more than five or six people opposing the execution and the friends or families of the victims. The Bundy execution was different; it had huge crowds. It was like a festival; people were selling electrocution lapels that had Old Sparky on it and T-shirts with the electric chair. Pick up trucks were driving around with stuffed Teds sitting in electric chairs. There were signs and posters, people selling champagne and doughnuts. I don't know of any sight like this before or since. Local deejays were promoting "Fryday" on the radio. People came from all over the country and almost everybody was in favor of the death penalty.[114]

After the Execution

The Bundy case continued to grab headlines for a week after the execution as more details came out about the execution and Bundy. Bundy had given an interview with religious broadcaster James Dobson, in which he blamed his urge to kill on pornography. Conservatives used this admission across the country to denounce the ills of pornography and immoral values. Over the years, Bundy was mentioned sporadically in the news media, most often in reference to other serial killers or problems with the capital system. The reporters who covered the case see that the Bundy story is not likely to be duplicated because of the right mix of circumstances and feelings that were brought together during his case. Lucy Morgan, a reporter for the *St. Petersburg Times*, states:

I don't think that there will be another Bundy. He incited a lot of emotion and destroyed the innocence that surrounded the college campus; before him college campuses didn't invite that type of crime. Today, there isn't the same revelry surrounding the death penalty. Even those who were in favor of the death penalty at Bundy's execution were a little uncomfortable with the celebratory mood.[115]

Tim Nickens, an editor with the *St. Petersburg Times*, agrees:

I don't see another case to the Bundy extreme. Nobody on death row could garner that much attention, not to that extent; Bundy came to symbolize the death penalty and everything evil. Plus, since then, there has been all the evidence against the death penalty; feelings aren't quite as strong.[116]

THE CASE OF JOHN WAYNE GACY

John Wayne Gacy is most well known for his crimes in Chicago, but he had trouble with the law in Iowa earlier in his life. In September 1964, Gacy was married and moved to Iowa to manage a Kentucky Fried Chicken restaurant owned by his father-in-law. He quickly became active in the community, and he and his wife had two children. Then in the spring of 1968, Gacy was indicted for committing sodomy with a teenage boy. The boy told the courts that Gacy had tricked him into being tied up while visiting Gacy's home a year earlier, and had violently raped him. Gacy plead guilty to the charges and was sentenced to 10 years in state prison. While in prison his wife divorced him. Gacy was a model prisoner and was released after 18 months.[117] After being released, Gacy moved back to Chicago.

After his return to Chicago, Gacy started a contracting company in 1974 and began to hire young males to work for him. On December 12, 1978, Robert Piest, 15, was outside of the pharmacy where he worked, when he was approached by Gacy, who offered him a job with his company. Piest's mother, who was waiting inside the pharmacy, started to worry when Piest did not return. His mother contacted the police, who after learning the name of the contractor who approached Piest, went to Gacy's house. The police took Gacy to the police station for questioning, but he was released after denying any involvement with the disappearance of the boy. The following day, police ran a background check on Gacy and discovered his prior conviction. A search warrant was issued for his home, but no evidence was found initially to connect Gacy to Piest's disappearance, and Gacy was a free man. Then, after further tests on the evidence taken from his house, police found the necessary evidence to connect him to the crime. They found a ring that belonged to a teenager who had disappeared a year earlier, discovered that three former Gacy employees had also disappeared, and came across a receipt for a roll of film, which one of Piest's coworkers had given him on the day he went missing. [118]

John Wayne Gacy's story became the focal point of the local newspapers starting in December 1978 when the police searched his house in suburban Chicago for a second time and discovered the remains of nearly 30 people. Gacy, who confessed to the police on December 22, attracted young males to his home and sexually abused and killed them, disposing of most of them under his home. He would lure the young males back to his house, where they would get drunk, and where Gacy would typically drug them. After drugging the victims, he would handcuff them and sexually assault them. To keep the victims from screaming, Gacy would put a sock or underwear into their mouths and kill them by pulling a rope or board against their throats as he raped them. Many of the autopsies of the victims revealed socks or underwear lodged in their throats.[119]

The Gacy story dominated the local media for years on end and overlapped with the national coverage of Ted Bundy. The Chicago newspapers had multiple stories about the case every day for a month after the discovery of the bodies. Daily updates on the number of bodies discovered under his house appeared on the front page. The Gacy body count would grow steadily until finally, in April 1979, the remains of Robert Piest were discovered in the Illinois River, making him the thirty-third victim. Gacy told police that the reason he disposed of the bodies in the river was because he ran out of room in the crawl space under his house. Along with the number of bodies, the media coverage featured pictures and maps of his house showing where the bodies were discovered.[120] The national newspapers became interested in the story once the body count began to rise; however, their coverage was much briefer.

Similar to Bundy, reporters' descriptions of Gacy compared him to a preconceived notion of what a killer was supposed to look like. This is evident in the headline of a *Chicago Tribune* article: "Danger Cited: Killers Don't Always Look the Part." The descriptions of Gacy talked about the two sides of his personality. They focused on the fact that he was a Democratic Precinct Captain, leader of the Polish Day Parade, and business owner, who was described frequently as a very nice man by those who knew him. Gacy also entertained children at parties dressed as a clown. There was a cover picture of him dressed as "Pogo" the clown on the front page of the *Tribune* on December 27, 1978, which was subsequently shown nationwide. Along with the picture of Gacy dressed as a clown, there is an equally famous picture of him with then first lady Rosalind Carter taken during a democratic fundraiser in Chicago. All of these images were in contrast to the fact that he killed 33 people. Like the stereotype being established of serial killers, he was consistently referred to as evil: "If the devil's alive, he lived here."[121] Additionally, like Bundy, the label of serial killer was not attached to Gacy until much later.

The Trial

On February 6, 1980, John Wayne Gacy's murder trial began in the Cook County Criminal Courts Building in Chicago, Illinois. He entered a plea of not guilty by reason of insanity. The local paper had daily coverage of all things Gacy. There were stories on the lawyers, judges, and witnesses that would be called. The trial coverage continued to focus on the duality of his personality, as evidenced by the headlines of the articles discussing the trial:

Witnesses at Sex Murder Trial: 2 Faces of Gacy: "Beast", "Nice Man"
John Wayne Gacy Jr.: A Model Citizen and a Mass Murderer [122]

His lawyer also played upon this idea, reading from Robert Louis Stevenson's *The Strange Case of Dr. Jekyll and Mr. Hyde.*

The prosecution's first witness was Marko Butkovich, the father of Gacy's victim John Butkovich. He was the first of many family members and friends of the murdered victims who testified. Reporters had plenty of information to write about, with most of the witnesses breaking down in tears on the bench, while others sadly recounted their last goodbyes to their loved ones. The jury was presented with testimony of over 100 witnesses over a period of five weeks. They deliberated for only two hours before rendering a guilty verdict. On March 13, 1980, he was found guilty of murdering 33 people, more than any other person in U.S. history at the time. He was sentenced to death for the 12 murders that were proven to have taken place since capital punishment was reinstated in Illinois, and he received life sentences for the other murders. [123]

Down Time

After the trial and death sentence, Gacy did not receive the daily coverage from the local papers that had followed him through the trial, although many stories would bring Gacy back into the news before this execution. The first was in 1982 when a play opened in New York called "The House Across the Street." The play dealt with neighbors of mass murderers. The neighbors are inevitably interviewed by the media after the arrest of their neighbor, and never seem to notice anything weird or have anything bad to say about him. A *New York Times* article summarized the play:

"House" is set in a Chicago suburb and is loosely inspired by the John Wayne Gacy case. It tells of a typical all-American family, the Fortunes, who wake up to discover that the nice man across the front lawn raped and strangled 31 boys and then buried them in every crevice of his home. Although the family's living room looks right into the murderer's house, no one ever noticed "anything out of the ordinary." [124]

The description of the play illustrates the ideas that were starting to pervade the country regarding serial killers at this time.

Attention to Gacy increased again alongside the growing interest in serial killers across the country. By 1985, the stereotype of the serial killer was cemented in the public mind and was frequently mentioned in any discussion of other serial killers. A *Los Angeles Times* article about the "Valley Intruder" (Richard Ramirez, later nicknamed The Night Stalker) discussed how Ramirez was different from the past profile of serial killers like Bundy, Gacy, and the Hillside Strangler, who "methodically choose victims with symbolic features." It continued noting how serial killing had received increased media attention and that people were beginning to recognize the differences between serial killers and mass murderers.[125]

Gacy was also mentioned frequently in the local papers in any story that discussed the prison system, death penalty, or murder. This was also true on the national level, where Gacy's name was cited in stories dealing with the problems with the capital punishment system.[126] Additionally, he became a political symbol both locally in Chicago's political races and in the national presidential politics. Locally, his name was used during the Illinois gubernatorial election:

Democratic gubernatorial candidate Neil Hartigan tried to portray GOP opponent Jim Edgar as soft on law-and-order issues Thursday, while Edgar's camp accused Hartigan of distorting comments made by the Republican secretary of state about the death penalty. "I deal in the practical effects of the law, and the effect of Mr. Edgar's action would be that John Wayne Gacy would not be put to death."[127]

Also, he became the center of a political debate between Democrats and Republicans when the Republicans used his picture on brochures discussing Democrat Michael Dukakis' policies.

Democratic presidential nominee Michael S. Dukakis angrily denounced Republic campaign tactics Wednesday, blasting a lurid brochure that suggests he would free Chicago mass murderer John Wayne Gacy.[128]

Throughout this time, Gacy would occasionally make the news with stories about his appeals. His story was in the news again in May 1992 when a five-part interview with local Chicago personality Walter Jacobson aired on television. It was aired during sweeps week coinciding with the made for television movie about him called "To Catch a Killer," with Brian Dennehy playing Gacy. At the same time, Gacy attracted media interest by starting a 900 number declaring his innocence.

The Execution

The local press focused on the execution for weeks before the actual date. A particularly noteworthy article in the *Chicago Sun-Times* titled "Death Penalty Debate Grows; Foes Face A Litmus Test As Gacy Execution Nears" discussed how he "is your poster boy for the death penalty" and that "even some of the activists who want to keep him alive admit that the worst serial killer in U.S. history might appear to be the perfect argument for capital punishment." The article continues with a discussion of various anti- and pro-death penalty activists regarding Gacy's pending execution. It states that there are problems with the death penalty system (executing innocent people, the mentally ill, those represented by a public defender, and racism), but "despite such horror stories, capital punishment has widespread support across the nation. Three quarters of Americans favor it as an option in murder cases, according to a 1991 Gallup Poll." [129]

In the week before the execution, multiple stories appeared daily, discussing everything and everybody involved with the case. The newspapers also, ironically, wrote articles about all the attention the case was generating. [130] The day before the execution, articles covered every step that Gacy would take over the next 24 hours: "after dinner, Gacy plans to confess his sins to a Roman Catholic priest, then attend a 9 P.M. mass in the prison." [131] This is consistent with the Bundy coverage. The newspapers covered every minute detail concerning the inmate's actions before and after the execution, highlighting his last words ("Kiss my ass") and last meal (which consisted of fried chicken, french fries, a cola, and fresh strawberries). [132]

On the day of the execution, May 10, 1994, the *Chicago Sun-Times* had 11 articles about John Wayne Gacy. Some of the headlines were:

Death Draws Crowd But Little Sympathy
The Curious Want To See The End
Forget Gacy, Victims Worth Remembering
Justice, Not Revenge, Is Concern Of Victim's Sister
It's Over For Gacy; Killer Not Remorseful, Felt "Wronged"

Much like Bundy, reporters detailed the scene outside the execution where many gathered both for and against the death penalty. The stories discussed everything from people selling T-shirts that read "no tears for the clown," people chanting "put the clown in the ground," and those speaking out against the death penalty. [133] Much greater weight was given to the anti-death penalty voices in the Gacy coverage than to Bundy's execution some five years earlier, but still an overwhelming amount of attention was placed on the pro-death penalty supporters.

The national articles also discussed the scene the day before the execution:

Earlier Monday, in downtown Chicago, hundreds of singing, laughing people, some wearing party hats, others dressed as clowns, marched through downtown in celebration of the impending execution.

The article notes that there were "1,000 death penalty supporters" and remarks that there were some people opposed to the execution.[134] Stephen Braun, a *Los Angeles Times* reporter, describes the scene during an interview:

But Gacy's stolid refusal to acknowledge any guilt—coupled with his uniquely psychotic weirdness—gave the stories an almost comic twinge. TV showed his killer clown photos repeatedly, and by the night of his execution, black humor was rampant among the reporters waiting for word that Gacy was gone. Gacy's only support came from doctrinaire anti-death penalty advocates marching outside—and even they didn't show much passion. Gacy's notoriety and his open enjoyment in reveling in his murderous past stripped him of any modicum of empathy that more anonymous death row killers might have received.[135]

After the Execution

During the execution, a malfunction in the execution procedure received continuing attention in the Chicago area. Chemicals clogged in one of the tubes leading to Gacy, and the tube had to be changed, which led to an 18-minute delay between administering the chemicals and the time of Gacy's death. Lawyers and anti-death penalty supporters used the malfunction to demonstrate the problems with the death penalty system in Illinois.[136]

The days after the execution continued to produce local attention dedicated to the Gacy story. An article in the *Chicago Tribune* discussed the highs and lows of the execution coverage by the local media describing the "circus" and "carnival-like" atmosphere outside the execution. It also mentioned the fact that the television coverage "seemed to give short shrift to protestors who gathered outside Stateville."[137] In the aftermath of the Gacy execution, you can begin to see the doubts that would eventually lead to Illinois' moratorium on executions.

THE CASE OF RICHARD RAMIREZ

A wave of murders swept across California in the summer of 1985 that caused widespread fear and panic. The murders were eventually connected to one man, initially called the Valley Intruder but then labeled the Night Stalker by the press (first attributed to the *Los Angeles Herald-Examiner*). His first murder occurred on June 28, 1984. Ramirez broke into Jennie Vincow's house by removing a screen in the window. After not finding anything valuable to steal, Ramirez turned his attention to 79-year-old Vincow, who was sleeping in her bedroom. He slashed her throat, stabbed her repeatedly, and then sexually assaulted her.[138]

He did not strike again for eight months. In February 1985, he kidnapped and sexually abused a six-year-old girl. Then on March 17, Ramirez came up behind Maria Hernandez as she got out of her car in the driveway to her condo. He shot her in the head and left her for dead. Hernandez had put her hands on her head and the bullet remarkably hit her hand and car keys ricocheting away from her head. Ramirez entered the condo and killed Hernandez's roommate, Dayle Okazaki. As he exited he encountered Hernandez, who had heard the gunshots and was running away from the scene. Hernandez said "please don't shoot me again," and Ramirez ran away.[139] That same night, he pulled up next to Tsai-Lian Yu in her car. Ramirez began to pull Yu from her car, and she screamed for help. He shot her twice. A driver passing by saw Yu crawling from her car; he stayed with her until the police arrived. She died later that night.[140] His attacks became more frequent, with five in March and two in May 1985. Between June and mid-August, nine more attacks were attributed to him. Yet it wasn't until August 8, 1985, that the police announced that they were after a serial killer who was responsible for killings from Los Angeles to San Francisco. Then on August 28, the police revealed the name of the wanted killer. The Night Stalker's identity, Richard Ramirez, was not known until the LAPD was able to lift a print from his abandoned car.[141]

The newspaper coverage consistently focused on the fact that he was a serial killer. Articles talked about his distinctive signature or "trademark" that was left at each of the crime scenes and frequently discussed the stereotypes that were associated with serial killers.

> At his press conference Tuesday, during which he stressed public awareness, Gates called the Stalker—also known as the Valley Intruder—"an unorthodox serial killer" and pointed out that "due to the Night Stalker's…random selection process, we do not know where he will strike next." But he said the serial killer generally "strikes in the early morning hours…near freeways" and advised citizens to take several precautions to "decrease the chance of a second incident."[142]

Early articles frequently talked about the "profile" of serial killers and differences in criminal work when one is looking for a serial killer. This can be seen in the August 29, 1985 *Los Angeles Times* article titled "Psychological Profile: Probing Killer's Mind," which discusses "Mind Hunters," the F.B.I.'s computer profiling operations in connection with the Ramirez case. The profilers "handle 300 referrals a year from local law enforcement agencies who are looking for serial killers or rapists—including the case of the Night Stalker."[143]

With daily features on the Night Stalker, widespread fear gripped California. Reporters discussed how residents were staying up at night looking for the serial killer and the many residents "mobilized by fear, who have joined the Police Department's Operation Night Watch."[144] Also, articles discussed the rise in gun sales and the need for gun safety. On August 30, the police released a description of Ramirez that was broadcast statewide and put on the front page of the paper. Ramirez was traveling back from San Francisco and was unaware that his picture was released.

The case took a new turn the next day when residents in an East Los Angeles neighborhood caught Ramirez. Ramirez entered the area looking to steal a car after being spotted in a convenience store. He found a car with the doors open and keys in the ignition. He jumped in and started to drive away. Faustino Pinon, who was working on the car at the time, started chasing after Ramirez. The two wrestled over the keys, and Ramirez told Pinon he had a gun. Pinon continued to fight with Ramirez, eventually throwing him from the car. He started to run away and attempted to steal another car. By this time, Pinon and other neighbors were chasing after Ramirez. They caught him in the middle of the street and knocked him to the ground with a metal pipe.[145] The police arrived shortly after his capture. The *Los Angeles Times* describes the scene:

Desperate and near exhaustion, Night Stalker Richard Ramirez made a wrong turn when he dashed onto Hubbard Street—unknowingly he had stumbled into a neighborhood of heroes. Four citizens grabbed and subdued the suspected murderer after a 20-second footrace, one of them pounding at him with a steel rod.[146]

The next day, six articles about the case appeared in the *Los Angeles Times* discussing everything from the chronology of the 16 murders (later reduced to 14 murders) to his connection with Satanism (eventually a popular topic in the media). When residents were the ones who finally caught Ramirez, the case became even more locally interesting with stories about all the individuals who took part in the capture and their anticipation of the reward that had been issued for the Night Stalker.

The *New York Times* detailed the capture and noted: "after Mr. Ramirez's arrest, hundreds of residents crowded outside the police station where he was being held and chanted, 'Kill him, kill him.'"[147] This was only the second time that the *New York Times* had written about the case, the first being a brief article on August 31, 1985, titled "Police Identify Suspect In 16 Killings On Coast." The *New York Times* followed the story for a third consecutive day when Ramirez's connection with Satanism was announced by authorities. At the time, Satanism was a hot topic. Stories of Satanic rituals and abuse had become popular topics on talk shows and in the newspaper, especially in California with the massive amount of attention surrounding the McMartin Preschool case, where the operators of a day care were accused of ritually abusing children.

The Trial

On September 4, 1985, Ramirez appeared in court for the first of many times to hear the initial charges against him. The newspaper coverage immediately picked up on the fact that he could face the death penalty. On September 27, Ramirez was arraigned on 68 felony charges including 14 murders; the prosecutor said that the death penalty would be sought in each of the murder charges. His trial would be delayed repeatedly. The first delay began in October when Ramirez was allowed to switch lawyers. It was not until October 24, 1985, that he entered his plea of innocent to the court. This moment made for the first of many where reporters would concentrate on Ramirez's courtroom antics. As he was led from the courtroom he displayed a pentagram with his hands and shouted "Hail Satan!" This was picked up by the national news as well. The preliminary hearing began on February 24, 1986. The hearing was covered in great detail by the local press. The testimonies during the hearing gave reporters plenty to focus on, as surviving victims and law enforcement officials testified about their experiences with Ramirez.

Jury selection finally started on July 21, 1988. The death penalty was discussed in the media regarding the potential jurors facing death penalty questions.[148] The trial again hit a snare with accusations of a juror talking about racist bias within the death penalty. The incident led to more discussion of race and bias regarding Ramirez, jury selection, and the capital punishment system. Additionally, the case started to become a political issue in California, as articles discussed the value of preliminary hearings, which in the Ramirez case took over a year. Also, articles examined the cost of the Ramirez case, along with the McMartin Preschool trial[149] and the Randy Kraft trial.[150]

Politicians also used the case to push forward a ballot initiative to speed up criminal trials in California.[151]

The trial began on January 29, 1989, after a three-year delay, with television cameras allowed to shoot parts of the trial. This was a disputed topic, as the judge originally banned cameras from the courtroom during the preliminary hearing.[152] The local newspaper provided daily coverage of the trial; the national newspapers did not follow the trial in detail. After 31 days, 137 witnesses, and 521 exhibits, the prosecution rested on April 13, 1989. Ramirez once again struck out at the media in the courtroom yelling, "Media: sensation-seeking parasites."[153]

The deliberations took until September 20, 1989, when the jury found Ramirez guilty on 13 murder counts and 30 other felony counts. Ramirez once again addressed the court, stating, "You maggots make me sick—one and all. I am beyond your experience, I am beyond good and evil."[154] The *Los Angeles Times* had six articles about the Ramirez case and six pictures of him on the day of the verdict.

The jury found that there were 19 special circumstances, such as the commission of a burglary along with murder, that make him eligible for the death penalty. The guilty verdict was then followed by the sentencing phase of the trial, which brought articles discussing the death penalty.[155] The jury returned with their recommendation for the gas chamber on October 3, 1989. Ramirez was then in and out of the news occasionally when the reward money was finally handed out to his captors and whenever there were appeals of his convictions. He was also in the news briefly when in 1996 he got married to Doreen Lioy at San Quentin, where he has been awaiting his execution.

THE CASE OF AILEEN WUORNOS

Aileen Wuornos had a troubled upbringing in Michigan. Her mother, who was 15 when she was born, left her in the care of her parents. Her father, who she never knew, was a convicted child molester who hung himself in prison. It wasn't until she was 10 that she learned that her "parents" were actually her grandparents. Wuornos had a child when she was 14, who she put up for adoption. Soon after, she was living on the streets and began a life of prostitution. After a few brushes with the law, Wuornos, who was now 20, hitchhiked to Florida in September 1976.[156]

Her early years in Florida included arrests for armed robbery, for which she served a year in prison, multiple weapons possession, forgery, and theft. She also began to use aliases including Lori Grody and Susan Blahovec.[157]

In June 1986, Wuornos met Tyria Moore who quickly became her lover. They traveled across Florida living off Wuornos' earnings from prostitution. Although their romance ended, they remained constant companions.[158]

Then on November 30, 1989, Richard Mallory, an owner of a Clearwater, Florida, electronics repair business, went missing. A few days later his 1977 Cadillac was found outside Daytona. On December 13, two men found his badly decomposed body, which had been shot three times, wrapped in carpet on a dirt road in Volusia County. Police had no leads.[159]

Between December 1989 and November 1990, six bodies were found in desolate areas along Florida's highways. The victims' cars were taken and many were naked or partially clothed. A seventh victim, Peter Siems, was also reported, but police did not find the body. Wuornos and Moore became suspects in the murders after they were in an accident in Siems' car and fled the scene. Witnesses were able to provide a sketch of the two women to police.[160] By this time, journalists had noted a pattern in the killings, but the police had not revealed them to the public. In late November 1990, the media exposure forced authorities to go public with their sketches of two women suspects believed responsible for the string of murders. By early December, the police located Lee Blahovec (Wuornos) in a motel outside of Daytona. She was put under surveillance while the police collected evidence connecting her to the crimes.[161] They found fingerprints on the victims' cars that matched Blahovec and also Lori Grody (Wuornos), and pawned items belonging to the victims, which were traced back to her as well.

Then on January 9, 1991, Aileen Wuornos was arrested at a bar for outstanding warrants under the name Lori Grody. Police did not mention the murders when they arrested her or alert the media that a suspect had been detained.[162] The following day, Tyria Moore was located at her sister's house in Pennsylvania. She was questioned about her involvement with the murders in Florida. The police agreed not to press charges if she would help their case against Wuornos. On January 14, Moore began a series of phone calls, which were recorded, to the jail. Wuornos slowly started to confess to the murders in order to protect Moore from any involvement.[163] Then on January 16, 1991, she summoned detectives and confessed to six killings, all allegedly performed in self-defense. The local newspapers immediately picked up on the story, after police announced that the suspect in the string of highway murders had been arrested.

The Trial

The Wuornos case continued to attract newspaper coverage through April when she was indicted in the first murder charge. Local coverage of the case continued as the pre-trial hearings began in June 1991. Articles in the local papers began to delve into the story much more deeply as more details of the case emerged. Reporters focused on her troubled past and sexual abuse as a child[164] and a videotape in which Wuornos allegedly admits to the crimes.[165]

Wuornos' trial for the murder of Richard Mallory opened on January 13, 1992, with jury selection. Newspapers noted that jurors were quizzed on their views on the death penalty and whether or not they could administer it to a woman.[166] Questions about whether or not they believed a prostitute can be raped were also asked. The local journalists covered the trial on a daily basis and frequently noted that she could face the death penalty. The beginning of the trial was also the first time that the *Los Angeles Times* wrote about the case. The *Los Angeles Times* published their first story on January 17, 1992, when Tyria Moore, Wuornos' "lesbian lover," testified against her.[167] The *Los Angeles Times* reported on the trial only three more times (Wuornos's confession, January 24, 1992, guilty verdict, January 28, 1992, and the death sentence February 1, 1992). The *New York Times* did not report on the trial at all.

On January 24, 1992, Wuornos took the stand as the only defense witness. She detailed her killing of Richard Mallory, which she said was in response to a violent rape and beating by him. She insisted that she shot him dead in self-defense, using her pistol only after he threatened her life. Three days later, the jury rejected her story, deliberating a mere 90 minutes before they convicted her of first-degree murder. Reporters took note of Wuornos' comments after the verdict was read:

Wuornos couldn't control her rage as the jury left the courtroom. As her attorneys tried to calm her, she yelled at the jurors: "I was raped. I hope you get raped—scumbags of America."[168]

The jury recommended death on January 30, 1992, and the following day she was formally sentenced to die. The *St. Petersburg Times* describes the courtroom scene as the sentence was announced:

The object of their debate sat sobbing like an injured child. Aileen Carol Wuornos, the woman who killed a Clearwater businessman and perhaps six other men, sat slumped in her chair, looking small. This was not the Damsel of Death, the female Ted Bundy, the Highway Hooker.

The article exemplified the two different points of views that were established throughout the case:

She is a remorseless, diabolical killer, State Attorney John Tanner argued, and a candidate for the electric chair if ever there was one.

She is a terribly depraved victim, defense attorney Tricia Jenkins would counter, and "a damaged, primitive child," a case for mercy if ever there was one.[169]

The debate surrounding Wuornos' motivation would continue long after this first trial.

In April, she pled no contest to the murders of three more victims; it is noted "a significant factor was that Wuornos, a self-described born-again Christian, wanted to 'get right with God.'"[170] Over the next couple of weeks articles continued to focus on her no contest plea and desire to be executed quickly. Then she requested to not be present at her own sentencing hearing in May 1992. The jury voted in favor of death. The newspaper remarked, "Wuornos' absence was just one oddity in what turned out to be a bizarre trip through the criminal-justice system."[171] On May 15, the judge upheld the jury's recommendation; she once again added some interest to the proceedings:

"I'll be up in heaven while you all are rotting in hell," Wuornos, a self-proclaimed Christian, told the court. She turned to the state attorney's table and glared. "May your wife and kids get raped," she told the two men. Walking out of the courtroom, Wuornos offered her final salute: an upraised middle finger and an obscene comment to the judge.[172]

The unique thing about the Wuornos case is that much of the attention, especially nationally, came to her after she was already sentenced to die. This was in part motivated by the numerous movie and book deals that attracted national interest in the case. From the very beginning, Hollywood was interested in the story. Wuornos and her attorney sold the movie rights to it within a couple weeks of her arrest (she would subsequently back out of the deal). At the same time, three sheriff's investigators on her case and Tyria Moore retained their own lawyer to look for offers for a Hollywood movie deal. The investigators noted, in their defense, that any money they received would go to the victims' assistance fund. The first movie that received large amounts of attention was *Overkill,* which aired on CBS. Most of the articles regarding this film focused on the fact that the movie paints Wuornos in a positive light. The movie also downplayed the relationship with Tyria Moore because, as the producer said, "we made a decision not to deal with that because we didn't want it out there that lesbians hate men and hate them enough to kill them."[173] He also stated that "if the men in her life had just treated her right, she wouldn't have killed them," which was not well received by the victims' families or victims' rights groups. The *New York Times* remarked that the movie "offers a not unsympathetic portrait" of Wuornos and Moore; the article notes the opening scene "showing the two women on a drunken joyride in a stolen car, suggests a nose-thumbing *Thelma and Louise* attitude toward society."[174] Additionally, reporters criticized the choice of a pretty actress to portray her. National interest also focused on the movie *Aileen Wuornos: The Selling Of A Serial Killer*, which details the commercialization of the case and suggests that Wuornos may have been sacrificed for the money.

The Wuornos case took an ironic twist on November 10, 1992, with revelations on the NBC news program *Dateline*. She had always claimed that she acted in self-defense, but neither her supporters, the media, nor Florida prosecutors were able to find any criminal record for Richard Mallory that would substantiate her claim of rape and assault. However, *Dateline* found out that Mallory had served 10 years for a violent rape in another state, information obtained by checking his name through the FBI's database. This added to the story because Wuornos claimed that she acted in self-defense and did not receive a fair trial. She also argued that everyone was rushing to make money off, and a movie about, her—and in reality that came true. The first TV movie about her aired one-week after the *Dateline* report.

The Execution

Wuornos was in the news only briefly as she was handed her sixth death sentence on February 6, 1993. She once again gave reporters something to write about when she addressed the judge: "'I can't believe that I'm the only female about to face her sixth death sentence,' she told Cobb. 'Ted Bundy killed 30 to 100 people, and he only got a death sentence every other time.'"[175] She would be in and out of the news over the next couple of years, as her appeals would approach. Even though she expressed a desire to be executed, and a judge on October 6, 1994, upheld three of her death sentences, "a state prosecutor noted that it could be 10 years or more before Wuornos dies for her crimes. The reason: she still has a bevy of state and federal appellate options ahead."[176] Her appeals continued throughout the decade, and in July 2001 she once again expressed her wish to die. She addressed the court: "I am a serial killer. I would kill again."[177]

Then on October 9, 2002, after passing on her last meal for a cup of coffee, she spoke her last words: "I'd just like to say I'm sailing with the Rock and I'll be back like *Independence Day* with Jesus, June 6, like the movie, big mothership and all. I'll be back." She was executed by lethal injection, which she requested instead of the electric chair.[178] There was both local and national coverage of the execution, and the tone had changed since Gacy and Bundy. No talk of celebrations outside the prison or any of the black humor that was common in the 1980s and early 1990s were found in the newspaper accounts. The *St. Petersburg Times* remarked that there were "death penalty protesters gathered outside the prison, one carrying a sign that read, 'Jeb Kevorkian' and that the execution brought some measure of peace to the families of her seven victims, but left questions for those who doubted her sanity or oppose the death penalty."[179] These descriptions are a marked change from the early execution scenes and show the changes in public sentiment regarding the death penalty since the 1980s and early 1990s.

THE NEWSWORTHINESS OF SERIAL KILLING

Between 1977 and 1994, reporters only chose serial killers to become high profile capital punishment cases. During the same years, American's support for the death penalty and their generally punitive sentiments were also explicitly on the rise. Yet the newspapers failed to cover Karla Faye Tucker's crime, trial, and death sentence in 1983, and Mumia Abu-Jamal's crime, trial, and death sentence in 1980–1981 (outside of some local coverage). These stories failed to become high profile and take hold of the public's attention during this period; they were not deemed newsworthy. This would change, as we will see in the next chapter, and seems to have done so around the same time sentiments regarding punishment began to shift again in the mid 1990s. Thus, reporters and editors cannot simply assert that some cases are newsworthy and others are not based on some fixed objective criteria. Rather, the timing of stories also seems to have affected which stories were seen as newsworthy. As David Von Drehle, a reporter for the *Washington Post,* states:

> The idea of newsworthiness, unusualness, man bites dog, can only take you so far, it goes beyond that; there is an appetite for certain stories at certain times. I have been in the newspaper business over half of my life and I can't say how and why it happens. TV producers and newspaper editors are closely linked to public appetite.[180]

Serial killers were the right stories at the right time. Yet not every serial killer during the 1980s and early 1990s received large amounts of newspaper attention. Only four serial killers sentenced to death attracted widespread national attention. What made Bundy, Gacy, Ramirez, and Wuornos stand out from the rest?

The Newsworthiness of Ted Bundy

Many newsworthy elements attracted journalists to the Bundy case. First, he came to be associated with a large number of murder victims. By the time he was arrested in Florida, there were few articles that did not mention that he was responsible for 36 murder victims. Second, it was not just the number of victims but their characteristics that must be seen as important. All of his victims were young women that were described as pretty and coming from good backgrounds, mostly college students. The two college students in Florida were frequently referred to as "two Chi-omega sorority sisters" or described as "coeds." Additionally, the victims were all white with brown hair parted down the middle. Third, the college setting was another important element in the coverage of the case. According to Lucy Morgan, reporter for the *St. Petersburg Times*:

The case attracted immediate attention because of the setting: the FSU campus and a sorority house. State-wide interest was focused because of the college campus setting and the fact that he killed co-eds.[181]

A fourth important element in the coverage of the Bundy case was his characteristics. His charm and seemingly all-American look fed the newspapers' interest in the case. He was consistently described as the ex-law student, bright, handsome, charming, and seductive. Reporters frequently noted that Bundy did not fit the mold of the typical murderer:

Bundy was different than your normal killer; he was a reasonably good looking, nice, educated person who was able to pass himself off to people, pick up victims with his personality. He had virtues that people could identify with, looks and charm.[182]

This focus was evident in a 14-page article in the *New York Times Sunday Magazine,* titled "All-American Boy on Trial." The article begins:

Here was a young man who represented the best in America, not its worst. Here was this terrific looking man with light brown hair and blue eyes, looking rather Kennedyesque, dressed in a beige turtleneck and dark blue blazer, a smile turning the corners of his lean all-American face, walking jauntily before the judge, but free of any extravagant motion that could lead one to think a swaggering—even dangerous—personality existed beneath that casual, cool exterior.[183]

Journalists consistently spoke of Bundy as smart, handsome, and a law student: "The suspect, Theodore Robert Bundy, is handsome, articulate and college educated. He has a flair and charm that makes him 'the kind of guy you'd want your daughter to bring home' as one investigator put it."[184] These descriptions are offered almost to suggest that someone college educated and smart could not be capable of these crimes. Mark I. Pinskey, a *Los Angeles Times* reporter, argues, "An issue I raised, from the beginning, was that if you are white, good-looking, and appear middle class you can become a successful predator because you do not fit the traditional 'criminal' profile."[185]

Next, the nature of Bundy's offenses also added to the newsworthiness of the story. Newspapers consistently gave the details of his crimes, including the sexual elements of the cases. He is said to have raped all of the women that he murdered. One of the key elements of the prosecution's case was the presentation of teeth marks found on one of the Chi Omega victims' buttocks and breast, which only added to the sexual overtones of the coverage. This was not lost on the reporters covering the case.

With Bundy you had sex and violence, two of the three legs that guarantee major media coverage, the third being race, which was in this case absent. Also, there was a handsome, middle class suspect and very attractive young, middle class women victims. Other, bizarre aspects of the case emerged later.[186]

Last, his trials were particularly attractive for the news media because of many novel elements that played out during it. Bundy acted as his own attorney, which in itself is an interesting story. This spectacle was only fueled with television cameras filming the trial, which was novel at the time. Additionally, he asked a witness to marry him during questioning, on the day that he was sentenced to die for the third time. All of these factors combined to create a very attractive story for the news media. The right mix of circumstances also came together with the newspaper coverage of John Wayne Gacy.

The Newsworthiness of John Wayne Gacy

Like Bundy, the media was fascinated with the number of victims for which Gacy was responsible. The daily coverage of the increasing number of bodies found under Gacy's home was extremely newsworthy. Along with the number of bodies, journalists immediately picked up on the sexual elements of the case. Gacy was a convicted sex offender, due to an arrest in 1968, and this is consistently mentioned both locally and nationally along with the sexual details of the murders. The typical description of Gacy in the early accounts read like this:

Gacy, a convicted sex offender, reportedly told investigators he had sexual relations with 32 young men, then strangled them, buried 27 under his home and threw five into the Des Plaines River.[187]

Reporters also frequently described how the victims were killed; detailing the sexual abuse and intricate self-strangulating chair to which Gacy tied them. Stephen Braun, a reporter for the *Los Angeles Times*, believes that the media was attracted to this story because of

the magnitude of the crimes, Gacy's lack of repentance and euphoric nostalgia for the act of murder. There was also a weird symmetry of a former clown and former Democratic Party apparatchik who had managed to get along so well in society while he blithely went about butchering 33 young men.[188]

Another important element was the Chicago location, which is home to one of the country's largest media. The local Chicago newspapers were consistently trying to outdo the other papers in reporting on him. Competition over interviews with victims who had survived their contact with Gacy, victims' families, and law enforcement officials fueled the story in the Chicago papers.

Additionally, many stories focused on the characteristics of the victims and the tragedy now facing their families. Since many of the boys were runaways, a quick linkage was also made with the Gacy story and runaways. The *Chicago Tribune* had two articles on December 30, 1978, dealing with the connection: "Few Contact Police About Missing Boys" and "Hotline Set Up For Runaways." This connection with other social problems was one of the keys, which contributed to the concern of serial killing during the 1980s.

Finally, a *New York Times* article subtly shows the class and gender biases that the newspapers held when speaking of Gacy's victims:

Some were male prostitutes, but many were high school-age youths who came to his home expecting work with his construction firm.[189]

The statement makes it seem like it is okay to kill male prostitutes but wrong to kill high school youths. These types of biases help explain differential amounts of newspaper coverage of particular murders and murderers. If Bundy had not killed "pretty girls from good homes," would he have received the same amount of attention? If Gacy had only killed male prostitutes, would the media have cared? The importance of the victims' characteristics in newsworthiness can also be seen clearly with the newspaper coverage of Richard Ramirez.

The Newsworthiness of Richard Ramirez

The number and details of the attacks, the Los Angeles setting, his connection with Satanism, and the characteristics of victims led to immediate interest in the case of Richard Ramirez. Reporters who covered the case indicated that the number of crimes and victims was the driving force behind the coverage:

> Simply, the number of crimes was the motivating force behind the interest in the case and then his capture, which led to lots of stories about his background. Race was never brought into the case overtly, Ramirez is obviously a Latino name and he was caught in a largely Latino neighborhood and if I remember correctly some of his defense lawyers were also Latino, but it was never a real issue. Satanism also added to the story newsworthiness; it added to his image.[190]
>
> Why the Ramirez case? That case became as big as it did, I think, because of the utter randomness, brutality and frequency of the crimes. Ramirez held Los Angeles in terror like no one else in the past 20 years, killing young and old in the middle of the night for no particular reason. He didn't even limit his killings to Los Angeles going up to San Francisco for a brief period of time and killing a man there.[191]

Reporters also focused on the graphic and sexual elements of the attacks as they noted "gouged eyeballs," "slit throats,"[192] and graphic descriptions of sexual abuse.

To understand the interest in Ramirez, one cannot overlook the characteristics of the victims. Describing the Night Stalker's victims, an article notes that he preyed

> upon businessmen, Asian immigrants, grandmothers and retired couples. He kidnapped children off streets and sexually assaulted them; he dragged one woman from her car and shot her repeatedly. Most often, he crept into tidy tract homes through unlocked windows and doors before dawn, cut telephone wires and attacked victims while they slept.[193]

The article also points out that this took place "in serene middle-class neighborhoods." The importance of Ramirez's victims to the newspaper coverage can be seen in an Op-Ed piece by Frank del Olmo in the *Los Angeles Times,* which read, in part:

> What made the crimes especially fearsome was the fact that they occurred not on Skid Row, where a serial killer called The Slasher was caught several years ago, but in

quiet suburbs. And the victims were not prostitutes, as were many in the Hillside Strangler case, but middle-class men and women asleep in bed. The Night Stalker captured our imagination as no other serial killer ever had. He was not killing "them" in a faraway, dingy place. He was killing people like "us" in comfortable, ordinary homes.[194]

The articles on the day of the verdict displayed many of the elements that led to the consistent attention on the case.

The crimes were especially chilling because they seemed so indiscriminate. His victims were not prostitutes or vagrants or hitchhikers. Rather they were middle-class men and women who lived peacefully in neatly-tended homes and condominiums and had simply gone to bed with a window or door unsecured on a warm, benign California night.[195]

The newspaper coverage of Ramirez shows that his crimes were seen as especially disturbing because of the social class of the victims.

Additionally, the connection with Satanism became one of Ramirez's more well-known attributes. Journalists frequently referred to him as a "Satan-worshiper" and discussed his fondness for the rock band AC/DC, which, articles state, "some believe is meant to be an acronym for 'Anti-Christ, Devil's Child.'"[196] Ramirez left satanic messages and symbols at a few of the murder scenes. The newspapers discussed how Satanism had also been linked with other killings recently: "Richard Ramirez, suspected by police in the 16 Night Stalker slayings, is the latest in a small group of American murder suspects whose crimes have been associated with Satanism."[197] The article noted that public awareness of Satanism had increased due to Christian groups' complaints about rock music lyrics and their role in recent crimes, also referring to the McMartin Preschool case. The interest in serial killing, more generally, was linked in the media with the moral panic concerning satanic ritual abuse and killings at this time; Ramirez became a symbol of this connection.

Other newsworthy events took place that kept the story in the papers. The *Los Angeles Times* discussed the attractiveness of the Ramirez trial:

For the less judicially minded, the Night Stalker case has all the trappings of a sensational murder trial: A defendant whose courtroom comportment has been less than predictable; opposing lawyers whose apparent contempt for one another has nearly led to fisticuffs; an easygoing judge whose patience is being severely tried. Earlier, the bickering attorneys caused another judge to threaten to throw them all in jail.[198]

Also, a juror was dismissed for sleeping during the deliberation[199] and was replaced, which meant that the jury had to start its deliberations over again.

Then, a juror was murdered by her boyfriend, which delayed the deliberations even more.[200] All of these events kept the Ramirez story in the newspaper for years.

The Newsworthiness of Aileen Wuornos

Journalists' continuing search for a fresh take on an existing story was met
with Aileen Wuornos, who was reported as the first woman serial killer. The
initial newspaper reports about the case appeared on January 18, 1991, in the
St. Petersburg Times, and set the tone for the coverage that would follow:

> As details of the life of Aileen Carol Wuornos emerged Thursday, so did a picture
> of a woman whose escalating private troubles and public crimes may win her a
> unique position in American criminal history: The first woman to commit classic
> serial killing.[201]

Reporters continued to focus on this unique serial killing angle by noting,
"Wuornos may prove to be, as one expert put it, the first 'female Ted
Bundy.'" The newspaper reports frequently discussed the differences between
Wuornos and other female murderers:

> While other women have been involved in multiple murders, none until Wuornos
> had killed in ways normally associated with male murder. Wuornos worked alone
> and used a gun to kill strangers, notes Boston serial-murder expert Jack Levin. For
> the most part, other female murderers used poisons to kill victims they knew. Levin
> and other experts have watched the Wuornos case closely because it appeared to offer
> a new wrinkle in the serial-murder phenomenon: a woman who killed like a man
> and seemed to enjoy it.[202]

The stereotypes surrounding serial killers were continually challenged and
rethought throughout the newspaper coverage of the case. Her story was seen
as novel by both criminologists and mainstream journalists.

In addition to her unique place among serial killers, women are also seen
as novel on death row. The day the judge formalized the death sentence,
newspaper accounts pointed out that she would join "a small but notorious
group of female killers on Florida's death row," and noted that "women are
seldom sentenced to death in Florida, and when they are, it is usually for a
particularly shocking crime."[203] Other newsworthy elements were also found
with the Wuornos story. While in prison, Wuornos found religion and
became friends with Arlene Pralle, a religious woman. Pralle began corresponding with her in jail and started giving interviews about her and

Wournos's relationship to the media. Pralle would eventually adopt her. Much like Ramirez, Wuornos was also known for her outrageous courtroom behavior. She once stated to judge and jury, "I hope you scumbags get raped," and "I will seek to be electrocuted as soon as possible. . .I want to get off this crooked, evil planet."[204] This was after she fired her attorney and hired an ex-rock musician and truck driver, whose telephone number spelled out "Dr. Legal." Like Bundy, Gacy, and Ramirez before her, there were many newsworthy elements to the Aileen Wuornos story that distinguished her from other serial killers.

THE UNATTRACTIVE SERIAL KILLERS: GERALD STANO, RANDY KRAFT, AND RONALD SIMMONS

After analyzing the newsworthy elements of the high profile serial killers, it is also valuable to look at serial killers who did not garner large amounts of newspaper attention. The idea that the number of victims and crimes will lead directly to the front page is mistaken. There were other serial killers during this time frame, like Gerald Stano, who reportedly killed 49 people, Randy Kraft, who was responsible for 16 victims, and Ronald Simmons, who killed 14 people. They killed as many if not more people than Bundy, Gacy, Ramirez, and Wuornos, yet did not become media sensations. Why were some killers chosen over others? A beginning answer to this question can be obtained by looking at the social context of the Stano, Kraft, and Simmons murders.

As mentioned at the start of the chapter, Gerald Stano was in the cell next to Ted Bundy on Florida's death row. He admitted to killing 41 young women between 1969 and 1980. He was convicted of 10 murders, and like Bundy, sentenced to death three times between 1983 and 1986. But his trial and sentence received little newspaper attention outside of some local Florida coverage. Stano was executed March 23, 1998, also without much media attention. Why was Gerald Stano not a media sensation like Bundy? Jan Glidwell, a reporter for the *St.Petersburg Times*, asks the same question:

> When people start recalling serial murderers, they talk about John Wayne Gacy and Aileen Wuornos and Charlie Starkweather, each of whom killed far fewer persons than Stano. They talk about Charlie Manson, Juan Corona, Jack the Ripper and Ted Bundy. But they almost never mention Gerald Stano. Why? [205]

To answer this, it is essential to look at the characteristics of Stano's victims. His victims were hitchhikers and prostitutes found along the Florida highway, who were not seen as being as newsworthy as college students or middle-class families. For example, Richard Ramirez received considerably more newspaper attention, in part because he killed men and women as they slept in their middle class homes. In one particular newspaper article, the reporter asks, would we have even noticed Ramirez if he had killed 15 people on skid row? The answer is a resounding "no."[206]

In an interview with Jan Glidwell, he indicated that the perception about Stano's victims was not even completely accurate:

> There was also the perceived social class of the victims. Stano's victims were assumed to be prostitutes and topless dancers but there were also honor students, captains of their high school swim team, and housewives. The original coverage was that the victims were prostitutes from the strip in Daytona and Tampa and the media never got past that. Myself and five other reporters interviewed the families of the victims and less than half fell into that category. But the perception was there.[207]

So it is not only the number of victims but also the characteristics (e.g. race, class, and gender) of the victims that are important for the media. Additionally, Stano did not have the charisma or fit nicely into the stereotype of the serial killer that was dominant at the time. Glidwell also points out:

> He was not a very sympathetic character. The cops themselves couldn't stand to be around him. He would talk about killing like it was a hobby, like working on his car. He never developed a following like Manson or Gacy, with the picture with him and Rosalind Carter. Stano had none of that, and he was a fry cook. Ramirez's victims were perceived as higher socio-economic status so he attracted attention. Maybe Stano's problem was that he had no catchy name.[208]

His execution did not attract worldwide attention like Bundy or Gacy. Stano received very little attention, and the attention he did receive can be explained, in part, by the fact that he was the first person electrocuted in Florida after the controversy over Pedro Medina (who caught fire during the execution). With the exception of his victims' families and some law enforcement agencies, journalists really did not notice Gerald Stano. Simply killing 41 people does not guarantee a spot on the front page of the newspaper, as many reporters would have you believe.

Likewise, Randy Kraft was arrested in 1983 and convicted of 16 murders in 1989. His victims were male hitchhikers and marines found along the California highways. He was known as the "Scorecard Killer" because of the list found by police in his car that referenced over 60 different killings. The Kraft trial attracted media attention in Los Angeles because it was the longest and most expensive trial in the city's history at the time. However, nationally, Kraft did not become as high profile as some of his fellow serial killers like Richard Ramirez, who was responsible for fewer victims in the same city. Once again, to understand this it is necessary to look at the characteristics of the victims. Ramirez's victims were middle class couples and families, whereas many of Kraft's victims were hitchhikers who were not deemed newsworthy by the reporters or the public.

Another killer not covered extensively by newspapers was Randall Simmons. On Dec. 28, 1987, Simmons went on the attack in Russellville, Arkansas, randomly shooting and killing two people and wounding three others. When police searched his home, they found 14 members of his family, all murdered. He was convicted and sentenced to death for the crimes. Simmons did not fit in with the stereotype of the serial killer that had been established by the media. His case barely even made a splash in the national newspapers.

Numerous other killers did not attract the same amount of newspaper attention as Bundy, Gacy, Ramirez, and Wuornos. One such example is Larry Eyler, who was convicted of two murders and was the suspect in the murders of 21 more young men in Indiana, Illinois, Kentucky, and Wisconsin from 1982 to 1984. He was sentenced to death but died in prison before his execution. Then there is Bobby Joe Long, who was convicted of two murders in Florida and confessed to eight others in 1984. His victims were primarily prostitutes. He has been sentenced to death and is still awaiting execution. Killing numerous people does not guarantee media stardom and fulfill the criteria for newsworthiness, as the reporters and editors indicated. The traditional newsworthiness criteria like novelty, importance, and drama cannot be understood in a vacuum. It is also necessary to look at the social context of the event to understand the selection of one story over another.

CONCLUSION

The death row cases that generated the most newspaper attention between 1977 and 1994 were those that concerned serial killers. All of the cases included discussion of the profile, methods, and stereotypes that came to be associated with this newly coined phenomenon. None of the cases raised too many questions about the fairness and justness of capital punishment. While each newspaper cited one source or mentioned a small group of protestors outside the execution of Gacy and Bundy, no widespread discussion against their executions was found in the newspaper accounts. The newspaper coverage of the Wuornos and Ramirez trials also displayed no questioning of the capital sentence. This is not surprising; support for and the number of executions rose throughout this time period. Society's sentiments were very much in favor of the death penalty, and the types of cases reporters chose to cover corresponded to that. Reporters made the choice of cases seem self-evident: commit a series of crimes, receive large amounts of media attention. This fails to account for the criminals who commit a series of crimes and do not attract large amounts of media attention. The journalists fail to acknowledge the importance of the social context of the event in determining the newsworthiness of the story.

The times began to change in the early 1990s, when support for capital punishment began to waiver, and with this, the types of cases reporters chose to cover also changed. No longer would serial killers and executions with celebrations dominate the headlines. Newspapers would now choose to cover cases that would evoke discussion about the fairness of capital punishment and protest about its use. The change did not happen overnight, but began to take shape in 1994.

4

Protest Cases 1994–2002

Bundy was the epitome of this thing (*serial killing*), there was a four-hour television miniseries starring *People* magazine's sexiest man. You would never see that today, having Brad Pitt star as the Green River Killer. Gacy and Ramirez were both variations on the same themes. Then you had *Silence of the Lambs*, all the attention was peaking. Nowadays how can a person be worse than Hannibal Lecter? Clearly a culture thing was going on that isn't going on now.

—David Von Drehle, *The Washington Post*[209]

Public opinion and mainstream newspaper coverage of capital punishment both began to change in the mid-1990s. Society's overwhelming pro-capital punishment sentiments were beginning to weaken. This was reflected in the death row inmates who took center stage during this period; Karla Faye Tucker and Mumia Abu-Jamal appeared in the newspapers more than any other inmates. These two figures cast a different image on the death penalty than their Bundy, Gacy, Ramirez, and Wuornos predecessors. Unlike the serial killers whose coverage coincided with overwhelming support for capital punishment, the coverage of their cases centered on the appropriateness of capital punishment. For Tucker, the issue was whether a religious white woman should be executed. For Abu-Jamal, the debate was over his alleged innocence and the fairness of his trial.

Newspaper coverage of death row inmates and executions provided another indicator of changing public attitudes. After the early 1990s, newspapers were no longer dominated by stories of serial killers and their anticipated executions. Rather, the most highly profiled capital punishment stories focused on Karla Faye Tucker and Mumia Abu-Jamal (the case of Timothy McVeigh, another high profile case during this period, will be discussed in the following chapter). Abu-Jamal's potential execution and the execution of Tucker generated protest internationally and across the nation.

The mainstream newspaper coverage of each case and interviews with reporters who covered the stories will now be analyzed, with a particular focus on differences between the local and national coverage, the evolution of the coverage over time, connections to larger political or social issues including the death penalty, justice, and public sentiments regarding punishment. Additionally, the newsworthiness of each case will be examined in order to understand what made these cases stand out from other death penalty cases during this period.

THE CASE OF KARLA FAYE TUCKER

Karla Faye Tucker's life of drugs and sex began very early. Her mom, who was a drug addict and prostitute, taught Karla the tricks of the trade as a teenager. Tucker was married by age 16. The marriage didn't last long, and Tucker was soon back working as a prostitute. When she was 20 years old she met Daniel Garrett, who was 14 years older, and soon moved in with him. They both engaged in a party lifestyle that included frequent drug use.[210]

On June 12, Tucker, now 23, and Garrett were hosting a weekend long party at their house in Texas. At the party was their friend Shaun Dean, who had recently broken up with her husband Jerry Lynn Dean. Shaun's nose and lip were swollen from physical abuse by her ex-husband. Tucker never liked Jerry Lynn Dean, who on their initial meeting had left a leaky motorcycle in her living room. Throughout the party, Tucker and others discussed getting back at Jerry Lynn Dean. The talk became more aggressive as the day went on and more and more drugs were taken. In the evening, Daniel Garrett left the party to go to his bartending job at a local bar. After his shift at 2 A.M., Tucker and Jim Leibrant picked up Garrett at the bar and began to discuss plans to steal Jerry Lynn Dean's prized motorcycle for revenge.[211]

The three drove to Dean's apartment, where Leibrant remained outside as a lookout. Tucker and Garrett, who had a .38 caliber gun in his boot, entered the front door with a key taken from Shaun Dean. Once inside, they saw that the motorcycle was in many parts, making it difficult to steal. Tucker also noticed that a three-foot pickaxe was leaning against the wall. As they decided what to do, Dean called out from his bedroom. Garrett rushed the bedroom, striking Dean, 27, with a hammer multiple times on the head. Tucker entered the bedroom swinging the pickaxe at Dean, who was struck more than 20 times. She noticed a woman hiding under the sheets next to Dean. Tucker swung the axe repeatedly into Deborah Ruth Thornton. She was an office worker who had met Jerry Lynn Dean at a pool party a few hours before the murder. The pickaxe was left embedded in her chest.[212]

Before leaving the apartment, Tucker and Garrett took the motorcycle and the keys to Dean's car. They drove Dean's car, with his motorcycle in the trunk, back to their house. They would eventually abandon the car and toss the motorcycle into a nearby river. The next day, Dean's landlord discovered the bodies and contacted the police. The police initially had few leads. That changed when Garrett's brother, along with Tucker's sister, contacted the police about what their siblings had told them about the crimes. They were fearful for their lives after hearing that Tucker and Garrett were threatening to "off" anybody who knew about the murders. Garrett's brother wore a wire, getting Karla Faye and Daniel to talk about their involvement with the murders.[213] On the tape, Tucker would claim to have received sexual pleasure with each swing of the pickaxe. The two were arrested on July 20, 1983. They were indicted on September 13, 1983, on capital murder charges. Jim Leibrant agreed to testify for the state and received a deal where he served 40 months for his involvement.[214]

The Trial

Tucker and Garrett were tried separately for the murders. Tucker's trial, which was first, began on March 2, 1984. Tucker entered a not guilty plea to the murder of Jerry Lynn Dean. The first trial focused exclusively on the murder of Dean. A jury was selected by April 11. There were nine days of testimony, including Leibrant's description of the night of the murder, the tape-recorded conversations obtained by Daniel Garrett's brother, and Tucker's sister, who testified regarding Karla Faye's involvement with the murders. Tucker's only defense was that she was "temporarily insane" due to the amount of drugs she had taken the night of the crime; she did not testify during the trial.[215] The trial ended on April 18; a guilty verdict was rendered the same day. The sentencing phase of the trial started on April 23. Tucker testified to her drug use, and experts testified to the effects of drugs on her state of mind. The jury was unconvinced and sentenced her to death after three hours of deliberation. With the conviction and death sentence in Tucker's first trial, the state decided not to pursue the second murder charge facing her. Garrett was subsequently found guilty and sentenced to death for the murder as well.[216]

When Tucker arrived on Texas' death row in 1984, she was its first woman resident. Garrett was also convicted of the crimes and placed on death row. He died in prison of liver disease in 1993. Tucker had generated some local newspaper attention during her trial, especially after the bizarre details of the crime were discovered, notably her claim that she experienced sexual gratification with each swing of the axe. As T.J. Milling of the *Houston Chronicle* notes:

Tucker's conviction was big news, but her death sentence handed down by a jury of eight women and four men on April 25, 1984, was even bigger. "Pickax murderess sentenced to die," the front-page headline declared in letters an inch high over a picture of Tucker wiping a tear from her eye. Since then, there has been sporadic media interest in Tucker.[217]

Interestingly, the story did not attract any national attention for nearly a decade.

After her sentencing in 1984, two years went by before the *Houston Chronicle's* first stories about the case. On March 28, 1986, though, two stories surfaced on the same day in the *Houston Chronicle*, detailing Tucker's transformation in prison. The articles were titled, "On Death Row; Pickax Murderer Finds A 'New Life'" and "The Embodiment Of Evil? Opinions Have Changed Over Pickax Murderer Karla Faye Tucker."[218] The second story chronicled Tucker's troubled past that led her into prostitution and drugs, but also discussed changes that were taking place during her imprisonment. According to reporter Christy Drennan, Tucker had found God and "managed to get her high school equivalency certificate. She spent mornings working—making quilts and dolls—and afternoons and evenings studying."[219] The newspaper coverage consistently described her "change" while in prison: "initial opinions of police, prosecutors and defense attorneys were that Tucker was the embodiment of evil. Many of those opinions have changed."[220]

After these articles appeared, the Tucker story was briefly covered whenever the courts heard one of her appeals. Also, in Texas, Tucker became a reference point in newspaper discussions of women on death row or in the prison system. Coverage did not become widespread or national, however, until her first execution date was set in 1992. This was the first time that the story attracted the interest of the *New York Times*, in an article reporting that the court had postponed the execution.[221] After this article, the *New York Times* did not report on the case again until six years later when Tucker's execution was only a month away; the *Los Angeles Times* first took note of the story at the same time.[222]

Predictably, the local coverage also became more frequent as Tucker's initial execution date approached (June 30, 1992). The *Houston Chronicle* concentrated on her reforms while in prison and discussed Tucker's religious conversion, her growing number of supporters, and her non-threatening appearance. One story describes Tucker in glowing detail, as follows:

Even today, her charcoal-colored eyes and thick tumble of hair give her a faint gypsy appearance despite a soft saddle of freckles on her nose, a white kerchief pulling her hair back from her face and light blue, jail-issue frock that makes her look somewhat like a housemaid.[223]

The picture and article were the subject of an editorial article the next day titled "No Sympathy For This Born-Again Murderess." The editorial read, in part,

I was astounded that you put a beautiful picture of convicted pickax murderer Karla Faye Tucker on Page One. Also, that you used four or five columns of newsprint on her behalf. My compliments to Carol Rust, she is a gifted writer. But I believe you should have given the bloody victims' pictures equal space and time.[224]

The attention that this case began to receive reflected the growing controversy that would surround Karla Faye Tucker's execution, including the debate over the execution of a woman and her religious conversion in prison.

The *Houston Chronicle* reported that the state Supreme Court granted Tucker a stay on June 23, 1992. After the stay, the Tucker story was in and out of the *Houston Chronicle* sporadically over the next five years. Local coverage focused on her appearance on *Prime Time Live* and the death of Daniel Ryan Garrett from liver disease, who was convicted along with her in the murders, on death row.[225] More execution dates (November 19, 1993 and June 13, 1995), which were postponed, and her marriage to the prison chaplain on January 28, 1995, also generated attention. But it was not until late 1997, as Tucker's fourth and seemingly final execution date approached, that the story became something of a sensation.

Beginning in December 1997, two months before Tucker's scheduled execution on February 3, 1998, the local newspapers covered the story almost daily. Like the serial killer death penalty cases, the Tucker case became the subject of political debate. The controversy, however, differed from the Bundy and Gacy executions. While in those cases the speed of the execution was at issue, with Tucker it was the execution of a woman that sparked debate. As summarized in a December 9, 1997, *Houston Chronicle* article:

> Within the next month, as Gov. George W. Bush mounts his re-election campaign, he is likely to be faced with an issue that no other Texas governor has confronted: Whether the state with the most active death chamber in the nation is willing to strap a woman to a gurney and pump her body full of lethal chemicals.[226]

The next day (December 10, 1997) two more articles dealt with the governor's decision: "Death Penalty; Governor Should Deal With Tucker Case Like Any Other" and an article by William F. Buckley, Jr. titled "Killer Leaves Gov. Bush a Tough Decision."

The national newspapers also followed the details of the case more closely as her pending execution date approached. Howard Rosenberg, a television columnist for the *Los Angeles Times,* wrote about the importance the media had played in bringing the Tucker case into the national spotlight:

> Television has made it possible for viewers themselves to assess Tucker's level of redemption, for she is the first condemned murderer in memory to present her life on national TV. Her case is....herself. She looked as demure as the girl next-door last week when CNN's Larry King faced her for an hour across a plexiglass barrier in prison, the same partition that separates her from her visiting husband, a prison minister she married in 1993.[227]

This quote demonstrates the many aspects that brought Tucker's case into the national spotlight. The description of her as being "as demure as the girl next-door" illustrates the gender issues that helped bring about support for her and the differential treatment she received because she was a woman. (These issues will be discussed in greater detail in the following section.) The growing debate surrounding Tucker's approaching execution was reflected in a *New York Times* article's headline on January 25, 1998: "The Nation: Ambivalence? Incompetence? Fairness? Behind the Death Row Bottleneck."[228]

The Execution

Texas's bloodthirsty criminal justice officials have a dilemma. A Bible-quoting, Jesus-loving, reasonably normal looking woman named Karla Faye Tucker has been sentenced to death. Ordinarily the death penalty is no big deal in Texas, where liberals are required to carry visas and compassion is virtually illegal. It is a state that has shown itself perfectly willing to execute the retarded and railroad the innocent. But the scheduled execution of Ms. Tucker is another matter. Even in Texas, government officials are squeamish about zapping a woman.[229]

As Karla Faye Tucker's execution approached, her case sparked national debates about the morality of the death penalty across the nation. She was on the cover of *People Magazine*, appeared on Pat Robertson's *700 Club*, and received a letter of support from Pope John Paul II. The case continued to be seen as a political issue:

For Governor Bush, considered a likely presidential candidate, Ms. Tucker's case has represented a political dilemma, since he has consistently sought to demonstrate his tough-on-crime credentials but he also has no wish to alienate Mr. Robertson and other Christian conservative leaders who have implored him to show mercy to Ms. Tucker.[230]

The political decision became tougher for Bush as results from various polls were released concerning the Tucker execution. For example, a *Houston Chronicle* poll found that because of her transformation in prison only 48% of Texans believed that Tucker should be executed, while nearly three-quarters of them supported the death penalty in general.[231]

As the execution approached, media attention became even more intense. On the eve of her execution, she was the topic of discussion on news programs nationwide and was mentioned in the *Tonight Show*'s monologue. The *Houston Chronicle* had seven articles dealing with the Tucker story covering every aspect of the case, including one titled "Many still fighting to stop Tucker's execution; Death penalty foes: 'World is watching,'" which covered the international support for Tucker.

The day of the execution, the Tucker story was front-page news across the country. Every detail of the execution was covered, including Tucker's last meal—which consisted of a banana, a peach, and a salad—and her last words "I would like to say to all of you, the Thornton family and Jerry Dean's family, that I am so sorry. I hope God will give you peace with this."[232] The *New York Times* had five stories about the case regarding the gender issue and demonstrations outside the execution. The *Los Angeles Times* had only one, but it was on the front page. *Los Angeles Times* reporter Jesse Katz described the scene outside the execution:

Hundreds of death penalty foes and supporters clamored for attention outside the Huntsville prison—surrounded by nearly as many camera crews and reporters—it was clear that Tucker had at least succeeded in putting a human face on the question of capital punishment and rekindling the debate over its morality, even in the home of the nation's most active death chamber.[233]

This description is much different from that of Bundy's and Gacy's execution, where most of the attention was given to those in favor of capital punishment. In contrast, reporters gave more attention to those against the death penalty outside Tucker's execution.

After the Execution

The following day, journalists covered the aftermath of the execution. The *New York Times* ran an article titled "Karla Tucker is Now Gone, But Several Debates Linger," which opened by noting, "Not since 1977, when a Utah firing squad shot Gary Gilmore, the first prisoner put to death after the Supreme Court allowed resumption of capital punishment, has so much attention been focused on an execution."[234] The *Houston Chronicle* continued its coverage with four stories discussing the Tucker case on February 5, three on February 6, and three on February 7 and 8, 1998.

The Tucker case continued to attract national attention when public opinion polls revealed changed death penalty attitudes in Texas since Tucker's execution. The *New York Times* noted that in 1994, 85 percent of Texans favored the death penalty, but after the execution support dropped to 68 percent. The article quoted the poll organizer regarding the changing sentiments in Texas: "That's still mighty firm support, but it nevertheless represents almost a 20-point drop from our last poll in 1994. People obviously have seriously rethought. Now let's see if that grows and spreads to other states."[235] Tucker has been referenced periodically in the newspapers in recent years whenever another woman was executed or in discussion of religious conversion in prison. Her case brought the anti-death penalty discussion into the national spotlight, where it has remained.

THE CASE OF MUMIA ABU-JAMAL

Mumia Abu-Jamal, who was born Wesley Cook, adopted the name after leaving the Black Panther Party in the early 1970s. As far back as high school, Abu-Jamal was outspoken and active politically. In 1970, he was expelled from Benjamin Franklin high school for passing out pamphlets promoting "black revolutionary student power."[236] Abu-Jamal worked as a journalist for WUHY in Philadelphia until he was asked to resign over what the station official called a "dispute over the objective reporting of the news." In 1981, to supplement his income as a freelance journalist, Abu-Jamal began driving a cab at night. He carried a .38 handgun for protection; while he had legal authorization to own the gun, he did not have a permit to carry it.[237]

On December 10, 1981, according to police reports, police officer Daniel Faulkner pulled William Cook over. Cook got out of the car, and Faulkner ordered Cook to stand against the car for a search. Subsequently, Cook threw a punch at Faulkner and a fight ensued. Mumia Abu-Jamal, Cook's brother, emerged from a parking lot across the street and began to run toward the two men with his gun. According to the police, he began firing. The police reported that while it was not clear whether Faulkner was struck by the first shot, as Abu-Jamal approached, Faulkner was lying on his back. Abu-Jamal fired three or four more shots at the prone Faulkner and, at some point during the incident, Faulkner managed to fire once at Abu-Jamal, striking him in the right side of the chest.

From the first day of coverage, the local newspapers wrote about the story in great detail; four stories appeared initially on December 10, 1981. Abu-Jamal was not a run-of-the-mill criminal, but rather a local celebrity of sorts. He was the outgoing president of the Association of Black Journalists, former reporter for public radio, and a freelance writer. *Philadelphia* magazine named Abu-Jamal one of its "People to Watch in '81." He also was an activist and a local supporter of the radical group MOVE, whose dreadlock hairstyle he adopted, and was active in the Black Panther Party while still in high school.

The Inquirer immediately recognized the newsworthiness of the Abu-Jamal story. The headlines the first day pointed to many of the elements that would bring his case international attention: "The Suspect, One Who Raised His Voice" and "The Accused: Friends Can't Fathom 'Brilliant' Newsman As Murder Suspect." Instantaneous support for Abu-Jamal came from the future president of Association of Black Journalists, Joe Davidson, who stated:

"We are going to continue to support Mumia," said Joe Davidson, who will become president of the local ABJ chapter in January. "The policeman's shooting is a terrible tragedy, but we feel anybody, regardless of the circumstances, is deserving of a complete and fair defense. We feel he is still our brother and we must stand beside him."[238]

Davidson was the first to take note of the racial and political issues that this case would come to symbolize.

"We are disturbed by disparaging news reports about Mr. Jamal's political and religious beliefs," Davidson said. "As an organization dedicated to truth and fairness in journalism, we will continue to monitor media coverage on this matter. We hope that Mr. Jamal will be tried in the courtroom and not in the press."[239]

Early coverage commonly referred to Abu-Jamal's organizational affiliations and radio commentaries against the "system." Race also was a major issue from the outset with discussion of Abu-Jamal's former association with the Black Panthers and his current support of MOVE. MOVE has a long and controversial history in Philadelphia, including a 1978 incident at their Philadelphia compound that resulted in the death of police officer. MOVE is a loose-knit, mostly black group whose members all adopt the surname Africa, advocate a "back-to-nature" lifestyle and preach against technology.[240] This added to the racial dynamics of the case.

After Abu-Jamal was denied bail on January 12, 1982, the story went away for a couple of months until the pre-trial hearings began. The media covered the hearings intensely, and the race issue continued to take center stage in large part due to Abu-Jamal and his lawyer Anthony Jackson's tactics. At several hearings, Jackson stated that the slaying and the arrest of Abu-Jamal had racial overtones that would "polarize the community."[241] Additionally, members of MOVE started to attend the hearings and interrupt the court. During an early hearing in April 30, 1982, Abu-Jamal was removed from the courtroom because of his behavior, which often included yelling at the judge and lawyers during the proceedings. These early tactics, which received considerable amount of attention from reporters, only foreshadowed the chaos that ensued during his trial.

The Trial

From the very beginning, the local newspaper covered every detail of the trial, including daily stories about jury selection. Mumia Abu-Jamal, who planned to represent himself, was quickly removed from the jury selection process. Judge Sabo indicated that he was taking too long and was "unsettling" many of the potential jurors. *The Inquirer* reported:

Several prospective jurors left the courtroom Tuesday saying they were too upset and afraid to serve after being questioned by Abu-Jamal, who wears his hair in the dreadlock style of the MOVE sect.[242]

The jury was selected after a week of controversy, and the *Philadelphia Inquirer* detailed the selection of nine whites and three blacks for the jury and the racial issues surrounding jury selection.[243]

The first day of the trial, July 18, 1982, began with the judge not allowing Abu-Jamal to act as his own attorney and a courtroom brawl involving Abu-Jamal's brothers.[244] Abu-Jamal insisted that John Africa, the founder of MOVE, represent him. The judge would not allow this because Africa did not have a license to practice law. There were 12 days of testimony during the trial, with various witnesses testifying to Abu-Jamal's role in the shooting. Neither Abu-Jamal nor his brother testified to the events the night of the murder. For years to come, the details of the trial would be a source of continued debate and controversy. Did Abu-Jamal get a fair trial? Was Judge Sabo just during the trial? These questions would be the cornerstone of the media sensation that would surround Mumia Abu-Jamal in the decades to come.

On July 2, 1982, Mumia Abu-Jamal was found guilty of murder, after the jury deliberated for five hours, and became eligible for the death penalty. Abu-Jamal added to his image of a political prisoner by shouting, "On a move, long live John Africa. This system is finished" as he was escorted from the courtroom.[245] The following day the jury sentenced him to the electric chair after listening to Abu-Jamal deny the killing for the first time. His statement also featured an attack on the judge ("Judge Sabo deserves no honor from me, this courtroom is run on force not honor. He is executioner, a hangman"), jury ("You are not a jury of my peers"), and political power in America coming from violence ("It's America who seized the land from the Indian race, and it was not done through preaching Christianity and civilization. I think that America has proven that quote to be the truth"). He did not offer any mitigating circumstances (for example, that he had never been arrested before, he had five children, or that it was not premeditated, a necessary condition of the death penalty) that may have saved him from a death sentence.

It was not until nearly a year later that the judge officially sentenced Abu-Jamal to die.[246] Abu-Jamal continued to make noise during this hearing by threatening the judge and once again praising MOVE. Marc Kaufman, who covered the case from the beginning for the *Philadelphia Inquirer*, discussed the problems with Mumia Abu-Jamal's defense:

He was known mostly for his connection with MOVE; that was how he was understood for the first decade. The death penalty was a kind of foregone conclusion from the way the trial was carried out. He never really made a case for mitigating circumstances. He never made a case other than the fact that John Africa was not allowed to be his attorney. He let his court appointed attorney question a few witnesses but he did not mount a vigorous defense. Sitting in the courtroom watching, I was surprised that he never argued the logistics of the shooting. He never discussed the details between how he and the officer were shot once.[247]

After this sentence, the Abu-Jamal case dropped from media visibility almost completely, only garnering references in conjunction with MOVE activities, the continuing racial problems in Philadelphia, and police officer shootings. In 1985, MOVE was again in conflict with the police. A police assault on a MOVE house in West Philadelphia was capped by the use of a rooftop bomb that ignited a blaze that took 11 lives and reduced 61 row houses to rubble. The whole episode was broadcast on television and covered nationwide. Abu-Jamal's connection with the group added to his status as a political outsider and to his growing number of supporters.

The groundswell of support surrounding the "free Mumia" campaign is first mentioned in the *Philadelphia Inquirer* on July 15, 1990, in an article entitled "Abu-Jamal Stirs Foes of Execution." This piece noted the growing support for Abu-Jamal after his trial:

> In the ensuing years, the very qualities that made Abu-Jamal's case so striking in the first place have turned the case into a sort of minor cause celebre for opponents of the death penalty in the United States, Canada and Europe. His supporters have written tens of thousands of letters and collected thousands of signatures on petitions urging Governor Casey to commute his death sentence.[248]

This is the only mention of him and his supporters for another three years. As Marc Kaufman indicated:

> The trial back in 1981 was big news in Philadelphia and Pennsylvania but it was not until the 1990s that it became a national story. Abu-Jamal was a bright, articulate guy who got together with the right people to get his message out. He wrote articles in different publications and got lots of attention for his book *Live From Death Row.* In late 1980s and 1990s he became huge on the web; he might be the first case where the Internet got the message out.[249]

But it was not until 1994 that newspaper attention once again focused on the case of Mumia Abu-Jamal. This time the attention was not just local, but national and international, and it would not go away. On April 13, 1994, with a death warrant on the horizon, the journalists firmly took note of the story with headlines like "Death Warrant at Issue for Casey. He Agreed to Meet With Backers and Foes of Mumia Abu-Jamal: The Inmate is on Death Row."[250] What is interesting about the headline is that the Abu-Jamal story happened so long ago that the reporter had to remind readers that "the inmate is on death row." Also around this time, the death penalty in general and Abu-Jamal more specifically started to become a political issue in Philadelphia and Pennsylvania. Reporters noted how "the case also promises to become a highly emotional moment in the nation's uneasy embrace of the death penalty."[251]

National attention to Abu-Jamal was slow to develop and only really took hold as his number of supporters, who believed he was unjustly convicted, grew. The *New York Times* first reported on the story on December 13, 1981, immediately after the crime happened, picking up on the racial elements of the case. The article started: "The arrest of a black radio reporter for the gunshot slaying of a white police officer has raised tensions between the police and some black groups." The coverage dealt explicitly with race, detailing Abu-Jamal's involvement with the Association of Black Journalists and talking about how the case had been turned over "to W. Wilson Goode, the city Managing Director, who is black."[252] The *New York Times* did not report on the case again, however, until May 15, 1994, when National Public Radio was about to broadcast Abu-Jamal's commentaries on the radio. The *New York Times* also reported on the NPR decision not to air the broadcasts because of pressure from victims and police organizations. On May 17, 1994, they reported that "over the last 12 years, Mr. Abu-Jamal's case has been the subject of an unusual amount of public attention,"[253] and listed the growing number of supporters and celebrities that backed him. After the NPR article, the *New York Times* did not report on the case for a year, but as the number of demonstrations and celebrities grew and an execution date was set for August 17, 1995, the coverage became more consistent. This, however, was more attention than Abu-Jamal received on the West coast.

The story was not reported at all by the *Los Angeles Times* until May 17, 1994, when the Entertainment Desk noted the NPR decision not to broadcast Abu-Jamal's commentaries.[254] The first news story dealing with the Abu-Jamal case was not until July 2, 1995, when the governor set his execution date.

National coverage, while scarce, focused much more heavily on the racial and political issues of the case. The coverage detailed the growing number of demonstrators involved with the case, Abu-Jamal's political background, and the racial makeup of the jury some 14 years prior. Additionally, the national coverage did not focus on the case until 1994, when public support for the death penalty had started to decline.

The attention Abu-Jamal and his supporters received led police organizations to become more vocal. Continued racial problems in Philadelphia only added to the story. Philadelphia was dealing with a long history of corrupt and racist cops that only inflamed the Abu-Jamal story in the newspapers. Marc Kaufman and Julia Cass, reporters for the *Philadelphia Inquirer*, discussed the importance of the Philadelphia setting in terms of attention to Abu-Jamal's case:

The image of Philadelphia justice plays a central role in the belief of thousands of people across the United States and the world that death-row inmate Mumia Abu-Jamal is innocent and did not get a fair trial. The Philadelphia police who arrested him in 1981 had a reputation, acquired especially during the years in which Frank Rizzo was police commissioner and mayor, for toughness bordering on brutality. Even today, scores of drug convictions are being overturned because Philadelphia police officers planted evidence on innocent people, then lied about it in court.[255]

This article exemplified the story's rebirth in the mid-90s. The story contained a point-by-point description of all the major players and points of contention during the history of the case; it also contained a graphic with a timeline of the case.

Abu-Jamal continued to stir political and social debate in 1995 because of his claim of innocence and unjust conviction. For one thing, several academics began to weigh in supporting Abu-Jamal. Various professors were quoted about the inequity of the criminal justice system and racial and economic disparities in sentencing; some even talked about their use of Abu-Jamal's writings in class.

Abu-Jamal's legal appeals for his approaching death continued to supply newspapers with more than enough fuel for ongoing coverage. Indeed, the newspaper coverage had a soap-opera-like feel to it. The first day of the hearing got off "peacefully enough," as the *Inquirer* described, but things returned to "normal" for the case as the paper described the scene:

By mid-afternoon, though, the hearing erupted with angry outbursts from two Abu-Jamal supporters in the audience, prompting Common Pleas Senior Judge Albert F. Sabo to eject them from the courtroom. One, an elderly black man, took a swing at a court officer as he was led away. "This is getting to be a circus," Sabo declared after the unidentified man had gone.[256]

The following day's headline continued to detail the craziness of the hearings: "Lawyer Overcome in Heated Dispute Under Cross-Examination, Abu-Jamal's Trial Attorney Lost His Breath. Also, A Fracas Made the Victim's Widow Run From Court." After a stay was granted, Abu-Jamal attracted national attention with his request for a new trial and his increasing number of supporters. The near-daily coverage went away when the judge refused to grant Abu-Jamal a new trial on September 16, 1995.

Local coverage continued to be much more detailed, describing the growing Abu-Jamal phenomenon and further pro-Mumia demonstrations in Philadelphia and around the world. One article in particular, titled "Abu-Jamal's Long Climb to a World Stage, from Death-Row Cell to Global Cause Celebre," reported on the demonstrations around the world:

"Mumia Abu-Jamal is a symbol," said the woman, Marie Agnes Comesque, a writer and organizer of the burgeoning Mumia movement in France. "He represents the opposition to the system. He is a Panther. It's unbelievable." And last Thursday in Greece, two bombs went off in American-owned banks. A group called to take responsibility for the blasts, saying they were in protest of Abu-Jamal's death sentence.[257]

The reporters went on to discuss groups all over the world who both supported Abu-Jamal and opposed the death penalty. The article appeared on the same day as an interview Abu-Jamal gave from prison. In the interview, "he says that he is baffled by the tide of support behind him, thinks the judge hearing his appeal is biased against defendants, and that America's death rows are filled with men unjustly convicted."[258] The reporter noted that not everybody was thrilled with Abu-Jamal's new celebrity status, including the police, Mrs. Faulkner, and Pam Lyncher, a Houston "housewife, mother and crime victim" who founded a group called Justice for All in Texas in response to the "Free Graham" movement (Gary Graham was executed in Texas in 2000 amidst protest). She remarked that Abu-Jamal was not the first, or the only, death-row inmate to become a cause celebre. Two years previously, many of the players now promoting Abu-Jamal's cause in Philadelphia were in Houston in support of convicted killer Gary Graham. "When I started reading about this Mumia thing, it was like complete déjà vu. It's the same Hollywood people, the same legal maneuvering, the same disregard for the victims of crime," said Lyncher.[259]

Abu-Jamal's name continued to be mentioned in the newspapers when demonstrations took place around the country, but coverage was not consistent. Then in 1996, the state Supreme Court ordered the judge to set a date within 30 days for legal arguments on whether to hear testimony from a key prosecution witness at Abu-Jamal's 1982 trial who now said she lied under pressure from police. The hearing started on October 1, 1996, and was covered intensely by the local press; Abu-Jamal's lawyers claimed he was framed by the police. The hearing only lasted a few days, and on November 1 the judge denied the request for a new trial, ending another chapter in Abu-Jamal's court battles.

Over the next couple of years, Abu-Jamal would be in and out of the news with more demonstrations around the world and his commentaries on prison being played on radios and at college graduations. The event that captured the most media attention during this period was a planned rock concert in New Jersey by Rage Against the Machine, Beastie Boys, and a variety of other artists. The proceeds from the concert were to benefit Mumia Abu-Jamal's defense fund. The concert stirred controversy in New Jersey and gathered national headlines when the police officers' unions tried to boycott working at the show. Their boycott was unsuccessful as they were ordered to work the concert; some 2,000 refunds were issued when the public learned that the proceeds from the concert would benefit Abu-Jamal, but the show went on to a full house.

On October 13, 1999, Governor Tom Ridge once again signed a death warrant for Abu-Jamal and set a December 2, 1999, execution date. The date would stand for only two weeks before another stay was granted. Then Abu-Jamal was allowed to fire his defense team. The new team took over in the spring of 2001 and supported the idea that the killing of Faulkner was a "mob-hit."[260] A new set of appeals started in August, with more rallies and intense local coverage. The appeals were dismissed on November 21, 2001, but this was not the end for Abu-Jamal's case.

On December 18, 2001, Mumia Abu-Jamal's death sentence was lifted. The judge ruled that the jury may have misunderstood sentencing issues. Lifting the death sentence made national news. The *New York Times* and *Los Angeles Times* covered the story on the front page. Abu-Jamal's lawyers continue to fight to have his conviction overturned, while police organizations and the victim's family remain outraged over his removal from death row. The newspapers reported on the story for a few days after the decision, but the story has since disappeared from the media. The removal of Abu-Jamal from death row would have been unthinkable during the 1980s and early 1990s, but times had changed. The newspapers were no longer filled with articles celebrating a serial killer's execution; it was the release of a black "radical," convicted of shooting a white police officer, that attracted headlines.

THE NEWSWORTHINESS OF PROTEST CASES

Among these "protest cases," the most publicized during the period from 1994 to 2002 were the cases of Karla Faye Tucker and Mumia Abu-Jamal. Interestingly, serial killing itself did not disappear between 1994–2002 when media coverage declined; rather, serial killers continued to commit multiple homicides. Compared to the hundreds of stories on Bundy and Gacy in the 1980s and early 1990s, they received scant coverage. This reflects a change in attitude by reporters, not a change in reality. For example, Maturino Resendiz was sentenced to death in May 2000 for the 1998 bludgeoning murder of a doctor in Texas. Resendiz asserted he was an angel on a mission from God to destroy evil and confessed to at least 19 homicides that occurred between 1997 and 1999. However, Resendiz's murders only led to six *New York Times* and 11 *Los Angeles Times* stories. Another serial killer overlooked at the time was Robert Lee Yates, Jr., sentenced to death by lethal injection for the aggravated murders of two women on October 10, 2002. At the time he was serving a 408-year sentence under a plea agreement two years prior with Spokane County. He admitted to murdering 13 other people since 1975, yet only two *New York Times* and nine *Los Angeles Times* articles discussed Yates. In Florida, Danny Rolling was sentenced to death in 1994 for five murders that terrorized the University of Florida in 1991, and he also accepted responsibility (in 2002) for another three slayings. Yet Rolling's murders were the subject of only three *New York Times* and four *Los Angeles Times* articles. Gerald Stano, discussed in Chapter 3, who was tied to over 40 murders, was executed in Florida to little fanfare in 1998. David Von Drehle argues that the media's interest had indeed changed:

> Look at the Green River Killer, who was allegedly just apprehended. In the 80s there was real serial killer mania and that was the big unsolved case. If that case was closed in 1985 every newspaper and television would have covered it, Ann Rule would have a book about it; competing books would be out there. Today, the story has gone nowhere in the mainstream press.[261]

Apparently, serial killers were no longer the high profile category of death row cases. Rather, the types of cases that generated large amounts of newspaper attention were those that expressed doubt about the death penalty's appropriateness and justice, thereafter generating noticeable protests and controversy. The Tucker case raised doubts not about the innocence of the soon to be punished person, but about the appropriateness of the death penalty itself. By contrast, the case of Mumia Abu-Jamal focused media and public attention on a debate over justice: had Abu-Jamal actually committed the murder of which he was accused?

The Newsworthiness of Karla Faye Tucker

Tucker was one of only 68 people executed across the nation in 1998, yet her story was voted the second most important in Texas in 1998 by the

Houston Chronicle, trailing only the racially motivated murder of James Byrd in Jasper. Reporters believed that newspapers were drawn to the case because she would be the first woman executed in Texas since the Civil War and only the second in the nation since the death penalty was reinstated in 1976. This would support the notion of novelty in explaining the media's coverage of Tucker. She was different from all those others who had been put to death in Texas in the last 100 years. For example, Carol Rust, *Houston Chronicle* reporter, explained that

Tucker stood out from all the other inmates in Texas; she was a woman, that made her different. In Texas, executions themselves no longer attract a lot of media attention; you need something different to get people talking. Then the fact that the religious leaders got behind her and all the national media attention just pushed the story more and more.[262]

Novelty definitely explained some of the Tucker case's appeal to the media, but alone this explanation is too simplistic. If gender was the sole factor contributing to the amount of newspaper coverage, more people would have heard of Velma Barfield, the first woman executed in the nation since the death penalty's reinstatement in 1984, or Judy Buenoano, who was executed shortly after Tucker.

Velma Barfield was the first woman executed in the modern era of the death penalty. She was executed in 1984 in North Carolina for poisoning Stuart Taylor, a friend. In addition, Barfield admitted to poisoning her mother and two elderly people she cared for as a nurse, although she was not convicted in these cases. Judy Buenoano, who was executed two months after Tucker, was a Latina who was given the name "Black Widow." She was convicted of fatally poisoning her husband, drowning her teenage son, and trying to blow up her fiancé with a car bomb—all for insurance money. She collected about one-quarter of a million dollars and stood to gain more than half a million more had her fiancé died. Neither of these cases generated much media attention. For example, the number of articles with references to Karla Faye Tucker in the Lexis/Nexis database was 498, compared with 47 for Velma Barfield and 44 for Judy Buenoano.

To understand the amount of newspaper coverage devoted to Tucker, then, we must examine the interaction of her race, class, gender, and religion, and how this may have made her story unique. As feminist scholar Elizabeth Spelman has noted, it is never the case that "the treatment of a woman has only to do with her gender and nothing to do with her class or race."[263] This interaction seems to have been the distinctive factor in the Karla Faye Tucker story. Tucker's case did not fit the stereotypes that many people have of prisoners, and especially murderers, in our society.

Journalists at the time made frequent references to Tucker's race and to the fact that her "whiteness" resulted in a good deal of the support for her. A Tucker supporter was quoted in the *Houston Chronicle* as saying, "she didn't fit what we thought people on death row were like."[264] Statements like these cannot be understood without reference to Tucker's race, which was an important factor in bringing her case into the national spotlight.

Additionally, media accounts of the case made frequent references to Karla's unfortunate upbringing; it was often used as a justification for her actions. Karla Faye Tucker's class background reads like that of an after-school television special. She was the youngest of three daughters whose parents divorced when she was eight. Tucker's mother introduced her to drugs when she was nine years old and forced her into prostitution when she was 14. She states that she and her mother shared drugs "like lipstick";[265] she subsequently became addicted to heroin and toured, as a groupie, with the rock band The Allman Brothers. At the time of the murders she was living a life of drugs and prostitution; the night of the murders she was said to have been taking drugs. Biographer Beverly Lowry concludes that Tucker was on a self-destructive course of drugs, bikers, fights, and prostitution that would have killed her.

Similarly, *People Magazine* wrote a story on Tucker's childhood, concluding, "how anyone could commit such a crime is hard to fathom, but Tucker's childhood may offer some clues."[266] But would wealthy women of privilege receive sympathy from the media if they had an unfortunate upbringing? Would people have been as sympathetic if she had been a black woman? Karla Faye Tucker's mother is described as the real criminal in many media accounts. Why did people feel sympathy for Tucker and not others with similarly rough childhoods?

Much of the newspaper attention surrounding Tucker focused on the fact that she was a woman. Reporters talked about "the prospect of executing a woman" as if it was something altogether different from executing a man. This belief is rooted in traditional gender roles and expectations for men and women that the media emphasized. Many saw Tucker's gender as the only thing that gave her hope in her appeals and the only thing that gave her case any newsworthiness. As Victor Streib, dean of Ohio Northern University's College of Law and an expert on female executions argued, "if it were Karl Tucker instead of Karla Tucker we wouldn't be having this conversation."[267] For one thing, women are infrequent on death row. They account for 10 percent of murder arrests but only 2 percent of death sentences imposed at the trial level, 1.5 percent of the persons presently on death row, and 1.1 percent (11 of 820) of those actually executed since its reinstatement.[268] Women, of course, do not kill as often as men, and when they do, their crimes tend to be explained by domestic conflict.

The fact that Tucker was a woman led reporters to discuss her appearance more often than in articles about male inmates. Almost all of the articles about Tucker contain some description of her looks:

Gender may not be an explicit component of her plea, but being a petite, photogenic, rosy-lipped woman of 38 with flowing brown curls has surely kept it from falling on deaf ears.[269]

Ms. Tucker has gained undeserved sympathy because of her sex and her doe-eyed good looks.[270]

The 38-year-old, 5 foot 3, 120 pound Ms. Tucker would be only the second woman executed.[271]

Tucker was a slim, fine-boned woman of 38 with artfully applied lipstick and rouge.[272]

This is contrasted with Barfield, who was a "portly, bespectacled grandmother"[273] and "a tough-looking broad," as a *Newsweek* correspondent put it.[274] Buenoano is described as a "slender grandmother in a blue-green prison uniform."[275] The fact that there is any discussion of their looks opens up the question of whether there would have been descriptions such as "slender" or "portly" or "attractive" if these were men being discussed. Are men's height, weight, hair, and lip color reported in stories about them? Why is it acceptable and even expected to discuss women's appearances as if it is somehow important to the story? The focus on women's appearance in the media should not be that surprising given the amount of emphasis that society places on their looks compared to men. Deborah Rhode details the media's focus on appearance of women:

A 1970 *Newsweek* account of a march on a prominent male-only public bar reported that the vice-president of NOW led the way in a purple jumpsuit. Ti-Grace Atkinson had a "dreamy, softly sexy style" and Germaine Greer had "lean good looks," while Kate Millet did not "wash her hair."[276]

Rhode notes that such gender stereotypes have declined in frequency, but have by no means vanished from the media landscape. She argues that this kind of coverage not only diminishes women's credibility, but it also marginalizes their substantive message.

It was not just Tucker's gender that was emphasized by reporters, then, but the fact that she was attractive; frequent references to her looks were made in newspaper accounts. She was described as having curly brown hair, rosy lips, girl next-door looks, fine bones, and a pretty face. As biographer Beverly Lowry states, "trying to imagine this attractive young woman as evil incarnate, I read the story again and again."[277] By contrast, both Barfield and Buenoano were described as grandmothers in their 50s. Barfield was described as an "unsympathetic, wizened, tough-looking older lady."[278] The media also picked up on the sexual elements of the case. Lowry described Tucker as having "direct, uncompromised, highly sexual charm." The fact that Tucker said she had sexual gratification with each swing of the pickaxe was the focus of much attention. Constant references to this in conjunction with her having been a prostitute also made her an extremely sexualized figure.

To explain why a former prostitute garnered so much sympathy, much of the newspaper coverage focused on Tucker's conversion to Christianity while in prison, a conversion complemented by her marriage to the prison chaplain and her work with prison-based ministry. Her religious beliefs were the focus for much of the support she received. The Pope sent a clemency-seeking letter to the governor on her behalf. Television evangelist Pat Robertson had Tucker on his television show *The 700 Club*, and she became a posterchild of Christian conservative groups' support; this is remarkable given that these groups typically support capital punishment.

Religion served as the intervening variable that transformed Tucker from being viewed as a sexualized double murderer to being portrayed as a sympathetic figure. This transformation was the motivating factor behind much of her support. The Christian Broadcasting Network's Pat Robertson first interviewed her in 1993 and caused some evangelical Christians to reconsider their support for the death penalty. Richard Cizik, a policy analyst at the National Association of Evangelicals representing 42,000 churches, wrote: "the execution could produce a certain moral revulsion among evangelicals because she is a woman of such obvious spiritual change."[279] One Christian columnist, F.M. Richborug of Dallas, described Ms. Tucker as "this miraculously sweet-spirited little soldier in the war against criminal wickedness."[280] Religious leaders were quoted as saying that she "puts a human face on the death penalty" and that "it gives people a life they can identify with." Supporters are quoted as saying that she "put a particularly human face on those condemned to death"[281] and "didn't fit what we thought people on death row were like."[282] These are the arguments religious leaders, who are normally strict death penalty advocates, gave for supporting Tucker, even though they disregarded many other inmates who said they found God. Here, a critical factor may have been that Tucker found not simply religion but Christianity.

Additionally, her supporters claimed it was the "authenticity and depth" of her conversion[283] that was so captivating; this implies that others who have found God have not been genuine. Pat Robertson has described Tucker as an "extraordinary woman" who deserves mercy because of her "authentic spiritual conversion."[284] Her conversion was also stressed because of where she came from; newspaper accounts discussed her transformation "from prostitute to missionary." This religious transformation was the necessary element that created the media event. The transformation from murderer to woman of God brought Tucker into a sympathetic light in many people's eyes. Religion, with its emphasis on repentance and forgiveness, provided the foundation for many people's support for Tucker and their opposition to capital punishment. Tucker's transformation made it seem unnecessary to many to execute her.

The fact that the case took place in Texas was also very important. The Tucker story cannot be looked at apart from the context of its traditional Texas surroundings. Quotes in the newspapers reflect this awareness:

> Texans just don't treat their women that way.
> She fit the mold of the pure Texas gal.
> She looked at demure as the girl next door.[285]

The setting of Texas, which is home to many conservative Christians, offered a contrast between traditional gender roles and the execution of a woman. The effect of the religious element and support in the Tucker case led Governor Bush to say he "sought guidance through prayer" in making his decision, and "may God bless Karla Fay Tucker and God bless her victims and their families."[286] Tucker was not the only woman executed who was religious. Buenoano and Barfield both found Christianity. Barfield was a devout Catholic all her life who received support from Reverend Billy Graham (Buenoano's religion never became an issue in the media). Their cases did not become media sensations like Tucker because it was not just one favorable characteristic (i.e. being a woman) that she had, but a combination of desirable qualities that helped her story in the press.

Consequently, one must look at the interaction of Tucker's race, class, gender, and religious characteristics to get a better understanding of why so much media attention was focused on Tucker. *Los Angeles Times* reporter Jesse Katz observed:

All these factors taken together, allowed her to do what very few death row inmates are able to do—convince the public that they are human beings, that they are something more than their crimes.[287]

If Tucker had possessed only one or two of these elements, the story would have still received coverage. However, the combination of all four elements led to well above average attention. Indeed, statements about Tucker that do not contain at least two or three of these references are rare: "kindly-looking, born-again-Christian woman," or "petite 38-year old inmate, a convicted pickax murderer who later declared herself a born-again Christian," or "a soft-spoken, gentle-looking, born-again Christian." [288]

Reporter Sam Verhovek quotes David R. Dow, a University of Houston law professor who has represented more than 20 death row prisoners. He explains why people saw the humanity in Tucker and refuse to see it in others:

Because the truth is that almost all execution victims are like Tucker. Most come to regret that they killed. Most have families who love them. Many find religion. Many are articulate. Some are even physically attractive. Dow argues that Tucker had five characteristics that made her a media sensation: she was a woman, white, attractive, articulate and a Christian. A lot of people on death row have three of those characteristics; some have four. But very few have all five, and I simply don't see another case commanding this amount of attention.[289]

Tucker broke the stereotype of the typical prisoner as black. Additionally, people seem to feel for and understand people who have had a rough childhood, especially when they are physically attractive. In addition, traditional gender ideologies frequently include protecting women from harm, and sometimes favor those who proclaim a belief in God. It was all of these factors working in combination that created the Karla Faye Tucker story. In comparison, Barfield and Buenoano were older, not physically attractive, and did not have childhoods that created sympathy. Buenoano also was Latina, a factor that may have worked against her in the media. The rest of the people executed in this country up to that point were men. Consequently, Tucker's case had the right mix of newsworthy elements to create the media sensation.

Six days after Karla Faye Tucker's execution, Steven Renfro was executed in Texas. The masses of anti-death penalty demonstrators present a week before were reduced to a group of two dozen. No celebrities spoke against Renfro's execution, and the media circus had left town. The media then turned to answer the question: what effect, if any, did the Tucker spectacle have on the death penalty? Karla Faye Tucker did manage to create renewed debate about the death penalty in Texas and across the nation. Polls indicated before the Tucker case that roughly 85 percent of Texans favored the death penalty. The polls after her execution found that only 68 percent supported the death penalty in the state.[290] Columnist Ellen Goodman argued, "This was a time when closed minds were reopened, however narrowly. A time when opinions cast in black and white—pro and con death penalty, tough and soft on crime —were suddenly shaded with Tucker gray."[291]

Many articles suggest that the support for Tucker and renewed debate about the death penalty arose because she was able to put a human face on the question of capital punishment. But why did so many people see Tucker's humanity while refusing to see it in so many others? Carol Rust of the *Houston Chronicle* points out that

> with all the attention that Tucker received both within Texas and nationally, it quickly dissipated after the execution. And we had another woman executed a few years later, Betty Lou Beets, and it didn't garner nearly as much attention...I guess you had to be the first[292]

Additionally, why did the human face have to be a white, religious, and attractive woman? Tucker's execution went forward amidst protest, but a black male convicted of killing a white police officer did not, which raises the question: what attracted the media to Mumia Abu-Jamal?

The Newsworthiness of Mumia Abu-Jamal

Unlike Tucker, Mumia Abu-Jamal did not have demographics working in his favor. Mumia Abu-Jamal was not novel like Tucker. He was a black male on death row, not a white woman. What made his case stand out from the rest? A good deal of the press that followed the Abu-Jamal case can be attributed to self-promotion in the form of books, speeches, and radio commentaries. Controversy also surrounded the case. Abu-Jamal's claims of innocence and an unjust trial rallied support around him. There is also no denying the importance of race in bringing his case into the national spotlight. Many saw a connection between his case and past racial injustices and social movements of the 1960s. The national press continuously referred to the social issues and conflicts that this case came to represent, describing how "in the nearly 14 years since, the case has become an international cause celebre and, for some, a battleground in the political and cultural wars stretching from the 1960s to the 1990s."[293] National reporters consistently made comparisons with Abu-Jamal supporters and the 1960s. This connection was helped by the fact that Abu-Jamal's lawyer for the hearings was Leonard I. Weinglass, who the *New York Times* noted was "a veteran of some of the most politically charged trials of recent decades, including that of the Chicago Eight after the 1968 Democratic Convention."[294]

Additionally, his supporters are referenced as "grass-roots community activists," suggesting a 60s-like movement. A *Los Angeles Times* article described them

in blue jeans and tie-dyed T-shirts, political activists all across the nation have joined arms with kinte-wearing African Americans to drum up grass-roots demonstrations reminiscent of 1960s anti-war protests. Their common shouted demand: "Free Mumia, Now!".[295]

The *New York Times* echoed these sentiments in their story on Abu-Jamal's stay of execution, which said that "the hearing, like the trial, has been haunted by the unresolved political and cultural conflicts of the 1960s and 1970s, pitting two sharply different views of the truth, from two sharply different patches of the United States."[296] The 1960s metaphors continued in an August 13, 1995, *New York Times* article: "The protests and passions of the 1960s made a comeback here today as more that 3,500 people rallied against the death penalty and demanded a new trial for a condemned radio journalist and former Black Panther, Mumia Abu-Jamal."[297]. The political nature of the case would be the driving force behind the continuing media coverage of Abu-Jamal.

The national coverage focused heavily on the social and political connotations of the case, supporting Chibnall's notion of newsworthiness. Even entertainment and popular culture columnists were taking note. For example, an article titled "Ideas and Trends; The Case That Brought Back Radical Chic" detailed the number of authors and celebrities who clung onto the Abu-Jamal case. The author noted the tradition of celebrities backing liberal causes and prisoners.[298]

The *New York Times* became active in the Abu-Jamal controversy, first publishing an essay against the execution on July 14, 1995, by writer E.L. Doctorow, which was subsequently published and cited across the country. Then on August 13, 1995, they printed an article by Lynne Abraham, the Philadelphia District Attorney, that tried to break down the myths and celebrity that had attached themselves to the Abu-Jamal case.[299] Additionally, the *Los Angeles Times* became involved and printed a column titled "Rallying

Round the Wrong Cause; Mumia Abu-Jamal's Supporters Should Consider That He Never Denied Shooting The Officer" on August 20, 1995, and another article titled "U.S. Inmate Has A Hold On Europe's Power Elite; Politicians, Philosophers Seek To Save Convicted Killer Mumia Abu-Jamal, Saying His Case Shows America's Racism And The Barbarism Of Capital Punishment" on September 6, 1995.[300] The *Los Angeles Times* continued to cover the controversy with articles titled "A Widow Fights Back; She Deplores Celebrity Support For Her Husband's Convicted Killer" and "Journalist's Death Sentence Has People Judging The Judge."[301]

Abu-Jamal's image as a political prisoner was strengthened when it was revealed that the F.B.I. had collected information about him since his youth. On June 12, 1995, the *Philadelphia Inquirer* ran an article reporting that ever since Abu-Jamal and 11 other youths protested the imprisonment of Black Panther leader Huey Newton in 1969, the F.B.I. had been following and collecting information about Abu-Jamal. The 700-page document was obtained by Abu-Jamal through the Freedom of Information Act and included a wide range of information that was released to the *Philadelphia Inquirer*:

> From 1969 to 1974, the government monitored the teenage activist, sending a steady stream of messages—"airtels" in FBI jargon—to headquarters in Washington about his speeches at public gatherings, his writings in the Panther newspaper and his comings and goings to Panther chapters in other cities. Agents knew what his high school principal thought of him ("promising") and what he majored in at college (Third World Studies). The file ranges from wiretaps of the people who answered the phone at Black Panther headquarters ("Right on, sister") to raising suspicions as to whether Abu-Jamal was involved in the murder of the governor of Bermuda in 1973.[302]

This type of information only added to the growing support for Abu-Jamal. In addition, his first book, *Live From Death Row*, was released to a national audience in 1996.

Celebrities and black activists continued to hold rallies for Abu-Jamal all across the country. Abu-Jamal's cause continued to grow, fueled increasingly by the Internet, which boasts hundreds of Mumia sites. The *Philadelphia Inquirer* reported on this trend:

> So the organizations promoting Millions for Mumia have been enlisting stars, staging hip-hop concerts, encouraging teach-ins at schools and, above all, using the Internet. "I think there are 1,000 Web sites for Mumia," said Pam Africa, a MOVE member who heads the main organizing group, International Concerned Friends and Family of Mumia Abu-Jamal. Two of the most important sites—

www.mumia.org and www.peoplescampaign.org—cast Abu-Jamal as a symbolic victim of a racist American political system.[303]

The Mumia Abu-Jamal phenomenon continued to raise debate and questions about his innocence and justice throughout the coverage of the case. The day after the announcement of the Abu-Jamal march, the *Inquirer* ran an article, which started, "Sacco and Vanzetti. The Scottsboro Boys. Alger Hiss. The Rosenbergs. Mumia Abu-Jamal?" The article continued the theme of 60s protest when it discussed the groups supporting Abu-Jamal:

Whether or not it ever succeeds in getting Abu-Jamal's conviction overturned, a quirky coalition of liberal Hollywood activists and East Coast literati, '60s activist graybeards, and goateed punk anarchists, Marxist propagandists and MOVE members has scored a strange success. The groups have made a convicted murderer into an international icon of victimhood and resistance.[304]

It states: "None of that has prevented his case from becoming a cause, a movement, a flashback to the '60s". The "Millions for Mumia" march took place on April 24, 1999. The *Philadelphia Inquirer* reported: "About 10,000 supporters of death-row celebrity Mumia Abu-Jamal jammed the west apron of City Hall yesterday in an emotional, almost-festive rally that paired fresh-faced high school students with veterans of Vietnam-era marches."[305]

How was Mumia Abu-Jamal able to attract so much media attention? While his demographics did not make him novel in death row, his speaking and writing ability, along with his charisma, were unique. Marc Kaufman, a reporter who covered the case for the *Philadelphia Inquirer*, states:

He was able to attract a lot of people independent of the death penalty issue. He was able to put the death penalty in a different light. Because he was bright and articulate, he did not fit the stereotype of someone on death row. His trial was incredible theatre; he understood how theatre could be a useful tool for him and his issues. The Fraternal Order of Police and many in Pennsylvania wanted him executed so it was a serious conflict and debate...I don't know how important race was, whether it operated for or against him. There was a racial component to the trial but I'm not sure race played too big a role in bringing the case to a national stage. I heard that in Europe the fact that he was African American helped increase his visibility.[306]

Additionally, Abu-Jamal worked at bringing attention to his case. As David Von Drehle notes:

He is a great promoter, very canny, never talks about details of case, never making statements that can be disproven. The case is factually open and shut, he has never said that he didn't do it; Chessman did the same thing. Mumia writes like a dream, is handsome, dreadlocks work great for him, has a face to put on a t-shirt, and there isn't a deep sense of menace, not like Gacy. Mumia is not likely to kill anyone if released.[307]

But Mumia Abu-Jamal was not able to attract such widespread support and attention during the 1980s, when the national media ignored his case. His case only began to attract national newspaper coverage when growing doubts started to surround the capital system. The country's uneasiness about the death penalty is reflected in the newspaper's coverage of the opposition to Abu-Jamal's sentence. With the racist history of the death penalty, it would have been unthinkable just a decade earlier for the possible execution of a black man who was convicted of killing of a white police officer to generate so much debate across the country. Public sentiments and media coverage had dramatically changed since the serial killers filled the newspapers.

CONCLUSION

The cases that received the most attention between 1994 and 2002 were those that generated debate about capital punishment. Mainstream newspaper coverage of both Karla Faye Tucker and Mumia Abu-Jamal included discussion of the appropriateness of capital punishment and the large number of people against its use. This is not surprising, since support for capital punishment decreased throughout this time period as crime dropped and the economy rebounded from recession. Serial killers, who dominated the prior years, all but disappeared from the mainstream newspapers.

Tucker and Abu-Jamal's stories coincided with decreasing support for capital punishment. Additionally, they fit into Chibnall's criteria for newsworthiness as they raised social and political debates, including debates about executing women and planned execution of what many saw as a political prisoner and innocent man. Their cases raised two different challenges to the capital system. Tucker's case created debate about executing women and executions themselves, whereas Abu-Jamal raised issues about the potential to execute the innocent and about justice itself. The newspaper coverage of Abu-Jamal and Tucker both displayed the nation's growing doubts regarding capital punishment; another case during this period brought up different emotions and arguments. The newspaper coverage of Timothy McVeigh will be analyzed in the next chapter.

5

Federal Cases and Terrorism

In 1994, opposition to the death penalty was growing, as evidenced by declining public support and increasing legal challenges. The Oklahoma City bombing and subsequent arrest of Timothy McVeigh arguably affected this trend by reinvigorating many people's support for capital punishment. In addition, the new threat of terrorism was used to justify the continued practice of the death penalty, and opened a window of opportunity for policymakers. Connecting the two, President Clinton signed the Anti-Terrorism and Effective Death Penalty Act of 1996 after the Oklahoma City bombing. The Act, which affects both state and federal prisoners, restricts review in federal courts by establishing tighter filing deadlines, limiting the opportunity for evidentiary hearings, and ordinarily allowing only a single habeas corpus filing in federal court. The 9/11 attacks on the United States would continue the public's focus on the terrorist threat. Similar to the moral panic with serial killers in the 1980s, terrorists now were the focus of the public. This heightened concern would also lead to changes in policy, most notably the Patriot Act.

As noted previously, public support of the state capital system began to decline in 1994. Yet, in the same year the federal death penalty expanded, and the United States continued to support capital punishment in the international arena. The most notable example of these trends was Timothy McVeigh, who was convicted of the 1995 Oklahoma City bombing. McVeigh was convicted of blowing up the Alfred P. Murrah Federal Building in Oklahoma City, killing 168 people. McVeigh was angry with the federal government for the raid at the Branch Davidian compound in Waco, Texas. His case would spark debate about the death penalty issue across the country. Timothy McVeigh was different than the people discussed in previous cases. He did not fit the same mold as the earlier serial killers, nor did he elicit the same sympathy as Tucker and Abu-Jamal. Rather, McVeigh's case was one of stark contrasts. He was the perpetrator of the worst domestic terrorist attack in history at the time. Overwhelming support existed for his execution, yet no rejoicing took place at its completion. Thus, McVeigh brings together two opposing strands surrounding the death penalty illustrated in previous chapters: he is a mass murderer, yet his case also raised controversial issues about the administration of capital punishment.

THE CONTEXT OF PUBLIC OPINION: THE FEDERAL DEATH PENALTY AND TERRORISM 1994–2002

Something in the zeitgeist has changed, you have the rise in terrorism as bogeyman in the closet that has replaced the serial killer, and a decrease in the murder rate has people less worried. In the mid 70s to early 1990s serial killers were the big story, but not anymore (David Von Drehle, *The Washington Post*).[308]

Following the 1994 crime bill and growing concerns surrounding terrorism, the federal death penalty was expanded to 60 different offenses, including murder of certain government officials, kidnapping resulting in death, murder for hire, fatal drive-by shootings, sexual abuse crimes resulting in death, car jacking resulting in death, and certain crimes not resulting in death, including continuing criminal enterprise. The number of defendants charged with offenses punishable by death increased dramatically after 1994. Its use has continued to increase in recent years from 12 in 1994 to 153 in 1997.[309]

When he first took office in 2000, Attorney General John Ashcroft started to actively push for the death penalty. In his first year in office, Ashcroft reversed the recommendations of federal prosecutors 12 times, ordering them to seek the death penalty in cases where they had recommended against doing so. He also approved capital punishment for one or more defendants in nearly half the eligible cases. To further complicate the issue, some of the cases came from Michigan, Vermont, and other states that have outlawed capital punishment, but where the federal death penalty can be applied under certain circumstances. Of the 273 defendants approved by the Attorneys

General for capital prosecution since 1988, 26 received death sentences (57 are still awaiting or on trial) with three being executed.[310]

The expansion of the federal system coincided with rising concern over terrorism even before the terrorist attacks of 9/11. Across the country, the death penalty began to be seen by both politicians and the public as a necessary weapon in the war against terrorism:

Mayor Rudolph W. Giuliani and Governor-elect George E. Pataki both used the firebombing of the No. 4 train this week as an opportunity to push for reinstatement of the death penalty in New York State. "This can be another reason for why New York State should have a death penalty," Mr. Giuliani said today. "So that if someone tries to unleash this kind of terror on the subway, we have the ultimate deterrent to prevent them with."[311]

In the type of carefully staged public ceremony that has become increasingly familiar this election year, Gov. Jim Florio flew to Liberty State Park here today to sign a bill that makes terrorists who kill anyone in New Jersey liable to the state's death penalty.[312]

Public opinion polls showed that even those normally against the death penalty make an exception when dealing with terrorists. Survey results show that Americans view terrorism with such abhorrence that about a fifth of those who usually oppose the death penalty would support the execution of a defendant convicted in this kind of attack.[313] These results point to the mixed feelings that McVeigh raised for many people. Andrew Kohut, director of the Pew Research Center for the People and the Press, noted in the *New York Times*:

Rising public opposition to the death penalty has been one of the few liberal social trends in recent years. But there is some reason to wonder whether the public's overwhelming enthusiasm for executing Timothy McVeigh will stall or possibly reverse this development. Every nationwide poll taken has found the vast majority of Americans favoring the execution. This comes at a time when the same nationwide surveys are finding diminishing support for capital punishment since the early 1990s.[314]

The Pew Center's polls show backing for the death penalty slipping from a high of 80 percent in 1994 to 66 percent in 2001. But the survey also found that 75 percent favored Timothy McVeigh's execution. A Gallup poll in April 2001 uncovered an even greater dissonance in opinion when fully 22 percent said they opposed the death penalty but wanted to see McVeigh die.[315] These numbers point to the ambivalence of opinions concerning the death penalty and grave concern over the terrorist threat. Timothy McVeigh would become a symbol of the death penalty debate and terrorist threat across the country.

Timothy McVeigh received more newspaper attention than any other person sentenced to death. The mainstream newspaper coverage of the McVeigh case and interviews with reporters who covered the stories will now be analyzed with a particular focus on differences between the local and national coverage, the evolution of the coverage over time, any connections that were made with larger political or social issues including terrorism, the death penalty, and public sentiments regarding punishment. Additionally, the newsworthiness of his case will be examined in order to understand what made him become the most covered death row inmate of all.

THE CASE OF TIMOTHY MCVEIGH

Timothy McVeigh became interested in guns at a young age. His grandfather gave him his first gun when he was 13 years old. He was an active hunter and outdoorsman during his teen years living in Pendleton, in upstate New York. His interest in guns would eventually lead him to the Army. He joined the Army on March 24, 1988, and was stationed at Fort Riley, Kansas. He flourished in the military environment and quickly became a standout. He met Terry Nichols and Michael Fortier, who quickly became close friends. In 1991, he served honorably in Iraq during the Gulf War, earning a Bronze Star. After returning to the states, McVeigh failed in his attempt to become a member of the Army's Special Forces. This failure left him disillusioned with the Army, and increasingly with the government overall.[316]

After leaving the Army, McVeigh returned home to his security job but quickly became bored in his hometown. His interest in guns would take him across the country to gun shows and visits with Nichols in Michigan and Fortier in Arizona. It was during these years that his hatred of the federal government began to grow. The main issue that motivated McVeigh was the government's increasing limits on guns. He traveled to Waco, Texas, during the standoff between the Branch Davidians, lead by David Koresh, and the ATF and FBI. The standoff started after the ATF raided the Branch Davidians' compound, Mt. Carmel, to serve warrants dealing with illegal firearm possession. In Waco, he distributed anti-government literature and bumper stickers.[317] When the standoff ended with a fire that burned the compound to the ground and resulted in the deaths of 76 Davidians, McVeigh vowed revenge.

With the help of Nichols, McVeigh began collecting bomb-making materials and stockpiling dynamite and fertilizer. Fortier, who accompanied

McVeigh on a trip to Oklahoma City to scout out the federal building, did not want to be involved with the bombing.[318] On April 16, 1995, McVeigh drove his 1977 Mercury Marquis into Oklahoma City, followed by Nichols. Parking it near the federal building, McVeigh took off the license plate and left a note on it indicating the battery was dead. Nichols and McVeigh then began loading a rented Ryder truck full of bomb components.[319] When they were done, Nichols returned home and McVeigh stayed with the truck.

On April 19, 1995, McVeigh drove the Ryder truck, which contained over 4,800 pounds of ammonium nitrate fertilizer, into Oklahoma City. He parked the truck just outside of the Alfred P. Murrah Federal building and walked away. He got into his car, still where he left it three day before, and drove off. At 9:02, the bomb exploded, destroying one-third of the seven-story building and killing 168 people, including 19 children.

McVeigh was 75 miles north of Oklahoma City when he was pulled over because his car did not have a license plate. The officer noticed McVeigh was carrying a gun and arrested him. He was charged with four misdemeanor charges: unlawfully carrying a weapon, transporting a loaded firearm in a motor vehicle, failing to display a current license plate, and failing to maintain proof of insurance.[320] While he was being held, investigators at the bomb scene found the rear axle to the Ryder truck. From the identification number on the axle they were able to trace the truck back to the rental agency in Junction City, Kansas. The employees at the rental agency were able to provide the FBI with a description of John Doe 1 and John Doe 2. The descriptions were shown around the area, where an employee at the hotel recognized John Doe 1 as Timothy McVeigh. The employee was also able to provide the FBI with the address McVeigh used to register at the hotel; it was Terry Nichols' address.[321]

The bombing was originally thought to be the work of foreign terrorists, but this quickly changed when the police arrested Timothy McVeigh and Terry Nichols in connection with the bombing. The first article about Timothy McVeigh by the *New York Times* ran with the headline, "Authorities Hold a Man of 'Extreme Right-Wing Views.'" The reporter described the scene as McVeigh was arrested:

"Murderer!" shouted people in an angry crowd of several thousand milling around the village green of Perry, Okla., a faded oil town of 5,000 inhabitants 60 miles north of here, as the 26-year-old man, identified as a suspect in the murderous truck bombing of the Alfred P. Murrah Federal Building here, left the courthouse. "Baby killer!" "Burn him!."[322]

From this description, it is clear that the McVeigh case stirred considerable emotion across the nation.

The first mention of McVeigh in the Oklahoma paper is on April 22, 1995, in an article that detailed his arrest and alleged role in the bombing under the running headline, "Terror in the Heartland." The following day *The Oklahoman* described McVeigh and Nichols as having "spouted anti-government rhetoric and prided themselves in making and setting off home-made bombs on a little farm in Eastern Michigan."[323] The government quickly stated in a news conference that McVeigh would be charged with the bombing and that the death penalty would be sought. Daily coverage of the bombing dominated the local media for months.

The death penalty was a consistent topic of discussion throughout the Oklahoma City bombing case, even before McVeigh was arrested. Attorney General Janet Reno announced in Washington shortly after the bombing that the government "would seek the death penalty against those responsible." President Clinton made a similar statement: "As I said on the day of the bombing, justice for these killers will be certain, swift and severe. We will find them. We will convict them. And we will seek the death penalty for them."[324] When the trial started, the prosecuting attorney made an argument to the judge that would be used throughout the case: "If the death penalty is not appropriate in this case, it's hard to imagine a case where it would be."[325]

McVeigh's connection with the militia movement and anti-government organizations received considerable attention in the press. While McVeigh was not a member in any militia organization, he held a similar worldview to many of the groups. Many in the militia movement held white-supremacist beliefs and used Christian theology as the basis of their organizations. The groups generally coalesced around a deeply shared antipathy to gun control, government intrusion on individual property and other rights, world trade, and the 1993 F.B.I. siege of the Branch Davidian complex in Texas. His feelings regarding Waco and Ruby Ridge were cited as his main motivation behind his actions. It was quickly noted that the Oklahoma City bombing occurred on the second anniversary of the raid on the Branch Davidians in Waco. The bombing put the spotlight on rural America and the burgeoning militia groups. Growing concern regarding militias across the country was detailed in articles about the increasing number of organizations.[326] President Clinton even took time out of a college commencement address at Michigan State University to denounce the growing militia movement.

On June 5, 1995, survivors of the Oklahoma City bombing went to Washington to promote the Omnibus Counterterrorism Act of 1995, which would end the lengthy appeal process for those sentenced to death under the federal system. It also included a wide range of provisions, many of them aimed at making it easier for the federal government to monitor the activities of suspected domestic and international terrorists. The bill authorized funding for 1,000 new federal agents and prosecutors to combat domestic and international terrorism. The government would get new authority to monitor suspected terrorists, to check their financial records, and to listen in on phone conversations. The bill would also require tracing agents to be added to dynamite and certain other commercial explosives. The bill was signed into law on April 25, 1996, with a large contingent of Oklahomans watching on the White House lawn. President Clinton signed the legislation and dedicated it to victims of terrorist acts.

Militia groups also became the focus of reporters during this time. A week after the bill was signed into law, militia leaders were in Washington to defend their actions and beliefs.[327] Growing concern over militia groups began to increase across the country, with attention directed at *The Turner Diaries,* which McVeigh admitted reading. The book, associated with the militia movement, details an apocalyptic race war with an overzealous federal government. Most notably, it contains a description of a federal building truck bombing, which is strikingly similar to the Oklahoma City bombing.

The Trial

In 1996, reporters began to turn their attention to the logistics of the trial. First was the question of whether or not the trial could take place in Oklahoma. Then questions arose as to whether or not cameras would be allowed in the courtroom; by law television cameras are not allowed in federal courtrooms. Additionally, McVeigh's lawyers argued for a change of venue for the trial, citing the thousands of newspaper articles covering the case. The judge agreed with the change of venue request, and Denver was chosen as the location of the trial. The announcement was not well received in Oklahoma, where victims and their families felt that their views would not be heard. Once the location was chosen, the presiding judge quickly announced that no cameras, even for closed circuit broadcast for victims' families, would be allowed in the courtroom.[328]

McVeigh was frequently the topic of the editorial page, either in the form of newspaper columnists' articles or readers' letters to the editors. He was used to speak about the administration of the death penalty in general. The problem with this, as the *Editorial Desk* of the *Los Angeles Times* noted, is that though these writers favored McVeigh's execution: "almost everything about the McVeigh case is the exception, not the rule. *The Times* continues to have serious concerns about the application of the death penalty. But none of those concerns are raised by the McVeigh case."[329] These contradictory feelings would characterize much of the coverage of the McVeigh case. McVeigh, for many people, was viewed as an exception to the norms of the capital system.

The trial, which lasted 11 weeks, began on April 24, 1997, in Denver, Colorado. The most damaging testimony against McVeigh came from Mike Fortier, who eventually received a 12-year prison sentence for failing to disclose McVeigh's plans to authorities. Fortier testified about McVeigh's hatred of the government and his trip to Oklahoma City to scout out the federal building as a bomb target.[330] His defense lasted only four days and was not able to dispute McVeigh's involvement with the bombing. Even though the mainstream press covered the trial closely, not televising the trial diminished the amount of news coverage it received across the country. It was still covered in great detail, but as the *Los Angeles Times* notes, "Thanks to no cameras, something that TV's promo kids easily could have inflated into 'Trial of the Century II' may not have been even the trial of the month."[331]

When the guilty verdict was rendered on June 2, 1997, after four days of deliberations, there were multiple stories in both the *New York Times* and *Los Angeles Times*. The verdict only prompted more discussion and debate over his death sentence. Editorial letters and columnists continued to fill pages of each of the newspapers arguing both sides of the issue. Those opposed to the death penalty saw McVeigh as a perfect chance to end capital punishment once and for all. They saw McVeigh as a shortcut on the path toward joining the world's democracies in cheating the gallows: "Stop his execution and every attempt that follows will be, to understate, greatly complicated"[332] because his crimes were so horrendous and deadly. Those in favor of the system saw McVeigh and his calculated murder of 168 people including 19 children as the perfect example of why the death penalty is necessary.

Then, after eight days of testimony, the jury voted for a death sentence on June 13, 1997. The McVeigh case was not regularly in the news for the next three years. This is typical of death row cases, as seen with Bundy, Gacy, Wuornos, and Tucker. Once the verdict was rendered, the case dropped out of the headlines until an announcement of a scheduled execution date. The media typically ignores the correctional system.[333] While the trial did not become a media sensation like the O.J. Simpson case, it was one of the most popular stories of the year. The associated press named McVeigh's conviction and sentencing as the second most important story of 1997, behind only the death of Princess Diana. Additionally, the *Los Angeles Times* did a series about "Stories that shaped the century" and included a story about Oklahoma City and Timothy McVeigh.[334]

McVeigh was also back in the news with the federal trial of Terry Nichols, which started on September 30, 1997. Nichols was found guilty of conspiring to bomb the federal building and eight counts (the federal workers killed in the bombing) of involuntary manslaughter. He was sentenced to life in prison after the jury could not agree on the death penalty. In 2000, Nichols was subsequently tried in Oklahoma on state charges for the murder of 161 victims. He was found guilty but was spared the death penalty and sentenced to 161 consecutive life sentences.

As the execution neared, McVeigh began to make headlines again with the release of the book *American Terrorist* (2001), which included interviews with McVeigh and his first confession. His confession made national news as he referred to the children who died during the bombing as "collateral damage" and said that he "has no sympathy for them." This set the stage for what some called the first "public execution" in a long time.

The Execution

He did become the poster boy for the death penalty debate across the country, often held up as the one who deserves it the most (Penny Owen, *The Oklahoman*).[335]

As McVeigh's execution approached, the death penalty was taking center stage across the country. In 2000, Illinois's governor placed a moratorium on executions because of flaws with the system. Additionally, President Clinton announced that he was postponing the first federal execution in nearly four decades in order for Juan Raul Garza to apply for clemency under pending guidelines. McVeigh made the process much quicker when, in December of 2000, he asked for his execution and said he would seek no more appeals, though he retained the right to ask for clemency from the president. McVeigh's execution date was set for May 16, 2001.

Once the execution date was set for May 16, 2001, discussion and controversy surrounded other details of the execution. It was touched off when the victims' families proposed a closed-circuit broadcast of the execution as a means of accommodating the large number who wanted to witness the execution. McVeigh then announced that he would like the execution to be televised nationally,

> because the closed-circuit telecast of my execution raises these fundamental equal access concerns, and because I am otherwise not opposed to such a telecast, a reasonable solution seems obvious: hold a true "public" execution—allow a public broadcast,[336]

he wrote in the two-page letter to *The Oklahoman*. On April 12, 2001, Attorney General John Ashcroft announced that the execution would be shown on a closed circuit broadcast to the victim's families in Oklahoma City. He noted that telecast would not be recorded. It would be "instantaneous and contemporaneous," leaving no permanent record for others to view.[337] Ashcroft's announcement did not end public discussion and debate surrounding televising the execution.

The execution was expected to draw thousands of media personnel. The warden of the federal penitentiary in Terre Haute, Indiana, anticipated a "media city" outside the prison.[338] Then, only five days before the scheduled execution, a 30-day postponement was announced after it was revealed that the F.B.I. had mishandled evidence in the case. The F.B.I. informed the attorney general that more than 3,100 pages of investigative material had not been given to federal prosecutors or McVeigh's attorneys before his 1997 trial. Newspapers criticized the F.B.I.'s handling of the case, while McVeigh's lawyers called for an indefinite postponement to sort through the new evidence, and the government stood by its 30-day delay.

As the new execution date approached, daily coverage surrounded the details of the execution, especially in the Oklahoma newspaper. Starting three days prior to the execution, the story dominated the newspaper. On June 9, there were six articles, and on June 10, seven articles. The day before the execution, the newspaper covered the anti-death penalty march that took place in Terre Haute (June 11, 2001) along with five additional articles covering the story. The day after the execution (June 12, 2001) there were 14 articles dealing with McVeigh in *The Oklahoman*.

National coverage was just as intense, with numerous articles in both the *Los Angeles Times* and the *New York Times* appearing the day before and day of the execution. Reporters detailed his step-by-step movements leading up the execution, covering the usual description of his last meal (two pints of Ben and Jerry's mint chocolate chip ice cream) and discussing those who would witness the execution. It was noted that McVeigh did not give any last statement before the execution but that he gave the prison warden a handwritten copy of the 18th century poem "Invictus," which ends with the lines: "I am the master of my fate, I am the captain of my soul."[339]

The day of the execution, the *New York Times* ran a series of articles discussing all aspects of the case, from "The reaction abroad" to the "Critic's Notebook: The Coverage." Describing the scene outside the execution, the *New York Times* noted, "only about 50 death penalty supporters were present at the time of the execution at the designated demonstration site, marked off by orange fencing." The reporter also noted, "about 150 death penalty opponents clasped hands and stood in a circle, singing 'We Shall Overcome' at the time of execution."[340] Compared to the Bundy and Gacy execution scenes, the scene was subdued. As Penny Owen of *The Oklahoman* remarked regarding the view of the execution held by many people in Oklahoma City:

Not a lot of Oklahomans traveled to the execution. A lot of people didn't go. Other than the seven that witnessed it, many stayed home. There were a few who were really hungry to have him executed and wanted to see and be a part of it, but I don't think overall many people wanted to rejoice in it. They weren't happy about it; it wasn't going to bring back their loved one. They just wanted justice. And not all of them were for the execution either.[341]

To many, the execution was not a time for celebration, but a reminder of the tragedy that had struck the country.

Newspaper coverage continued to display the conflicting feelings that the death penalty arouses in the description of the scene outside the prison:

The demonstrators who came to oppose or endorse the death penalty were also reined in, relegated to separate city parks during the day on Sunday and bused just after midnight to orange-fenced pens separated by hundreds of yards of grass. The contrast to that day six years ago when the 7,000-pound bomb Mr. McVeigh detonated ripped apart the lives and limbs of 149 adults and 19 children in Oklahoma City could not have been starker. Perhaps the most jarring contrast was Mr. McVeigh's death-chamber demeanor: calibrated, emotionless, blank. So much so that some of the 10 bombing victims and relatives of victims who were allowed to witness the execution found their relief at his death tempered by frustration that their need to understand or communicate to Mr. McVeigh would never be fulfilled.[342]

McVeigh's execution demonstrated that the public's feelings toward the death penalty are extremely complex and often contradictory. Demonstrations occurred on both sides of the issue. The coverage highlighted the chaos of the crime against the sterility of the sentence and the emotion of the victims against the calm of the offender. None of the cases examined thus far demonstrated this more than that of Timothy McVeigh. His execution was widely supported during a time when many were turning away from the capital system. The public's feelings toward his case demonstrate the complexity of the death penalty issue across the country.

The Newsworthiness of Timothy McVeigh and Terrorism

Mr. McVeigh, who said he carried out the attack on the building to punish the United States for federal raids at Ruby Ridge, Idaho, and near Waco, Texas, had eclipsed the crimes of other death row inmates, perhaps in all of American history. His crime was so immense that his execution became a national spectacle. It drew more than 1,400 reporters, filled newspapers, newscasts, talk shows, and chat lines, delighted pro-execution factions, and horrified anti-death penalty ones.[343]

Timothy McVeigh is a household name across the country for a variety of reasons. First and foremost, he perpetrated the most deadly domestic terrorist attack in our country's history (until September 11th, 2001). An enormous amount of attention was dedicated to the attack itself, which meant that whoever was found to be responsible would be the subject of wide public scrutiny. It was initially thought that Mideast terrorists were to blame for the attack, but when it was discovered that the attack was perpetrated by one of the country's own citizens, the story became something unlike anything people had seen before.

Chibnall's criteria for newsworthiness, introduced previously, included political connotations and individual pathology; McVeigh had both criteria working in his favor. His crime had political connotations unlike any other case discussed so far. His crime was committed against the government because of their actions in Waco and Ruby Ridge. The attack was a direct assault against the state, which clearly added to the amount of attention he received in the news media. Also, discussion around the type of person who could commit such a horrendous crime was prevalent in the newspaper coverage. He was a mass murderer and yet seemingly normal, a contrast that intrigued reporters and the public as they searched for answers to his motivations and psychology. People were disgusted that one of its own citizens could be responsible for the attack. McVeigh's upbringing was surprisingly normal. He joined the military after high school and won medals during the Gulf War before failing to make the elite Special Forces. The problem with much of McVeigh's background is that it is all too normal, with nothing that would point to this type of attack. Rick Bragg, of the *New York Times,* took note of his apparently normal upbringing:

It is an American story, if not a happy one. "It is so fearful because he was so all-American," at least on the surface, said Samuel Gross, a law professor at the University of Michigan and an expert on executions. "He was not a demented, crazy person like Ted Kaczynski. He had led an ordinary life, just an ordinary ex-G.I., come home. There was nothing about him that would stand out at a church picnic in Oklahoma City."[344]

Penny Owen a reporter for *The Oklahoman* agrees:

The magnitude of the crime made it newsworthy and the fact that he was one of us, in a way, made it more newsworthy. He had no prior criminal record. He wasn't an international terrorist, wasn't insane. He could have been the boy next door to many people. Some called him a monster but he wasn't a monster and that's what made it intriguing and frightening. He was not so removed from society; he was a loner but was part of society, kind of ordinary.[345]

When speaking with reporters and editors about the newsworthiness of McVeigh, they often referred to it as a "no brainer." Penny Owen of *The Oklahoman* believed:

No matter who it was it would have been huge. Timothy McVeigh or Terry Nichols didn't make it any more special. Even if it was international terrorists and it went to trial it would have been the same because the victims were so vocal and the crime so huge.[346]

For the most part this is true. Due to the very nature of the crime and amount of victims it was going to be a huge story. However, there was also novelty to the story once McVeigh was identified as the alleged perpetrator. McVeigh, a white male, does not fit into our notion of a terrorist, and this added an important element to this story. The fact that McVeigh did not fit our stereotypical view of a terrorist fueled the story. If the perpetrator were of Mideast descent, as originally thought, would his or her name have become a household one? Did the perpetrators of the first World Trade Center bombing or September 11th bombings become household names? While this is not to suggest that the only reason McVeigh was newsworthy was because of his race and ethnicity, they definitely contributed to the amount of coverage. The crime occurred as more and more attention was being given to the militia movement across the country, a movement made up primarily of white males. McVeigh would become a symbol of this movement and their beliefs. When looking at newsworthiness, race becomes a relative concept. McVeigh's race was seen as novel compared to the stereotypical notion of terrorists, which added an element to the story. Additionally, race was an important part of the militia movement, of which he became the symbol in the media. The organizations were based upon white supremacist beliefs, not widely discussed in the mainstream newspapers. The newspapers instead focused on the anti-government motivations of the groups.

The impact race has on the newsworthiness of a story is not fixed. It must be viewed in light of the surrounding circumstances. For example, Abu-Jamal's race helped elevate his story because of the race of his alleged victim. Abu-Jamal is black, and the police officer that he was convicted of shooting was white. This racial dynamic added an important element to the story. Likewise with Karla Faye Tucker, the fact that she was white added to the newsworthiness of her story. Many people saw her as "different" than those typically associated with death row; this is in part explained by her race.

Another novel element, which added to the story's newsworthiness, was the fact that he was the first federal prisoner to be put to death since 1963, when Victor Feguer, a kidnapper and murderer who was described by his lawyers as retarded, died on a gallows in Fort Madison, Iowa. In state prisons, there have been more than 1,000 executions in the past 30 years. This was a national execution, unlike all previous executions since reinstatement, which were state sanctioned. Timothy McVeigh was responsible for a national tragedy, and his punishment was a concern of the entire nation.

A FIRST HAND ACCOUNT OF THE SURROUNDING EXECUTION SCENE

The McVeigh execution—originally scheduled for May 16, 2001, and then postponed to June 11, 2001—was my opportunity to see an execution scene. The execution gave me an opportunity to see the demonstrations, supporters, and media that have become associated with high profile executions such as those of Bundy, Gacy, and Tucker. By visiting the site, I wanted to look more closely at public opinion and at individuals' personal feelings on capital punishment. People's thoughts and feelings regarding McVeigh's execution provided invaluable insight into the complex and volatile nature of the death penalty issue. I was able to document both sides of the issue, visiting both demonstration sites established for the execution, those in favor of the execution and those opposed. I interviewed many of the participants and organizers at both sites and observed the events of the day, keeping notes throughout the night. The execution occurred at the U.S. Penitentiary in Terre Haute, Indiana.

The Anti-capital Punishment Demonstration

I arrived in Terre Haute the day of the execution right before midnight expecting a circus-like feeling in the city of 60,000. I was mistaken; there was not a single hint of the impending execution to be found as I drove down the main highway in town. I decided to go to the anti-capital punishment rally being held in a park near the prison grounds first. When I arrived, about 50 people were watching anti-capital punishment activists speaking on a stage with "www.abolition.org" and "No More Victims" hanging on banners behind them. Speakers talked about "remembering the victims, but not with more victims" and how the death penalty "deepens the culture of violence in our society."

Karen Berkhart, head of the Indiana chapter of Amnesty International, spoke about Timothy McVeigh and suggested that the attention he had received was due to "the heinous nature of his crime, 168 people makes people notice. It is also the first federal execution in years." She believed public opinion was "tending towards abolition." The McVeigh execution "is just continuing the circle of violence, it is a retaliation."

One of the more compelling speakers, a tall, dark-haired man named George Wright, began his talk by describing in vivid detail the night when his wife was murdered and he was shot three times. He described the long process by which he was accused, tried, and found guilty of the crime, before being exonerated years later. He spoke about how pro-death penalty proponents always say, "Well, you would feel differently if it happened to you." He was in the position to reply, "It has happened to me and I am still against the death penalty." He was the founder of the Journey of Hope and Healing, which is a non-profit organization that travels around the country promoting education and abolition of capital punishment. He believed that public opinion was swinging towards abolition because it "is now much easier to engage in dialogue" with people he met around the country. His organization raised awareness to the injustices and ineffectiveness of the death penalty; he thought that they were making progress. During his speech he argued that the "moratorium in Illinois, the number of innocent people being released from death row, and the increased use of DNA" were bringing the needed attention to the cause. He said, "If one innocent life is lost, that is one too many." He predicted that the media would play an important role in "disseminating information and making the death penalty a major issue. Information and education will cause change, and make people realize that the death penalty is not working, not ending crime."

Bill Wilke, another member of the Journey of Hope and Healing who had also suffered a loss of a family member from murder, also expressed his belief that views were changing. He pointed to Bob Curly in Boston, who was a proponent of capital punishment until changing his mind. He also pointed to Bill Babbit, Bud Welch, and Ted Kazinski's brother, who were all against the death penalty. They all felt "rage and hurt but have decided that the death penalty is not the solution to end their pain." The Journey Hope bus had just returned from the Murder Victims and Family Conference at Boston College where many people were "just looking for something to grab onto, and at first, many grab vengeance, but this changes over time."

George argued that the issue here "is not whether Timothy McVeigh deserves to die. It is whether we should kill." He asked: "Society doesn't have a better response? McVeigh is not a normal human being, but the issue is how we respond. We would better spend our time trying to figure out what makes him tick, whether something happened to him." He continued: "Is society safer at 7:01 today? No, society was safer when he was arrested. This is simply a staged political event. An expression of rage and anger, completing the circle."

George responded to the other side's argument of an eye for an eye. "We do not adhere to all these laws from biblical days, in their days you needed two eyewitnesses to convict somebody, we don't kill people for stealing bread." Wilke and George spoke of the 1998 faith statement against the death penalty by the Pope and the fact that the Journey of Hope banner led the procession. The Pope called for worldwide abolition. George felt that in fact religious people, especially Christians, were responsible for the continuation of capital punishment in the country.

The leaders have heard the message, but there is a hierarchy of levels and it doesn't translate to the masses. Pastors know the pulpit affects the collection plate and many of their members are in favor of capital punishment so they avoid the issue.

George continued:

All killing is not the same; I would have killed the man who killed my wife. I was shot, which is different than what is going on here; I had no choice. We have a choice. I stress "we." What is going on today is society is killing a man; we are all responsible.

He points to misconstrued ideas about the criminal justice system that promotes the death penalty.

Many people still think murderers get out in seven years, even if they get life without parole. Many people don't believe in the system. The movement has to be grass roots and raise awareness; politicians perceive that they need support. Bush, when speaking about capital punishment in the presidential debates, referred to deterrence as his reason for support. I almost lost my mind. Deterrence, no one still believes in that.

Wilke and George cited an international conference they had just attended in Brussels, Belgium, hosted by the European Union where they were treated as heroes. The leaders wanted to know how they could help; they found the United States' continued capital punishment incomprehensible. "Politicians in our country are not leaders, they are followers; their agenda is to get reelected, and they stick to their rhetoric." As if stating the obvious, he continued: "Bush knows very little; the most time he spent deciding on clemency on any death row case was 15 minutes." We ended our discussion with George stating, "things are changing as more debate and dialogue comes out."

The Pro-capital Punishment Demonstration

At 3:40 A.M., I arrived at the pro-death penalty area, which was far from the federal building and outlined with temporary orange fencing. There were only a handful of people, but many cameras and media. A few people sat on the bleachers. They were holding signs: "An Eye for an Eye, McVeigh Must Die" and "The Right Stuff, Enforce the Death Penalty." There were two men attracting most of the attention from reporters, standing with lights on them from the media cameras and holding sandwichboard-like signs. The first man, Mark Hynes from Frankfurt, Kentucky, had a sign which read, "God Hates Sin Prov. 6:16 Rom. 9:13." He told me he was "a Bible-believing Christian." He supported the idea of an eye for an eye and completely supported the death penalty because "I am convinced it originated with God, Genesis 9:6—'Whoever sheds the blood of man, by man shall his blood be shed; for in the image of God has God made man.' God instituted capital punishment, God supports it." I engaged him about the idea of forgiveness, which is also in the Bible, to which he responded: "God will forgive, not sure if McVeigh has met the conditions for forgiveness." Mark followed with his argument: "I believe in civil government. He (McVeigh) has forfeited his life. There is a difference between personal forgiveness, it is a different thing." He was a pastor in a non-denominational church and believed that support for the execution had been growing in recent weeks. He outlined his argument about the differences between personal forgiveness, vengeance, and civil government, which he stated many people don't understand: "I can forgive from my heart, that is not the message, but it would be hypocritical. I am only one, there are 168 that have lost their lives so he has forfeited his life." He restated his argument,

If I steal your car, you can forgive me, but I still must be subject to the law, and in this case the law says he must die. Murder is such a heinous crime that it calls for the death penalty. The Bible states in Genesis 9:6, the penalty must fit the crime, God is right, justice can be served.

I thanked him for his time and moved on to his partner.

Robin Israel, a pastor for the Bible Believers Church (Harris, California), displayed a sign stating, "The Image of Sin is Death." He was wearing a black jacket which stated, "Study the Bible, 2 Timothy 3:16." He believed the caliber of McVeigh's crime deserved the death penalty, and that "there may be more McVeighs out there, and they don't have a political license to bomb buildings." Once prodded about the death penalty, he began a long answer, which built momentum with his booming voice: "This is not a bad country. This is not Iraq, McVeigh is not a hero. He should not be likened to Jesus, which some are doing because they are both single and 33 and other nonsense. He is not a patriot, he's a murderer." He continued, "At 7:00 he pays the price, warning to other McVeighs." When asked about society's feelings about the death penalty, he said, "Society is about the same; people who are against this, they discuss it at home or next to the water cooler. They are not here; at home is where they are the experts." He paused to catch his breath before the big ending,

Most people want justice. 7:00 will not be a party; there will be no confetti. 7:00 will be sad, but he murdered 170 people. That is wrong. Some people believe in conspiracy theories, the bogey man, the x-files; this decision is out of my jurisdiction, this is the law. The victims should decide how he should die. This should not be a shameful act. He scouted out the building. He knew there was a nursery. This should be at noon. It should not be a shameful act. It is a worthy act.

I thanked him for his time and moved over for another media figure to step in.

A few more people showed up with more signs: "Enforce the Death Penalty, Without Justice There Can Be No Freedom," and "Today is a Great Day for Victims and Justice. A Message to the Men on Death Row, Your Time is Coming." A sign held by an older woman from Ohio, whose daughter was murdered, read, "Remember Belinda, Her Killer is on Death Row." Another sign read, "1 Life for 168, Is that Justice?" and "For Every Action There Must Be a Reaction, Die McVeigh Die."

At 5:00, a candlelight vigil was held. All the demonstrators went under a circus-like tent and lit candles. They were hoping for 168, but their numbers were nearly a third less than that. A college student spoke first about the execution, saying, "This is justice, not revenge. These are murders, not accidents. Don't lose sight of that. Support the government's decision." They were then silent for 168 seconds. This was about the same time that those at the anti-death penalty camp, some 1,000 yards away, were beginning 168 minutes of silence in remembrance of the victims. After the silence, another college student led a prayer "for the family of the victims, for all those affected by the tragedy, for Timothy McVeigh's family," at which point a lady interrupted and said that she does not pray for them. The moment did not amount to much, but there was an awkward silence before the prayer was ended. The vigil ended with everybody saying the "Lord's Prayer." As people left, I approached the woman who didn't want to say a prayer for McVeigh's family. She was J. J. Jackson from Oklahoma City, and was an assistant to the medical examiner who worked on victim's bodies. She said that she did not agree with the prayer: "His family doesn't deserve the same prayers as the victims and their families do. They must have known something." She said that she was there to "go along with the system" and that "it is the right thing to do." When asked about the death penalty more generally, she informed me that her brother was murdered but that she looks at it on a case by case basis. She said, "This is as close as I can get to it—I'm not here to be seen, just to do the right thing."

I looked back towards the bleachers and saw two young teens, brother and sister, with American flags draping them. There were more signs: "Bye Bye Baby Killer, McVeigh Meets *His* Maker," and "Sleep Easy OK City." Another man held a sign containing a collection of Bible verses that started, "Share the Gospel of Jesus Christ." He was Tim Blakely from Indianapolis, Indiana, and was with the Church of Jesus Christ. He said he had been to four or five executions, which were very low-key affairs. He began his discussion with me: "Is capital punishment of God or not? It is. God is multifaceted. He is just, he is mad sometimes, he can be angry, gentle, and he has wrath. He has a loving side, but also has a vengeful and wrathful side." He pointed to Genesis 9:6: "Whoever shed the blood of man, by man should his blood be shed." Asked about any changes in capital punishment recently, he said, "God is unchanging, doesn't change, the verse still applies today. You are not the governing authority, God is and is vengeful." He spoke of Romans chapters 12 and 13, where it talks about God's vengeance: "Vengeance is mine. The state, in this case, does it for us. They carry out God's wishes. There is justice, there has to be a price to pay." He argued: "McVeigh is a true warrior for justice and truth, but did it the wrong way. Just as he was, he was wrong and now must pay." He looked around and said, "This is an international event happening in Terre Haute. Big things make big news." I encountered Tim later on and we discussed society; he began with a condemnation of television and the Internet as the forces behind the problems in society: "You put garbage in, you get garbage out." However, he believed that "there is a strong revival happening, many people coming to know Jesus Christ." He then made his attempt to make me one of them with his proselytizing.

Next, I talked with Madge Burton, President of Victims Unite, a nonprofit organization that serves as an emotional support group for the families of murder victims during trials and executions and in general. She was from Ohio, where they have over 400 members. She spoke about anti-death penalty demonstrators;

I value my child's life; if they don't value their child's life, that is their judgment. For me, my children are worth more; I will work until I die to get the person executed who killed my child. This is what freedom is all about.

When asked about the execution providing closure, she said, "This is not about closure, you can never get over it. It's not revenge, it is about justice. There is no true revenge." Regarding the small turnout, she said she "is always surprised about the small number of people who show up."

As there was less than an hour to the execution, a collection of teens and a truck driving couple from Washington State began to get more excited; one of the girls yelled, "No more mint chocolate chip ice cream. Cold-hearted meal for cold-hearted man." The sun was shining brightly, but almost in conjunction with the impending event, a downpour occurred for a few moments, which sent everyone running for cover under the tent. Two men from a local morning radio show arrived and got a small group to do some chants. The 10 of them chanted, "Rot in hell, McVeigh." One held up a sign: "Justice in the U.S.A., An Eye for an Eye."

The clock counted down to seven o'clock. One of the radiomen received information about the execution from his phone. The small group cheered as they got word of each detail. We heard that he was pronounced dead at 7:14 A.M. A couple of cheers were heard, but for the most part everybody was left standing around waiting for something to happen. There was no announcement, no sign, and no party. The demonstrators and journalists lingered around in hope that something would happen, and then slowly began to wander back to the buses to return to their cars and lives. The demonstrators who came to support the execution were a small, diverse bunch, some showing support for the death penalty, some because of a personal tragedy, some for something to do (as evidenced by one high school student holding a "Go Cougars" sign up all night). Many were there for religious devotion, and many more because they worked for the media. The feeling walking away from the sight was disappointment.

The execution site demonstrated the conflicting feelings surrounding capital punishment and the continued importance of religion in the capital punishment debate. McVeigh's execution scene did not have the festive atmosphere that has been described at Bundy and Gacy's executions. The pro-capital punishment demonstrators were few in number compared to those protesting against capital punishment. This was surprising, given the magnitude of his crime. It led me to believe that while most people favored his execution, people were becoming more and more uneasy about the capital system. Speaking with those protesting the execution, even though this execution was moving forward, they sensed the momentum turning toward their side. On the other hand, those at the pro-capital punishment site were much more on the defensive about their views.

Religion was the consistent thread that ran through the demonstrations. Both those for and against capital punishment used the Bible when justifying their beliefs, particularly those in favor of the execution. Religion has historically played an important role in the capital punishment debate, and it continues today, as evidenced by the religious references and arguments found on both sides of the issue.

CONCLUSION

Timothy McVeigh was the most discussed death penalty case since its reinstatement in 1976. His story demonstrated the continuing ambivalence surrounding capital punishment in the United States. In a time of declining support for the death penalty, most people supported his execution. Terrorism brought another element to the already complex understanding of public opinion. While many supported McVeigh's execution, it did not have the type of blood lust and celebratory mood that was evident during the executions of Bundy and Gacy. So, as the state capital system continues to come under increased scrutiny, the federal system is alive and well and seen as more necessary than ever because of the threat of terrorism. This is another example of the conflicting feelings surrounding the death penalty, of which the Timothy McVeigh case became a symbol.

6

A Focus on the System: Moratorium, DNA Cases, and the Supreme Court

Media attention to the death penalty in the beginning of the twenty-first century has focused more on the capital system than individual cases. Rather than the high profile serial killers or a religious woman facing execution, the headlines have focused on innocent people being released from death row and the Supreme Court banning executions of the mentally retarded and juveniles. These issues have continued along with decreasing support for capital punishment among the public. Even lethal injection, which was started in part as a more humane way to execute criminals, has received criticism for being "cruel and unusual" punishment after it took two tries and more than a half hour to execute an inmate in Florida.[347] This, along with a number of Supreme Court challenges dealing with the constitutionality of lethal injection, caused most death penalty states that use lethal injection to put a temporary stay on executions until the issues can be worked out. The public has grown noticeably wearier of the death penalty, and it is evident in the issues that have attracted large amounts of media attention since the beginning of the new century.

Much of the recent concern regarding capital punishment has dealt with the increased use of DNA by the courts to determine guilt or innocence. This issue has particular appeal for death row inmates who are facing execution. The case of Earl Washington demonstrates the ultimate concern facing the capital system: executing an innocent person. Earl Washington was removed from Virginia's death row after DNA evidence cast doubt on his guilt in a rape and murder conviction in 1983. However, he was not released from prison until 2001 after more DNA tests were done to prove his innocence. Washington's case was a cautionary tale to all other states. Legislation has been brought forward as a result of the case to require more funding and support for DNA testing in capital cases.

After Washington's release from prison, Illinois became the center of the death penalty discussion when 13 inmates were released from death row after being found not guilty of the charges. The most notable case was Anthony Porter, who was just 48 hours from execution before he won a stay. Porter's case, along with the cases of the other inmates released, spurred Governor Ryan to issue a moratorium on executions in Illinois in 2001. Then in January 2003, Governor Ryan pardoned an additional four death row prisoners and commuted all 167 other death sentences in Illinois. Ryan's moves would push other states to examine their capital system as well, including New Jersey, which, in 2006, issued a moratorium on executions.

Following the increasing concern about the administration of the death penalty across the country, the Supreme Court decided to look into two issues involving capital punishment. In 2003, the Supreme Court issued a ruling that would receive media attention around the world. In *Atkins v. Virginia,* the court ruled that it is cruel and unusual punishment to execute those found to be mentally retarded. While this decision received substantial media coverage, the court's next ruling would garner much more attention. In 2005, the court used the same logic in prohibiting executions of the mentally retarded to forbid the execution of those younger than 18 at the time of the offense in *Roper v. Simmons.* Similar to the previous high profile cases, public sentiment played a role in these cases. This time it was not that public sentiment affected the amount of news coverage, but rather that public sentiment affected the court's decisions. The justices ruling for the majority cited society's "evolving standard of decency" as the major factor in determining their opinion. While experts are unsure what the future holds in terms of executions, the recent cases that have attracted the media's attention demonstrate an increasing uneasiness with the death penalty across the country.

DNA EVIDENCE AND THE CASE OF EARL WASHINGTON

The Crime

On June 4, 1982, Rebecca Lynn Williams, a 19-year-old mother of three, came home and opened the door to her Culpeper, Virginia, apartment. Once in the door, a black man came up behind her, pushed his way in, raped her, and stabbed her 38 times while two of her children, ages six months and two years, were in another room. Blood was smeared from the back bedroom down the hall to the front door where Williams fell and cried for help. Before Williams, who was white, was taken to the hospital, she told a neighbor, an off-duty police officer, that her attacker was a black man who acted alone. Police said the killing left the town in a state of fear.[348]

Almost a year passed without any strong suspects. Then, on May 21, 1983, after a night of drinking, Earl Washington, 30, got into a fight with his brother over a girl. He ran next door and broke into Hazel Weeks' home to steal a gun he knew she kept on the refrigerator. When she surprised him in the kitchen, he hit her with a chair. Washington grabbed the gun and returned to continue the argument with his brother, who he eventually shot in the foot. Later that night, drunk and running wild through the woods, he was arrested by sheriff's deputies in Fauquier County for assaulting Weeks. Under questioning from sheriff's deputies, Washington, who has an IQ of 69, confessed to the Weeks' attack and went on to say he had sexually assaulted her. He went on to confess to committing four other unrelated crimes, including the 1982 rape and murder of Rebecca Lynn Williams in neighboring Culpeper County. Investigators later concluded that Washington could not have committed three of the crimes, and prosecutors had to drop an attempted rape charge in the Weeks' case when she said Washington had not tried to sexually assault her. [349]

According to the notes taken by the Fauquier detective during the two days of questioning, after admitting to the Weeks' sexual assault, the detective wrote that

Earl still seemed nervous; as though there was still something else he kept from us. Because I felt that he was still hiding something, being nervous, and due to the nature of his crimes that he was already charged with, we decided to ask him about the murder which occurred in Culpeper in 1982.

"Did you stab a woman in Culpeper?" the state police detective asked. Washington nodded.

"Was this woman white or black?"

"Black." A few questions later, Special Agent C. Reese Wilmore tried again. "Was she white or black?" This time Earl Washington said, "White."[350]

That answer was enough for Washington to be charged with Williams' death, even though no witnesses, fingerprints, or biological evidence ever connected him to the crime.

The Trial

The trial lasted from January 18 to January 20, 1984, and was not covered by the press except for a brief mention of the verdict and sentence in the local newspaper. The case would not attract any substantial media attention until his execution date approached, and then again when DNA tests would begin to point to his innocence. The evidence presented at the trial was based mostly on Washington's statement to the police, which contained many inconsistencies. Washington told investigators he "stuck her...once or twice," but Williams died from 38 stab wounds. Also, he said she was alone, when, in fact, there was a baby in a playpen and a toddler roaming through the small apartment. The defense made no mention of these inconsistencies during the trial.[351]

The judge ruled that Washington's statement to the police was admissible after hearing from a state mental health expert that a man with an IQ of 69 and the mentality of a 10-year-old was competent to waive his rights to a lawyer during initial questioning, even though it was demonstrated that Washington didn't know what the words "waive" and "provided" meant.[352] Washington later recanted his confession, but he had no alibi for the Williams' murder. Additionally, during the trial, no witnesses or physical evidence put Washington at the scene. His blood type did not match a semen stain found in Williams' apartment, and police instructed the state lab not to test key hair evidence.

Washington was found guilty after the jury deliberated for just 50 minutes. The jury took only another 90 minutes to recommend a death sentence. After his conviction, Washington could not find a lawyer willing to handle his appeals. On May 13, 1985, following the lead of the Virginia Supreme Court, the U.S. Supreme Court upheld Washington's conviction. Virginia officials then set a September 5, 1985, execution date, even though Washington had no lawyer. He came within five days of being executed, but was spared only because another death row inmate alerted a large New York law firm about his situation, and those lawyers agreed to take the case.[353]

While his execution was postponed, six courts rejected his claims of innocence, including a panel of federal judges who determined that Washington's trial attorney had failed to meet minimal standards but upheld the conviction anyway. Virginia's appeals judges, who overturn fewer death sentences than in any other state, ruled that Washington's confession was properly admitted and that the blood evidence was inconclusive.[354] On December 19, 1991, the U.S. Circuit Court of Appeals sent the case back for new hearings after learning that Washington's blood type did not match the blood type of semen found on a blanket at the victim's house. Then on September 17, 1993, after the lower court decided that the blood type evidence was inconclusive, the Circuit Court upheld his death sentence.

Then things started to take a different direction for Washington. On October 25, 1993, a DNA test done by the Virginia state laboratory found genetic material on Williams's body that could not have come from Washington. But Virginia's "21 day rule" on admitting new evidence prevented Washington from going back to court. Twenty-one days is the shortest limitation in the country, and would come under national scrutiny in the press.[355]

The DNA test raised questions about the guilt of Washington. Yet two months later, Governor Wilder maintained that the release of the mentally retarded man from death row was anything but certain.[356] The DNA test, which wasn't available until 1987, conducted by the state on sperm found in the victim, identified a genetic characteristic that could have come from Washington. But it also found another trait that could not have come from Washington, the victim, or the victim's husband, which lead the Attorney General to state that he had doubts about Washington's guilt. The test did not necessarily point to Washington's innocence, but it did find:

> Neither Earl Washington Jr., Rebecca Williams nor Clifford Williams (the victim's husband), individually or in combination, can be the contributor(s) of the 1.1 allele (a genetic trait) detected on the vaginal swab. However, none of these individuals can be eliminated as contributing to the mixture if another individual possessing a 1.1 allele is also present.[357]

This meant that the only way Earl Washington could have been the rapist was if he had a partner in the crime. This didn't necessary prove his innocence but it contradicted the prosecution's argument that there was a lone assailant. Rebecca Williams did not die right away, and her dying statement was read into evidence at the trial. Her statement to investigators at the hospital supported the lone attacker: "I asked her if she knew who her attacker was, and she replied, no. I asked her then if her attacker was black or white and she replied, black. I then asked her if there was more than one, and she replied, no."[358]

The DNA test contradicted the prosecution's theory and Washington's confession that he alone attacked Williams. On January 14, 1994, state officials reduced Washington's sentence from death to life in prison but did not clear him of the crime. Washington's acceptance of this conditional pardon from the governor meant that he could never get a new trial and, ultimately, his freedom.[359]

There was very little action in the Washington story for over six years. Washington continued to plead his innocence, but without the specter of an execution, the momentum in his case slowed. However, with the election of a new governor and the increasing concern about the operation of the capital system across the country, most notably in Illinois, Governor Gilmore, on June 1, 2000, ordered a new round of DNA tests, which found no trace of Washington's DNA at the crime scene. This was the first time the governor had ordered post-conviction DNA testing.[360] The results of this test led the governor to pardon Washington of capital murder on October 2, 2000.

With Washington's exoneration, the investigation of Rebecca Williams' murder was reopened. Interestingly, the governor announced that a convicted rapist's DNA was found on a blanket at the crime scene; he did not identify the source of the matching DNA, saying the state lab could not confirm that evidence from the blanket was connected to Williams's death.[361]

Even with the exoneration for Williams' murder, Washington still was not set free. He still had time remaining on his 30 year sentence for the attack on Weeks. The decision to have Washington continue to serve the Weeks' sentence received national scrutiny. Part of the issue was that inmates on death row are not eligible to receive time off their sentence for good behavior. If Washington had received time off for good behavior, he would have served enough time to satisfy his sentence. After the news and criticism of Washington possibly being held in prison longer, Virginia state officials quickly announced two days later that they would grant Washington time off his prison sentence for good behavior.[362]

The case continued to generate debate and reform. Washington was the 75th U.S. inmate and the fifth Virginian to be exonerated by post-conviction DNA testing. A month after Washington was exonerated, Virginia decided to undertake a study of the fairness of their capital system. Then the State Crime Commission proposed allowing Virginia inmates to preserve evidence from their trials for future testing in the event that new technology became available that could clear them.[363] Finally, on February 13, 2001, Earl Washington walked out of prison after serving over 17 years. Like everything else in this case, controversy surrounded his release. Washington had planned to go straight to Washington, D.C., where he was to meet with at least two members of Congress and the media. Then he was supposed to celebrate with family members he hadn't seen since he went to prison. However, Virginia's board of probation told Washington that he was not to leave the state, or he would be in violation of his parole.[364]

Washington's story reached a climax with his release from prison. The story then slowly faded from the press, but it would reemerge a few times throughout the next few years. In October 2002, Washington would file a civil lawsuit against the police and prosecutors involved in his conviction.[365] On May 6, 2006, a federal jury ruled that a now-deceased Virginia State Police investigator fabricated the confession that sent Washington to death row. The jury awarded $2.25 million to Washington in his lawsuit against the estate of Curtis Reese Wilmore, who died in 1994.[366]

Then in August 2006, Kenneth Maurice Tinsley was charged in the 1982 rape and murder of Rebecca Williams. Tinsley, a serial rapist, was already serving life in prison, and was connected to the Williams' murder by DNA testing.[367]

THE CASE OF ANTHONY PORTER AND MORATORIUM IN ILLINOIS

The Crime

On August 15, 1982, Marilyn Green, 19, and Jerry Hillard, 18, were shot to death in the bleachers overlooking a swimming pool in Washington Park on the South Side of Chicago shortly after 1 A.M. Police originally believed that the crime had been an armed robbery, but it is now known to have resulted from a dispute over drug money. The *Chicago Tribune* reported on the crime the next day.[368] The murders received brief mention in the newspaper and again on August 17, when an arrest warrant was issued for Anthony Porter, who was a known South Side gang member and had been identified by witnesses. It was also mentioned in the newspaper that Porter was sought in connection with a gang related shooting on August 1 where a man was shot on the street.[369] The *Chicago Tribune* continued with the story the next day when Porter surrendered to the police.[370] However, the newspaper did not report on the story for another 15 years until Porter's execution date approached.

All the details surrounding the crime and Porter's trial would not receive substantial newspaper coverage until Northwestern University journalism professor David Protess, a private investigator that he hired, Paul Cilolino, and Protess' journalism students began to look into the crime. What they learned would eventually lead to Porter's release. They found out that immediately after the shooting, police interviewed William Taylor, who had been swimming in the park pool when the murders occurred. Taylor at first said he had not seen the person who committed the crime. However, later at the station, he said he saw Anthony Porter run by right after he heard the shots. After another 17 hours of interrogation, Taylor told police that he actually saw Porter shoot the victims.[371]

Once Taylor identified Porter, he became the only suspect, even though the police had been given information about other possible shooters. The mother of the female victim told the police that she suspected that the murders had been committed by a man named Alstory Simon, who had been in a heated argument with Jerry Hillard, one of the victims, over drug money. Police did interview Simon, but according to statements Protess and his students obtained years later from him, the police just showed him a photograph of Porter and asked if he had any information about the crime. Simon responded that he had not been in the park that night and said he was asked nothing further and never heard from the police again. A few days later, Alstory Simon moved to Milwaukee.[372]

After hearing that his name had been mentioned in connection with the double murders, Anthony Porter went to the police station. Despite his denying any involvement and the lack of physical evidence connecting him with the murders, he was arrested and charged with both of the murders.

The Trial

During the two day trial in September 1983, Porter's defense attorney did not put up a vigorous defense. Porter's family hired a private attorney, thinking that he would have a better chance than with a public defender. They retained a defense attorney, agreeing to pay him $10,000; they were only able to pay him $3,000. The attorney would later say that, due to lack of funds, he stopped investigating the crime. Additionally, during the trial, Porter's attorney fell asleep; the transcript shows that the judge had to wake him up. He only called two alibi witnesses and a photographer who had taken aerial shots of Washington Park. The jury deliberated nine hours before convicting Porter on all counts.[373]

The next day, his attorney waived Porter's right to a jury for sentencing, and a bench sentencing hearing began before the judge. At the end of the first phase of the sentencing hearing, it was determined that Porter was eligible for the death penalty. At this point, Porter's attorney informed the judge that he had learned that one of the jurors and one of the victims' mothers attended the same church. Since the juror had failed to disclose this relationship during the jury questioning, the defense attorney moved for a mistrial. The judge questioned the juror about the relationship. The juror responded that she did know the victim's mother but didn't realize it until after the trial had begun and that it did not affect her decisions. The jury was discharged and the judge denied the motion for a mistrial. The next day the judge found no mitigating factors and sentenced Anthony Porter to death.[374]

In February 1986, the Illinois Supreme Court denied Porter's appeal, which claimed that he had been denied a fair trial before an impartial jury. Porter next appealed to the United States Supreme Court, which upheld the conviction the following October. Then Porter filed a post-conviction petition, alleging he had been denied effective assistance of counsel by his attorney. The appeal detailed his lawyer's failure to locate and call four trial witnesses who could have testified that Alstory Simon and Inez Johnson actually committed the murders. This appeal was also denied, and in January 1995, the Illinois Supreme Court unanimously affirmed the ruling. The following years were followed by more appeals, but his execution was set for September 23, 1998.[375]

The next chain of events would prove critical for Porter's case. A new team of lawyers took over his defense and had his IQ tested. It was measured at 51, which meant that Porter was likely mentally retarded.[376] Although at the time it was legal in Illinois to execute the mentally retarded, his lawyers filed a last-minute petition with the Illinois Supreme Court. The petition argued that Porter's mental capacity rendered him incapable of understanding his punishment and, therefore, that he should not be executed. Two days before Porter was scheduled to die, the Illinois Supreme Court granted a stay while they gathered further evidence of his mental retardation. They ordered the Cook County Circuit Court to hold a competency hearing to determine whether Porter was fit to be executed.[377] It wasn't until after the stay was granted that Protess, Ciolino, and the journalism students started investigating the case.

While the stay was granted solely to investigate Porter's possible retardation, the Northwestern team was able to collect enough evidence to prove Porter's innocence. In December 1998, William Taylor, who identified Porter as the shooter, recanted his testimony to Ciolino and one of the students. He said in an affidavit that police had pressured him to name Porter as the murderer. On January 29, 1999, Alstory Simon's now-estranged wife, Inez Jackson, told Protess, Ciolino, and two of the students that she had been present when Simon committed the murders. She said she did not know Anthony Porter, but that he most certainly had nothing to do with the shootings.[378] Four days later, Alstory Simon confessed on videotape, stating: "Before I knew anything I just pulled it up and started shooting, I must have close to busted off about six rounds." The videotape was broadcast on the local Chicago news that night.[379]

Then on February 5, 1999, two days after the Simon confession, Porter was released from prison after spending 16 years on death row, and the murder charges against him were officially dropped the next month. Porter became the thirteenth person sentenced to death in Illinois under the present capital punishment law to be released based on innocence.[380] In September 1999, Alstory Simon pleaded guilty to two counts of second degree murder and was sentenced to 37 years in prison. (He has since recanted his confession.)[381] Porter was awarded $140,000 from the state for wrongful imprisonment but lost a lawsuit filed against the Chicago police for misconduct.[382]

The national media was fascinated with the Porter case after the involvement of the professor and students from Northwestern became known. The novel aspect of students freeing prisoners from death row became the lead in national and international articles about the case. The *New York Times* ran a story titled "Class of Sleuths to Rescue on Death Row," while the *Washington Post* article was called, "Students' Probe Ends 16 Years on Death Row for Illinois Man."[383]

Illinois' Moratorium on Executions

Illinois Governor George Ryan was affected greatly by the near-execution of an innocent man. Ryan, a death penalty supporter, began to look more closely at the state's death row and realized that Porter's case was far from unusual. The *Chicago Tribune* ran a five-part series in November 1999 titled "The Failure of the Death Penalty in Illinois." The series looked at all of the nearly 300 capital cases in Illinois since reinstatement in 1976. The newspaper found that of the 260 which had been appealed, half had been reversed for a new trial or sentencing. It also found that, in over 30 cases, inmates were represented by lawyers who were disbarred or suspended from practice, and that many of the cases relied on jailhouse informants to convict the defendants. In numerous other cases, recanted testimony by prosecution witnesses, improper rulings by the judge, or misconduct by the prosecutors resulted in convictions that had to be reversed.[384] As a result of the 13 freed death row inmates and mounting public pressure, Ryan issued a state moratorium on the death penalty, stating: "I have grave concerns about our state's shameful record of convicting innocent people and putting them on death row." Illinois had executed 12 people since reinstating the death penalty in 1977. During the same period, 13 Illinois death row prisoners were found to be innocent.[385]

Ryan's decision was national news, and had huge ramifications for the death penalty across the country. After Illinois' moratorium, a number of other states examined their own capital systems. Then in January 2003, Illinois' moratorium would take on greater significance when Ryan pardoned an additional four death row prisoners and commuted all 167 other death sentences before he left office.[386]

THE MENTALLY RETARDED AND THE DEATH PENALTY

The issue of executing the mentally retarded was examined in 1989 in the case, *Penry v. Lynaugh*. By a 5-4 margin, the Supreme Court ruled that it was not against the Eighth Amendment's ban on cruel and unusual punishment to execute the mentally retarded, because no national consensus existed against the practice. However, the justices kept the possibility open for future examinations.[387] After their ruling, changes came quickly among the death penalty states. At the time of the Penry ruling, only two states, Georgia and Maryland, and the federal government excluded the mentally retarded from execution. When the court decided to reexamine the issue in 2001, 18 states prohibited the practice.[388] The case would attract national attention to a crime involving a virtually unknown offender, Daryl Atkins.

The Case of Daryl Atkins

The Crime

On the afternoon of August 16, 1996, Daryl Atkins and his friend, William Jones, were drinking and smoking crack at Atkins' home in Hampton, Virginia. At around 11:30, they walked to a nearby 7-Eleven store to buy more beer. In the parking lot of the store, Atkins told Jones that he did not have enough money and would beg to get the money for the beer. After being unsuccessful, they robbed Eric Nesbitt, a 21-year-old airman from nearby Langley Air Force Base. Nesbit was on his way home from his part time job at an auto parts store. Unsatisfied with the $60 they found in his wallet, Atkins and Jones drove Nesbitt in his pickup truck to a nearby bank and forced him to withdraw an additional $200. The two then drove him to a remote area west of Yorktown.[389]

According to testimony at the trial, Nesbitt was ordered out of the truck and Atkins started firing. Jones and Atkins began fighting over the handgun. In the struggle, Atkins was shot in the leg. Jones then drove Nesbitt, who had been shot eight times, to the emergency room and left him there. He died soon afterwards. Interestingly, the *Richmond Times-Dispatch* reported on

August 22nd that Atkins had been arrested based on tips from the public. In the article, they reported that a "motorist found" Nesbitt's body and brought it to the hospital. It would not be until later that they discovered the motorist was William Jones. Nesbitt's stolen vehicle was discovered in front of a motel in Newport News.[390] However, the murder weapon was never recovered.

The Trial

During the investigation of the crime, video of Atkins and Jones in the vehicle with Nesbitt was found on the bank's surveillance camera, and further forensic evidence implicating the two was found in Nesbitt's abandoned vehicle. In custody, each man claimed that the other had pulled the trigger. Atkins' version of the events, however, was found to contain a number of inconsistencies. Doubts concerning Atkins' testimony were strengthened when a cell-mate claimed that Atkins had confessed to him that he had shot Nesbitt. A deal of life imprisonment was negotiated with Jones in return for his full testimony against Atkins.[391]

The most sensational testimony against Atkins during the 1998 trial was that of his accomplice William Jones. He told the jury that Atkins had been the shooter, which Atkins has always disputed. For Atkins' defense, a mental health expert appointed by his attorneys said he had an IQ of 59. Additionally, they testified that he had a long record of violent crime but had never lived on his own or held a job. Backed by its own expert witness, the Virginia attorney general's office said Atkins was intelligent enough to understand and plan a crime.[392]

The jury decided that Jones' version of events was more believable, and convicted Atkins of capital murder despite learning that Atkins was "mildly retarded and high on crack cocaine and alcohol at the time of the murder."[393] During sentencing, the jury found both the future dangerousness and the vileness of the crime as aggravating factors. The trial judge accepted the jury's recommendation and sentenced him to death. However, in January 1999, Virginia's Supreme Court granted him a resentencing after he appealed his first death sentence because the judge had given jurors an improper sentencing form. It was concluded that the written jury instructions in his first trial in York County Circuit Court did not list all the sentencing options.[394] Then in October 1999, a second jury also recommended the death penalty.

In September 2000, the Virginia Supreme Court split five to two on Atkins' appeal, with two justices saying Atkins' sentence should be commuted to life without parole. However, the majority upheld his death sentence. Justice Kinser, writing for the majority, noted that experts testified that an IQ score "is not the sole definitive measure of mental retardation," and that "Atkins was able to appreciate the criminality of his conduct and understood that it was wrong to shoot Nesbitt."[395]

The murder trial of Daryl Atkins was not widely covered in the press. The *Richmond Times-Dispatch* covered the murder of Eric Nesbitt, the arrest of Atkins and the death sentence.[396] The details of the trial were left uncovered until the case started to move up the appellate courts. National coverage of the case was nonexistent until the Supreme Court began looking into revisiting the issue of executing the mentally retarded in 2001. This decision by the Supreme Court received national attention as it was the first time since 1988, in *Thompson v. Oklahoma*, that the court would look at excluding a group of people from the death penalty. In Thompson, the court ruled that it was cruel and unusual punishment to execute those younger than 16 at the time of the crime.

*The Supreme Court (*Atkins v. Virginia*)*

The U.S. Supreme Court agreed to hear Atkins' case in 2001, after it dropped a North Carolina death-row inmate's case that became moot when that state passed a law abolishing execution of the mentally retarded. Oral arguments were heard on February 20, 2002. Arguments centered on whether or not a national consensus existed against the execution of the mentally retarded. Atkins' attorneys pointed out that 30 (18 death penalty states and the 12 states that do not have the death penalty) out of the 50 states prohibited the practice, while the state's attorneys, along with some justices, argued that you should not count the non-death penalty states in the equation. They argued that not even half of the death penalty states banned this type of execution.[397]

On June 21, 2002, the court announced its decision. By a six to three margin, the justices held that a recent wave of statutes banning the practice showed that a national consensus against it had formed, a consensus strong enough to warrant classifying all death sentences for the mentally retarded as cruel and unusual punishment prohibited by the Constitution. The decision attracted worldwide attention and was the front page story in newspapers across the country. The *New York Times* headline read, "Citing 'National Consensus,' Justices Bar Death Penalty for Retarded Defendants."[398] With their ruling, the Supreme Court imposed one of the most significant restrictions on who can be given the death penalty since the court permitted states to resume capital punishment in 1976. The decision also represented a change from a position the court had taken in 1989, when the justices, by five to four, gave executions of the mentally retarded their approval. At that time, only two death-penalty states banned executions of the retarded.

However, the justices believed times had changed among the states and the federal government, which bans the execution of the retarded. Additionally, the court believed that mentally retarded offenders were different in a number of important factors. For the majority, Justice John Paul Stevens wrote:

Those mentally retarded persons who meet the law's requirements for criminal responsibility should be tried and punished when they commit crimes. Because of their disabilities in areas of reasoning, judgment and control of their impulses, however, they do not act with the level of moral culpability that characterizes the most serious adult criminal conduct.[399]

Thus, the court said, the purposes of the death penalty, deterring murder and exacting retribution for it, do not apply to mentally retarded offenders. Additionally, the court indicated it had taken notice of cases like Earl Washington and other DNA exonerations of death-row inmates. The justices said that "impairments (of the mentally retarded) can jeopardize the reliability and fairness of capital proceedings against mentally retarded defendants," increasing their risk of wrongful convictions. Justice Stevens added a footnote to the ruling, mentioning the cases of two retarded former death-row inmates in Illinois (Anthony Porter) and Virginia (Earl Washington) who were convicted of murders that later DNA evidence proved they did not commit. [400]

The media did not do a comprehensive job of explaining the exact impact of the ruling, especially in regards to which inmates were affected by the decision. The court had previously ruled that profound mental retardation, a condition that is so debilitating it would disqualify someone from execution, was not at issue in the case. Rather, the Atkins case focused on mild mental retardation. This condition is defined by mental health professionals as those who have an IQ between about 50 and 70 and have experienced difficulty adapting to school and social and family life since before the age of 18. Since 1976, 35 such people have been executed, and there were 200 to 300 retarded inmates among the death row population of more than 3,700 convicted murderers at the time of the ruling.[401]

The Supreme Court's decision did not dictate how the states were to handle the new prohibition. The justices said it would be up to the states to develop precise standards and procedures for determining who should qualify for the new exemption from execution. Ironically, although Atkins' case and ruling may have saved other mentally retarded inmates from the death penalty, a jury in Virginia decided in July 2005 that he was intelligent enough to be executed. They found that the constant contact he had with his lawyers had intellectually stimulated him and raised his IQ above 70, making him competent to be put to death under Virginia law. The prosecution argued that his poor school performance was caused by his use of alcohol and drugs, and that his lower scores in earlier IQ tests were tainted. His execution date was set for December 2, 2005, but was later stayed. Then, the Virginia Supreme Court reversed Atkins's death sentence again, although not because of the mental retardation issue but rather on state procedural grounds. However, his case will once again go back to a jury to determine his sentence.[402]

THE JUVENILE DEATH PENALTY

The Atkins ruling had ramifications not just for the mentally retarded but for other death row inmates as well. Many death penalty experts saw a connection between the reasoning used by the justices in the Atkins decision and the issues present with juveniles on death row. The juvenile death penalty would be the next issue to attract national attention as the Supreme Court decided to take up the issue again.

In 2005, there were 71 people on death row for crimes committed when they were under the age of 18. They made up about two percent of the total death row population. All of these persons were male and either 16 or 17 at the time of their crimes. However, by 2005, their ages ranged from 18 to 43.[403]

The juvenile death penalty has been a controversial issue for many years. Arguably the most famous case that dealt with the issue was the murder trial of Leopold and Loeb (discussed in Chapter 2). While neither would be considered juveniles by modern standards, the issues raised in their case are relevant to the modern debate regarding the juvenile death penalty. Many involved in the Leopold and Loeb trial believed that the juvenile death penalty was a relic of the past and would eventually be done away with in our "civilized" society. No one at the trial could have imagined that it would take another 80 years for this to occur.

The Case of Christopher Simmons

The Crime

In 1993, Christopher Simmons, who was 17 at the time, and Charles Benjamin, age 15, were looking to commit a robbery in a nearby Missouri neighborhood. At around 1:30 A.M., they found a back window cracked open at the rear of Shirley Crook's home. They opened the window, reached through, unlocked the back door, and entered the house. Simmons turned on a hallway light. The light woke Crook, who was home alone. She sat up in bed and asked, "Who's there?" Simmons entered the bedroom and recognized Shirley Crook as a woman with whom he had previously had an automobile accident. Crook apparently recognized him as well, which made Simmons believe he had to kill her to avoid getting caught.[404]

Simmons ordered Crook, who was a married mother of two grown children, out of her bed and on to the floor. He found a roll of duct tape, returned to the bedroom, and bound her hands behind her back. He also taped her eyes and mouth shut. Simmons and Benjamin walked Crook from her home and placed her in the back of her 1988 Ford Aerostar. They drove from her home in Jefferson County to Castlewood State Park in St. Louis County.

At the park, Simmons drove the minivan to a 40-foot high railroad trestle that crossed the Meramec River. He and Benjamin began to unload Crook from the van and discovered that she had freed her hands and had removed some of the duct tape from her face. Using her purse strap, the belt from her bathrobe, a towel from the back of the minivan, and some electrical wire found on the trestle, Simmons and Benjamin bound Crook, restraining her hands and feet and covering her head with the towel. Simmons and Benjamin walked Crook to the railroad trestle. Simmons then pushed her off the railroad trestle into the river below. Simmons did not argue these facts during the trial.[405]

At the time she fell, Crook was alive and conscious. The medical examiner determined the cause of death to be drowning. Simmons and Benjamin then threw Mrs. Crook's purse in to the woods. The *St. Louis Post-Dispatch* reported the next day that "the burglars took $6."[406] They drove back to the mobile home park across from the subdivision in which she lived, where Simmons bragged about the murder. Crook's husband returned home later that night from his truck driving job and reported his wife missing to the police. Her body was found later that afternoon by four fishermen. Simmons was arrested the next day at his high school from a description the police received of a young man seen near Crook's abandoned van. Police read Simmons his Miranda rights, but he waived his rights and, after a little less than two hours of questioning, confessed to the murder. He also agreed to videotape a confession and to take part in a videotaped "reenactment" of the murder at the crime scene.[407]

The *Post-Dispatch* reported on the crime with a small article in the middle of the newspaper with the headline: "Teens Killed Woman, Got $6, Police

Say."[408] The story continued to gain attention as the paper described the crime in grim detail the following day:

Before Crook, 46, hit the cold water early Thursday, her abductors had made sure she couldn't swim for freedom. Her wrists had been bound with a leather dog leash. A cloth belt from her robe or nightgown ran from the leash to her ankles, which were tied with an electrical cable. Her body, clad in underwear and cowboy boots, was pulled from the Meramec River 12 hours later. Police, who have arrested two teens, say the restraints indicated that the gruesome murder was well-planned.[409]

Coverage disappeared for almost a month until it was announced that Simmons would be tried as an adult and when it was announced that the state would seek the death penalty three weeks later.[410] It was announced a month later that Benjamin would be tried as an adult as well.[411] Benjamin was tried first for first degree murder and found guilty. He was sentenced to life in prison without the possibility for parole.

The Trial

The Jefferson County prosecutor charged Simmons with first-degree murder, burglary, kidnapping, and stealing. The trial court removed the last three charges for trial purposes. The *St. Louis Post-Dispatch* reported on June 6, 1994, that Simmons sought a change of venue because of pretrial publicity.[412] A week later the trial court denied the change of venue request but agreed to transfer a jury from Cape Girardeau County into Jefferson County to hear the case due to the substantial publicity the crime had received in Jefferson County.[413]

The trial was very brief (only one full day of testimony), but the evidence against Simmons was overwhelming. The *Post-Dispatch* reported, "In a full day of testimony Wednesday, prosecutors called 13 witnesses in the death of Shirley Ann Crook, 46. The witnesses included the victim's husband, Steven Crook. No witnesses testified for the defense."[414] Additionally, Simmons had confessed to the murder, performed a videotaped reenactment at the crime scene, and there was testimony from Brian Moomey against him that showed premeditation (he discussed the plot in advance and later bragged about the crime). The following day the jury returned a guilty verdict.[415] The next day, June 17, the jury considered the sentence. There was testimony from relatives and friends of both Simmons and Crook. The jury deliberated for six hours, considering mitigating factors (no prior criminal history, sympathy from Simmons' family, and most significantly for the later appeal, his age). Nonetheless, the jury recommended a death sentence.[416] The trial court formally imposed the death sentence two months later.

Simmons made several appeals. The first was for the trial court to set aside the conviction and sentence, citing, in part, ineffective assistance of counsel. The trial court rejected the motion, and Simmons appealed. The case worked its way up the court system, with the courts continuing to uphold the death sentence. In 2000, the United States Supreme Court refused without comment to hear Simmons' appeal.[417] Simmons was scheduled for execution on May 1, 2002. Then on April 25, the newspaper reported, "High Court Delays Execution That Was Set for May 1; No Explanation Is Given; Neither Side Had Sought A Postponement."[418] Then on May 28, Simmons (who was scheduled for execution on June 5) was awarded a second stay of execution in light of the U.S. Supreme Court decision to hear *Atkins v. Virginia,* which would decide the constitutionality of executing the mentally retarded.[419] The media began to follow the case much more closely after the second stay of execution. The potential implications of the Atkins' case for the juvenile death penalty became a national focus.

When the Supreme Court ruled, banning the execution of the mentally retarded, Simmons filed a new petition for state post-conviction relief. After hearing Simmons' case, the Missouri Supreme Court on August 27, 2003, concluded that "a national consensus has developed against the execution of juvenile offenders" and that it was unconstitutional to execute those who were 16 or 17 years old when they committed capital crimes. After the decision, Simmons was re-sentenced to life imprisonment without parole. The State of Missouri appealed the decision to the U.S. Supreme Court.[420]

On January 28, 2003, the Supreme Court stopped speculation that it might reconsider its precedents permitting the death penalty to be imposed on those who were 16 or 17 when they committed their capital crimes. The *New York Times* reported that "without comment, the court turned down an appeal on behalf of Scott A. Hain, an Oklahoma death- row inmate who was 17 when he and a 21-year-old acquaintance killed two people in the course of a carjacking and robbery in 1987."[421] This was surprising to many because three months prior, four justices signed a joint statement calling the death penalty for juveniles a "shameful practice."[422] Additionally, many people saw a connection between the juvenile and mental retardation issue. The rationale of that decision, *Atkins v. Virginia,* should apply "with equal or greater force to the execution of juvenile offenders," the four justices wrote in October.[423]

Then just one year later, the Court changed course again. On January 27, 2004, the Supreme Court announced that it would review the execution of those offenders who were 16 or 17 at the time of the crime and hear the case of *Roper v. Simmons*. Donald P. Roper, the superintendent of the correctional facility where Simmons was held, was a party to the action because it was brought as a petition for a writ of habeas corpus.[424] The Supreme Court had previously examined the death penalty for juveniles in a 1988 Supreme Court decision, *Thompson v. Oklahoma*. Thompson, 15, murdered his brother-in-law, who was allegedly abusing his sister. Thompson was convicted as an adult and sentenced to death before the Supreme Court ruled on the case. The ruling barred the execution of offenders under the age of 16, ruling that the punishment would violate the Eighth Amendment's prohibition against cruel and unusual punishment.[425] In 1989, another case, *Stanford v. Kentucky*, upheld the possibility of capital punishment for offenders who were 16 or 17 years old when they committed the capital offense.[426] Interestingly, on the same day in 1989, the Supreme Court ruled in the case *Penry v. Lynaugh* that it was permissible to execute the mentally retarded.[427] However (as previously discussed), in 2002, that decision was overruled in *Atkins v. Virginia*, where the Court held that evolving standards of decency made the execution of the mentally retarded cruel and unusual punishment and thus unconstitutional.

On October 14, 2004, oral arguments were made before the court. The arguments presented were similar to those presented in *Atkins v. Virginia*, focusing on the increasing number of states banning executions of juveniles, the decreasing number of juveniles executed across the country, and the differences between juvenile and adult offenders. Then on March 2, 2005, the Supreme Court announced its decision prohibiting the execution of those under 18. The ruling moved 72 people off death row in 12 states. It represented an about-face for a court that only 16 years earlier had rejected the argument that the execution of those who kill at the age of 16 or 17 violated the Eighth Amendment's prohibition against "cruel and unusual punishments."[428] The justices cited "evolving standards of decency" in reaching their decision, which has been the basis of their interpretation of what constitutes "cruel and unusual punishment." International law was also taken into consideration. It was noted that since 1990, only seven countries outside the United States have executed people for crimes they committed as juveniles, and all seven—Iran, Pakistan, Saudi Arabia, Yemen, Nigeria, China, and Congo—have disavowed the practice. Within the United States, there have been 19 such executions in the United States since 1990, most recently in 2003.[429] Once the Supreme Court agreed to hear the Simmons case, all executions that stood to be affected by the decision were put on hold.

The court also concluded, citing a body of scientific and sociological research, that there are fundamental differences between adult and juvenile offenders which preclude them from being classified among the worst offenders. The differences were: "a lack of maturity and an underdeveloped sense of responsibility; vulnerability to peer pressure; and a personality that is still in formation, making it less supportable to conclude that even a heinous crime committed by a juvenile is evidence of irretrievably depraved character."[430] In drawing the line at 18 years of age for actions with death eligibility, the Supreme Court considered that 18 is also where the law draws the line between minority and adulthood for a multitude of other purposes, including voting, serving on juries, and marrying without parental consent.

In support of the "national consensus" position, the Court noted the increasing infrequency with which states were applying capital punishment for juvenile offenders. At the time of the decision, 20 states had the juvenile death penalty on the books, but since 1989 only six states had executed prisoners for crimes committed as juveniles. Only three states had done so in the past 10 years: Oklahoma, Texas, and Virginia. Furthermore, five of the states that allowed the juvenile death penalty at the time of the 1989 case had since abolished it. The Court also noted that only the United States and Somalia had not ratified Article 37 of the United Nations Convention on the Rights of the Child (September 2, 1990), which expressly prohibits capital punishment for crimes committed by juveniles.[431]

The media was quick to point out the ruling's implications for another high profile case. Lee Boyd Malvo is no longer eligible for the death penalty for his role in the Beltway sniper attacks that terrorized the Washington, D.C., area in October 2002. At the time of the attacks, Malvo was 17 years old. He had already been sentenced to life in prison without the possibility of parole, avoiding the death penalty, in his first murder trial in Virginia. However, he still had to face trial for two other murders in Virginia, as well as in Maryland, Louisiana, and Alabama. In light of the Supreme Court decision, prosecutors in Virginia decided not to pursue the charges against Malvo for the two other murders. The primary reason for extraditing the juvenile from Maryland, where he was arrested and where the greatest number of murders occurred, to Virginia, was the differences in how the two states deal with the death penalty. While the death penalty is allowed in Maryland, it is only applied to persons who were adults at the time of their crimes, whereas Virginia had also allowed the death penalty for offenders who had been juveniles when their crimes were committed.[432]

CONCLUSION

The cases discussed in this chapter at first glance look discrete and unconnected; however, as you look at the underlying issues, the similarities emerge. Concern about the fairness of the capital system is a theme that runs through each of the cases, whether it is death row exonerations, state moratoriums on executions, or prohibitions against executing juveniles and the mentally retarded. While the majority of people in the United States still support capital punishment, there is evidence that people are concerned about its administration. At this point, it is uncertain whether the public and lawmakers will be satisfied with continuing to tinker with the system in order to make it "foolproof" or whether all the concern about its administration will lead to the abolition of the death penalty.

7

Society's Ambivalence: Changing Notions of Punishment and Newsworthiness

Throughout this work, I looked at the seven high profile death row cases that have garnered the most newspaper attention since capital punishment was reinstated in 1976, along with the recent developments with DNA technology and the Supreme Court's rulings outlawing executions of the mentally retarded and juveniles. I examined local and national mainstream newspaper articles for each case along with interviews with reporters and editors from the various papers. The coverage was analyzed with three questions in mind. First, do the types of death row cases that become high profile during a particular timeframe seem to correspond with public sentiment regarding punishment? Second, why are some death row cases within each category selected to become high profile over other similar types of cases? Lastly, how can the relationship between public sentiment and the media be better understood? What are this book's implications for crime policy and society?

CHANGING PUBLIC SENTIMENT 1977-2005

Evidence of changing public opinion toward the death penalty over the last 30 years exists in the form of varying public opinion polls, political speeches, and changing laws and practices. As discussed in Chapter 3,

Americans began embracing more punitive sentiments in the 1970s. The economy was in a recession, the nation's crime rate climbed, and a punitive mentality took shape after years of more rehabilitative ideals and practices. Support for capital punishment also started to rise after historic lows in 1966, with only 42 percent supporting its use.[433] The social unrest of the late 1960s and early 1970s were visible signs of a loss of social control for many.

Throughout the 1970s, support of capital punishment rose: according to the General Social Survey over 70 percent favored its use in 1977. In 1976, after 35 states and the federal government reinstated capital punishment, the Supreme Court ruled that, in view of new statutes designed to reduce the arbitrary imposition of the death penalty, it was no longer cruel and unusual punishment, and executions began again in 1977.

In the 1980s, crime issues became a major focus for politicians; it was imperative for them to be seen as tough on crime as fear of crime replaced the economy as American voters' chief worry. Public support of capital punishment continued to increase throughout the 1980s and early 1990s. This time period saw a steady increase in executions in a growing number of states. This movement toward "getting tough on criminals" extended into the early 1990s, with many states expanding their death penalty statutes to include more offenses and additional categories of victims. Interestingly, rising punitive sentiments during this period in the United States coincided with the introduction of the serial killer in both the news and entertainment media.

Serial killing broke into American popular culture starting in the late 1970s and early 1980s. Media coverage of serial killing proliferated from 1977 onward, with intense reporting on several cases that attracted immense public interest. These helped shape perceptions of the emerging problem. During the early 1980s, legitimate concerns over crime meshed with separate issues of missing and exploited children, organized pedophilia, and ill-defined concerns about the prevalence of homosexuality to create an aura of "moral panic." Serial killing was very prominent in popular fiction, where true-crime books, novels, and films fueled the public's imagination.[434] However, the strict punitive sentiments and focus on serial killing had peaked.

Following more than a decade of tougher penalties for criminals and increasing public support for the death penalty, sentiments began to change across the country in the mid-1990s. These changing feelings came along as the country was beginning the most dramatic decrease in crime in the nation's history and as the economy was in the midst of unseen prosperity. The public's confidence in the capital punishment system began a dramatic decline, something unimaginable just a few years earlier.

Public support for the death penalty between 1994 and 2004 would shift drastically. According to the General Social Survey, public support for capital punishment was 79.7 percent in 1994, its highest peak since reinstatement. After this peak, public support declined continuously over the next ten years until finally leveling off in 2004 with 68.6 percent. While two-thirds of the country was still in favor of capital punishment, this number was the lowest in 20 years.

A large part of the public's changing feelings regarding capital punishment arose from emerging accounts of DNA testing that proved that innocent people were on death row and would possibly be executed. The case of Earl Washington is the most notable example of this when he was released from death row after 17 years in Virginia's death row. This was followed by the most significant event in the death penalty debate, which occurred when Illinois' Governor Ryan issued a moratorium on executions in January 2000 after 13 inmates were released from death row. They were released as a result of new evidence found by Northwestern College students that proved their innocence.

In June 2002, public concern about the fair administration of the death penalty helped prompt the court's change of heart in *Atkins v. Virginia*, one of two decisions within a week limiting the death penalty. In *Atkins v. Virginia*, the court ruled by a six to three margin that executing mentally retarded inmates is unconstitutionally cruel. Justice Stevens quoted Chief Justice Warren in explaining his ruling that executing a mentally retarded person was cruel and unusual punishment: "The basic concept underlying the Eighth Amendment is nothing less than the dignity of man...The Amendment must draw its meaning from the evolving standards of decency that mark the progress of a maturing society."[435] Then in January 2003, Governor Ryan commuted the sentences of all 156 inmates on Illinois' death row. Ryan's actions were covered worldwide as the death penalty debate continued to gain momentum. This was followed by another significant Supreme Court ruling, *Roper v. Simmons* in 2005, where the court continued to rely on evolving standards as it prohibited the execution of juveniles.

Thus, a general movement away from the state death penalty had emerged across the country. However, the Oklahoma City bombing and subsequent arrest of Timothy McVeigh in 1995 and execution in 2001 challenged this trend. With increased concerns over terrorism, the federal death penalty expanded its scope and use in recent years. Overall, two conflicting trends took place during this period. There was lessening support for and increasing legal challenges to the state capital system. On the other hand, the expansion of the federal system coincided with rising concern about terrorism. This concern led many to support the continued use of the capital system. The federal death penalty began to be seen as a necessary weapon in the war against terrorism by both politicians and the public. For example, a Gallup poll in April 2001 found that 22 percent of respondents said they opposed the death penalty but wanted to see Timothy McVeigh die.[436]

Ambivalence continued to surround the death penalty. Two bills came before the New Mexico legislature in 1999; one called for speedier executions, the other proposed banning them altogether.[437] McVeigh's case demonstrated the delicate balance that surrounded the death penalty. People's opinions on the subject were often conflicted and uncertain. While many people across the country were growing weary of the death penalty because of the number of innocent people being set free and lessening of punitive ideals, most people supported McVeigh's execution. McVeigh was a mass murderer, similar in many ways to the serial killers of the 1980s, yet he did not attract the same sense of celebration in his death. Bundy's and Gacy's executions brought parties and celebration; McVeigh's was seen as a necessary evil. It was more about the victims and sadness than a time to revel in the death sentence.

While McVeigh was only one case, his case highlighted the terrorist threat well before September 11th. Articles about that day drew comparisons with Oklahoma City. McVeigh became a reference point for future terrorist attacks and federal death penalty cases. He is often cited when arguments arise over the need for the death penalty. His case brought to light many of the issues that are still facing the country surrounding capital punishment. The September 11th attacks and a renewed focus on terrorism across the country may prove to help stabilize the death penalty debate. Very few people have stepped forward to protest when the government speaks of the death penalty for terrorists. This focus on terrorism and the death penalty may serve to split the capital punishment debate between the state system and federal system. Increasingly, the state system is coming under attack, yet the federal system seems to many to be more necessary than ever. This is another example of the complexity and ambivalence that surrounds this issue. Public sentiments regarding the death penalty have changed considerably over the past 30 years, but has this change been reflected in the media coverage of the issue?

THE MEDIA AND NEWSWORTHINESS

As discussed in Chapter 1, to understand why some death penalty cases attract a large amount of news coverage, it is necessary to look at the internal reasoning newspapers use to determine which stories to cover. After examining the studies of the media and story selection, it is apparent that most of them rely on the idea of newsworthiness in determining the criteria used by journalists and editors to select particular stories. There are a number of recurring criteria that are mentioned, including the importance and interest of stories, novelty, and trends.[438] The studies that focus specifically on crime point to the seriousness of the offense, "whimsical" circumstances, sentimental or dramatic circumstances associated with the offender or victim, and the involvement of a famous or high status person in any capacity.[439] Only a few studies have looked specifically at the death penalty, finding large amounts of media attention based on novelty of executions after reinstatement, claims of innocence by defendants, flaws in the execution, and the inmates' position of power in society.

These traditional criteria for newsworthiness illustrate that newsworthiness often involves more than just story content. Editors and reporters inherently make judgments about society that result from values built into the news industry. They decide what is normal, novel, and newsworthy in connection with capital punishment. When journalists decide that something is new or novel, they must also make assumptions about what is old and routine and therefore no longer newsworthy; when they report what is wrong or abnormal, they must also decide what is normal. The type of death row stories that are covered will affect people's perception about who is the typical death row inmate and who is deemed novel or more newsworthy.

Interviews with reporters and editors reveal that they too fell back on these traditional criteria in talking about newsworthiness. Reporters continually indicated that they made decisions simply on the basis of a story striking them as "interesting." Reporters and editors convey a sense that why a particular story was covered is self-evident. The Bundy and Tucker stories were referred to as "no brainers" when discussing why they became high profile. Or the reporters would put it back on the public with statements about giving the public what they want; however, why a particular story is covered in great detail is not self-evident. Other criteria also influenced the selection of certain stories over others. It was found with death row cases that these decisions were affected by interest in serial killing and cases that raised political implications. Also driving their selection was the social context of the event, making decisions based on the race, class, and gender of the offenders and victims.

The most useful discussion of what makes some death row stories "newsworthy" while others are not is from Chibnall in his book *Law and Order News,* where he provides professional imperatives that lead to "informal rules of relevancy in the reporting of violence." Two of his criteria, sexual and political connotations and individual pathology, proved extremely relevant to the high profile cases examined in this book.[440] These two distinct categories correspond with the two types of cases that were high profile during this time period. First, the protest cases (Karla Faye Tucker and Mumia Abu-Jamal) were newsworthy in part because of their sexual and political connotations. Additionally, the serial killer cases (Bundy, Gacy, Ramirez, and Wuornos) were newsworthy in part because of the pathology they displayed, often being depicted as monsters. Timothy McVeigh's case brought together both of these two ideas: raising issues about the social political connotations of the execution and interest in his mindset and pathology.

To obtain a more complete understanding of which cases become high profile, it is necessary to add to Chibnall's criteria the social context of the offender and victims involved. An examination of the race, class, and gender of those involved reveals much more about why a particular case attracted large amounts of media attention compared to other similar ones. It is necessary to look at the characteristics of the offender and his victims to understand why one particular serial killer is a household name while another is not well known. For example, Ted Bundy was very newsworthy in part because of his victims' characteristics. They were all attractive, white, middle-class college-aged girls, with the exception of Kimberley Leach, who was 12 years old. These are all favorable characteristics for attracting media attention. There were other serial killers like Gerald Stano who did not receive nearly as much newspaper attention, even though he is thought to be responsible for more victims than Bundy. This can be explained in part by looking at the characteristics of his victims. They were prostitutes and hitchhikers and thus less newsworthy to the media.

The same is true with the protest cases. Karla Faye Tucker is the woman who made national headlines; however, she was not the first or the only woman to have been executed during this time period. She was white, attractive, well spoken, and Christian, all of which made her story more newsworthy. Velma Barfield was executed in 1984 in North Carolina and attracted a good amount of attention, being the first woman executed since reinstatement; however it was nothing like the Tucker case. Barfield was 54 years old and became known as the "Death Row Granny," a very different image than that of Tucker. Barfield was a born-again Christian much like Tucker, but did not receive the same level of sympathy and support. Judy Buenoano, dubbed "The Black Widow," was executed less than two months after Tucker. She was the first woman executed in Florida since 1848 and the first woman to receive the electric chair since 1957, yet her story went virtually unnoticed. Obviously, some of the novelty had worn off after Tucker was executed, but just as important was that Buenoano was Hispanic and like Barfield, she was 54 years old. Thus, the race, class, or gender of those involved directly affects the newsworthiness of a case. Some victims or offenders are seen as more newsworthy because of their race, class, or gender characteristics. A newspaper's story selection is thus dictated by their internal criteria, which are influenced by the social context of the event. Additionally, I have found that these decisions coincided with changes in public opinion.

ASSESSING HOW MEDIA CRITERIA AND CHANGING PUBLIC SENTIMENT ARE RELATED

With the reinstatement of capital punishment in 1976, the first few executions received widespread attention (Gary Gilmore, John Spenkelink, and Joseph Bishop). After these first executions, some of the novelty of the practice wore off and there was only sporadic attention given to death row cases and executions. However, a few death row cases attracted substantial mainstream newspaper coverage and can be labeled high profile. After locating the cases that received the most mainstream newspaper attention over the past 30 years, it became apparent that the cases fell into distinct categories: serial killer cases, protest cases, and terrorism cases. It was further discovered that all of the similar cases occurred during the same timeframe. An association existed between public sentiment and the types of cases that were seen as newsworthy at different time periods.

Public sentiment during the late 1970s through the early 1990s was increasingly more punitive and supportive of capital punishment. During this time, serial killer cases, which included Ted Bundy, John Wayne Gacy, Richard Ramirez, and Aileen Wuornos, were the ones that became high profile. All of these individuals' crimes, trials, and executions occurred between 1977–1994 (with the exception of some of Bundy crimes, which occurred earlier, and Wuornos' execution, which occurred in 2002). These cases all focused on serial killers and were driven by public interest in the phenomenon. At the same time, the public was overwhelmingly in favor of capital punishment and increasingly concerned about crime. This led to a desire to see these inmates executed across the country. Both Bundy's and Gacy's executions were scenes of celebration with very little attention dedicated to any anti-death penalty demonstrators or issues.

The serial killer phenomenon was created in the 1980s in large part due to the media concentration on a few high profile cases.[441] Serial killing was tied to a variety of social problems during this time period, including rising crime, missing children, and Satanism. Interest in serial killing was at an all-time high, which increased the amount of media attention dedicated to Bundy, Gacy, Ramirez, and Wuornos. While serial killing attracts some media attention at any time, given the number of victims, surrounding violence, and fear that they cause, serial killer cases at later time periods did not receive the same level of media scrutiny as they did during this period.

The second category of stories are protest cases; based on my research, these consisted of the Karla Faye Tucker and Mumia Abu-Jamal cases, which received news attention between 1994–2002. While both cases began before this time period, with Tucker's crime taking place in 1983 and Abu-Jamal's in 1981, neither received national attention until much later. These cases received consistent local coverage, but did not become high profile until a time period when public sentiment began to change. At the same time that support for capital punishment declined, Tucker's execution and Abu-Jamal's supporters began to make national headlines. Both of these cases raised doubts about the practice of capital punishment across the country, something that was absent from the previous category of cases. Both cases attracted high profile supporters and put a different face on the capital punishment debate than the serial killers.

This suggests that it is not certain fixed criteria alone that drive story selection, but rather that the media is dynamic and changes in a dialectical interplay with public opinion. Otherwise it is hard to understand how and why public sentiments and media-highlighted death row cases were changing in a similar direction at around the same times. Indeed, media coverage and public underwent broadly parallel changes over these decades. As Stephen Hawkins, Director of National Coalition to Abolish the Death Penalty, observes:

> The media coverage has changed considerably over the last fifteen years; the media has become much more sophisticated. They used to be just concerned with the facts, demographic information and the offense, but now they talk about legal counsel and go much more in depth, with discussion of DNA. They have changed considerably from the mid 80s and Bundy where it was just observations. The press is doing more of their own investigating, like with innocent people on death row. This is in part due to the fact that editors don't want the same old thing; they need new angles. Some reporters have asked me, "Can you give me a new take on this?"[442]

As Hawkins indicates, media coverage has also become increasingly more complex and conflicted. Indeed, the types of cases that have become high profile suggest this complexity and conflict. Newspapers have dedicated large amounts of coverage to what can be categorized as two decidedly different types of cases; one set fostering a pro-capital punishment mentality and the other seemingly raising questions that cast doubt on the practice.

How can we explain this broad observation of parallels between the kinds of capital punishment cases the mainstream media selected for high profile treatment and altering public opinion? No doubt the media influences people's ideas and beliefs about the world. Without the media, people would not learn about the events that are taking place around them. But is this a one-way street with the media influencing public opinion? Or is there a mutual relationship between public sentiment and the news?

Based on the interviews with reporters and analysis of high profile death row cases, it seems that the media and public opinion are complex in their interaction. Rather than a linear cause and effect relationship, the relationship is reciprocal and interactive. They have multidirectional effects on each other with the media affecting public opinion and public opinion in turn affecting the media. This interaction does not take place without other factors influencing them. Politicians, activists, and changing laws also affect and are affected by public opinion and the media.[443] The media is the center of this relationship, serving as the connector between the different groups. Politicians and activists look to the media as an indicator of public opinion and also must rely on them for their voice to be heard.

While it is difficult to assess the amount of influence that each institution has on the others, interviews with reporters and editors have revealed that they are aware of public sentiments. They talk about the "public appetite" at a particular time and the "give the public what it wants" edict. As David Von Drehle, a reporter for the *Washington Post*, argues:

The idea of newsworthiness, unusualness, man bites dog, can only take you as far as it goes. Beyond that, there is an appetite for certain stories at certain times. I have been in the newspaper business over half of my life and can't say how and why it happens, but television producers and editors are closely linked to public appetite.[444]

As demonstrated by looking at public opinion regarding the death penalty, the "public appetite" changes and journalists respond with different types of stories. However, public opinion is also being conditioned by the media, which raises a difficult question. How does the media influence public opinion and at the same time public opinion influence the media? A way to begin answering this question is to look at the other factors that affect this relationship. Public opinion is driven by more than just the media, being conditioned by actual events (independent of the media reporting on them), changing laws, and political speeches. Likewise, the press is affected by more than just public sentiment. They have their own internal criteria for news-worthiness, economic concerns, and influences from politicians and activists. Thus, the media and public opinion influence one another, but this interaction is not independent of other social forces and institutions. Additionally, this interaction between the media and public sentiments has an impact on penal policy, and the taken-for-granted-notion regarding the increasing punitive nature of the United States.

If public policy is shaped in part by public opinion, and that opinion is shaped by the media, then it is important to understand the content of the media and the effect it will have on public sentiment. The news influences people's perception of crime. Even more importantly, the media plays a role in affecting criminal justice policies through the very assumption that they reflect the "true" nature of public opinion. The news is seen by both the public and politicians as a source of information about what "others" are thinking. Newspapers are then in the position to shape public opinion through the way crime is covered and also by suggesting or describing what the majority of us believe or support. The media has a powerful role in setting the crime and punishment agenda.[445]

Politicians may be unwilling to go against perceived public opinion, which has been shaped in part through the news. With newspapers presenting a heavy dosage of crime news, politicians are unwilling to back less punitive policies, although the public may be more receptive to them than media coverage would have us believe. Roberts, Stalans, Indermaur, and Hough, in their book *Penal Populism and Public Opinion*, argue that the news' overall effect is to convey a more punitive message to the public by devoting so much time to violent crime, which contributes to many people's desire for stronger punishment for criminals. The media concentrates on dramatic, unusual, and violent crime, which distorts the public's perception of crime in society. The public perception is influenced not by actual crime rates and trends, but rather by the amount and type of crime depicted in the media. This suggests that the death row cases that receive large amounts of attention will have a large impact on opinions and more importantly public policy.

The changing sentiments that have been demonstrated regarding capital punishment provide some evidence that, contrary to what many assume,[446] we are not an increasingly punitive society. Rather, public support regarding the death penalty has been decreasing at a rapid rate over the last decade. This decreasing support has also been reflected in more and more legal challenges to the capital system. This is not to suggest that the death penalty can represent punitive sentiments as a whole, but it does demonstrate the complexity of opinions regarding punishment, which could have implications for the future of penal policy. Politicians who look at public opinion more closely may discover more ambivalence than certainty when it comes to punitive policies and capital punishment.

Appendix: Research Methods

To ascertain which death row cases received the most attention, I used the Lexis-Nexis database. This allowed me to see which cases appeared most frequently during the period from 1980 to 2002. A complete list of all inmates who have been executed since the reinstatement of the death penalty in 1976 (820 as of December 31, 2002), as well as those more well-known inmates awaiting execution, were entered into the "General News" search engine, which contains articles from 135 newspapers nationwide. I used the number of articles that contained the inmate's name to isolate a subset of cases that received the most coverage, measured in the number of newspaper articles devoted to the case.

Note that Gary Gilmore does not appear on either of these lists. Gilmore's case has been well documented (see Mailer's *The Executioner's Song*) and was unique since he was the first person executed after the reinstatement of the death penalty. Yet, he did not appear in the database because his crime and execution occurred prior to 1980 when Lexis-Nexis data began to be stored; thus the Gilmore case is not included in this study. Likewise, John Spenkelink and Jesse Bishop's executions took place before Lexis-Nexis began storing data and were not included in the analysis.

Based on this analysis, I found that these high profile cases fell thematically and for the most part chronologically into distinct clusters: *serial killers/mass murderers* (Timothy McVeigh, Ted Bundy, John Wayne Gacy, Richard Ramirez, and Aileen Wuornos) and *protest cases* (Karla Faye Tucker and Mumia Abu-Jamal). According to the theories summarized in the

Total Number of Articles Containing Name

Timothy McVeigh	+1,000
Ted Bundy	687
Karla Faye Tucker	516
Mumia Abu-Jamal	514^
John Wayne Gacy	464
Richard Ramirez	458*
Aileen Wuornos	196

Number of Articles Within a Month of Execution+

Timothy McVeigh	+1,000
Mumia Abu-Jamal	514^
Karla Faye Tucker	482
Richard Ramirez	458*
John Wayne Gacy	346
Ted Bundy	287
Aileen Wuornos	196

*indicates person still on death row
^indicates person has been removed from death row
+indicates the number of articles that include the name of the individuals from the beginning of the story to a month after their execution. This number represents references to the person regarding their own case and not for references to them in the future.

previous section, though, these two categories are seemingly at odds with one another. The serial killers and mass murderers fit into a strict punitive ideal, as society demands their execution, and in many cases, celebrates its carrying out. The *serial killers and mass murderers* correspond with the contemporary notion within punishment of being tough on crime. Garland (1990) notes that there has been a reemergence of moral arguments that claim that punitive measures are a proper and defensible form of reaction to crime. This notion was absent from most twentieth-century penal discourse (p.8). The *protest cases* do not fall within the norm of punitive sentiments and challenge these more typical notions; they generate debates and protest about the practice of capital punishment. These cases challenge our cultural and political sensibilities, such as "get tough on crime," in part due to the political and social debates revolving around their race, class, and gender.

In the first category, Timothy McVeigh, known to many as the "Oklahoma City Bomber," was found guilty of killing over 168 adults and children. He was executed in June 2001 in Terre Haute, Indiana. Ted Bundy, whose name has become associated with serial killing, was executed in Florida on January 24, 1989, while hundreds of citizens outside the prison celebrated. Bundy confessed to murdering more than 30 victims across the country, mostly young women, between 1974 and 1978. John Wayne Gacy, known as the "killer clown," was executed in Illinois on May 10, 1994. Gacy was convicted of killing 33 young men; 27 bodies were found buried under his house. Richard Ramirez, nicknamed the "Night Stalker," terrorized Southern California during the summer of 1985, committing 14 murders. Ramirez, also recognized because of the satanic overtones of his crime, is awaiting execution on California's death row. Aileen Wuornos, known as the "hitchhiking prostitute" in Florida, received four death sentences and is responsible for the deaths of seven men, the first in 1992. She is often described as the "first female serial killer" and was executed October 9, 2002, in Florida.

The *protest cases* are Karla Faye Tucker and Mumia Abu-Jamal. Tucker was the second woman executed since the reinstatement of the death penalty and the first in Texas since the Civil War. She was executed on February 4, 1998, amidst much support for her clemency due in large part to her religious conversion. Mumia Abu-Jamal was sentenced to death for the 1981 murder of police officer David Faulkner in Philadelphia. Abu-Jamal has written several articles and books from death row that raised questions about the fairness of his trial. His writing has attracted many supporters; benefits for his defense fund have been held across the country in places like Madison Square Garden. Celebrities have also come to his defense, and rock groups like Rage Against the Machine have put on benefit concerts on his behalf. Abu-Jamal's death sentence was lifted on December 18, 2001, because the judge ruled that the jury misinterpreted the sentencing instructions. His conviction was upheld, and he is currently serving a life sentence.

These high profile death row cases were able to break through the more typical Foucauldian notion of private punishment where the public no longer "watches" as outside spectators. Yet, most death row cases receive scant amounts of news attention, with some executions receiving only a small mention in one paper, and conform to Foucault's expectation of punishment's increasing invisibility. Why then, do particular death row cases start to be seen as "newsworthy" by the press and public? I researched this question using mainstream newspaper accounts of death row inmates and interviews with the reporters and editors who covered the cases. I analyzed these cases in light of conflicting and simultaneous trends that exist within punishment in late twentieth century America.

CONTENT ANALYSIS AND INTERVIEWS

The cases selected for more detailed analysis were investigated using content analysis of mainstream newspaper articles and in-depth interviews with both reporters who covered the cases and capital punishment activists. For each of the cases, I examined all of the *New York Times* and *Los Angeles Times* articles along with a major local daily paper. For example, the analysis of Karla Faye Tucker includes articles from the *New York Times*, *Los Angeles Times*, and *Houston Chronicle*. For Mumia Abu-Jamal, the *Philadelphia Inquirer* was examined, along with the *New York Times* and *Los Angeles Times*. This strategy was used in order to get an understanding of both the national and local coverage of the cases. The *New York Times* and *Los Angeles Times* were chosen because of their high status and national audience, and because they are often picked up and sourced by other newspapers. The local papers were investigated because they had the most detailed coverage of the cases.

Content analysis was used on the articles to detect recurring themes and ideologies transmitted by the articles. The articles were coded for references to other current events or social problems, individual race, class, and gender characteristics, references to serial killing/mass murder, violation of cultural sensibilities, and general trends within punishment. Content analysis can enable the researcher to observe recurring patterns in the newspaper and find a structure in its content. The structure is not solely a figment of the researcher's interpretations. The reporters do not write about all the possible death row stories; they must select some cases and neglect many more. The result is a recurring pattern of news about a fairly small number of actors and activities. This does not mean that the picture of society that emerges from my analysis is the only one that could emerge. According to Herbert Gans, "News, like other kinds of symbolic fare, consists of innumerable bits of explicit and implicit content, and no single content analysis can grasp them all." I used newspaper articles, rather than television coverage, because they are easily attainable, more detailed, and inexpensive.

Building on the content analysis, interviews were conducted with reporters and editors who covered the high profile cases to gain an understanding of the rationale for the large amount of attention dedicated to the cases. Reporters and editors were asked questions in a loosely structured format that covered topics such as: What made this story newsworthy? What made this story stand out from others on death row? Was this story related to any other issues or events in the news at that time? Who decided to dedicate the large amount of attention to this particular case? What are your impressions about the media's attention or lack of attention to the death penalty? Major reporters and editors for each of the seven cases were interviewed.

Interviews were also conducted with members of anti-death penalty groups, like the National Coalition to Abolish the Death Penalty, and pro-death penalty groups, like Justice for All, to get their perspectives on general trends of punishment and cases that draw national attention. They were conducted in a loosely structured format and asked questions like: How do you feel about the media's coverage of death row inmates? Why do you believe some cases become national spectacles? Why do you believe that many people ignore most of the executions in this country? Do you notice more or less attention in the media to death row cases in recent years? Additionally, field research was done at Timothy's McVeigh's execution site on June 11, 2001. I conducted interviews at both the pro-capital punishment and anti-capital punishment demonstration sites at the federal penitentiary in Terre Haute, Indiana.

Notes

1. Linebaugh, P. (1992). *The London hanged: Crime and civil society in the Eighteenth Century*. Cambridge: Cambridge University Press.

2. Fishman, M. (1978). Crime Waves as Ideology. *Social Problems 25* (June): 531–543.

3. Surette, R. (1998). *Media, crime and criminal justice: Images and realities* (2nd ed.). Belmont, CA: West Wadsworth, 7.

4. Ibid.

5. Haines, H. (1992). Flawed executions, the anti-death penalty movement, and the politics of capital punishment. *Social Problems 39* (2), 125–138.

6. Ferrell and Sanders. (1995). Cultural Criminology, 308.

7. Bohm, R. (1991). *The death penalty in America: Current research*. New York: Anderson Publishing, p. 115.

8. Schwed, R. (1983). *Abolition and capital punishment; the United States' judicial, political, and moral barometer*. New York: AMS Press, p. 95.

9. Marquart, J., Ekland-Olson , S. & Sorensen, J. (1994). *The rope, the chair and the needle: Capital punishment in Texas, 1923–1990*. Austin: University of Texas Press, p. 190.

10. Rimer, S. (2000, October 31). Support for a moratorium in executions gets stronger. *The New York Times*, p. A18.

11. Kaminer, W. (2002, July 7). The way we live now. *The New York Times*, p. F7.

12. Tonry, M. (2004) *Thinking about crime: Sense and sensibility in American Penal Culture*. New York: Oxford University Press.

13. Roberts, J., Stalans, L., Indermaur, D. & Hough, M. (2003). *Penal populism and public opinion*. New York: Oxford University Press; Garland, D. (2001) *The*

Culture of control: Crime and social order in contemporary society. University of Chicago Press: Chicago, p. 172.

14. Gans, H. (1979). *Deciding what's news: A study of CBS evening news, NBC nightly news, Newsweek, and Time.* New York: Pantheon Books, p. 146.

15. Ibid, p. 174.

16. Katz, J. (1987). What makes crime 'news'? *Media, culture and society* 9, pp. 47–75; Ericson, R., Baranek, P. & Chan, J.(1987). *Visualizing deviance : A study of news organization.* Toronto: University of Toronto Press.

17. Cohen, S. &Young, J. (1973). *The Manufacture of news: Deviance, social problems and the media.* Beverly Hills, CA: Sage Publications, p. 34–35.

18. Frayn, M. (1973). The complete stylization of news. In Cohen, Stanley, and Young, Jock (eds.), *The manufacture of news: A reader* (pp. 81–84). Beverly Hills: Sage Publications.

19. Graber, D. (1980). *Crime news and the public.* New York: Praeger, p. 21.

20. Ibid, p. 42.

21. Barak, G. (Ed.). (1994). *Media, process, and the social construction of crime: Studies in newsmaking criminology.* New York: Garland Publishing, p. 10.

22. Chibnall, S. (1977). *Law-and-order news.* London: Tavistock.

23. Ericson, R., Baranek, P. & Chan, J.(1987). *Visualizing deviance : A study of news organization.* Toronto : University of Toronto Press; Surette, R. (1998). *Media, crime and criminal justice: Images and realities* (2nd ed.). Belmont, CA: West Wadsworth.

24. Cohen, S. & Young, J. (1973). *The manufacture of news: Deviance, social problems and the media.* Beverly Hills, CA: Sage Publications, p. 33.

25. Masur, L. (1989). *Rites of execution: Capital punishment and the transformation of American culture, 1776–1865.* Oxford: Oxford University Press, p. 114.

26. Surette, Ray. (1998). *Media, crime and criminal justice: Images and realities* (2nd ed.). Belmont, CA.: West Wadsworth, p. 70.

27. Graber, D. (1980). *Crime news and the public.* New York: Praeger, p. 45.

28. Ferrell, J. (1998) Criminalising popular culture. In F. Bailey & D. Hale, *Popular Culture, Crime and Justice.* Belmont, CA: West/Wadsworth, pp. 71–86.

29. Lifton, R. & Mitchell, G. (2000). *Who owns death? Capital punishment, the American conscience, and the end of executions.* Harper Collins: New York,. p. xi.

30. Surette, R. (1998). *Media, crime and criminal justice: Images and realities* (2nd ed.). Belmont, CA.: West Wadsworth.

31. Kaminer, W. (1995). *It's all the rage : crime and culture.* Reading, MA: Addison-Wesley.

32. Bailey, W. (1998). Deterrence, brutalization, and the death penalty: Another examination of Oklahoma's return to capital punishment. *Criminology.* (Nov).

33. Lipschultz, J., & Hilt, M. (1999). Mass media and the death penalty: Social construction of three Nebraska executions. *Journal of Broadcasting & Electronic Media* 43 (2), p. 239.

34. Ibid, p. 249.

35. Kaminer, W. (1995). *It's all the rage: crime and culture*. Reading, MA: Addison-Wesley, p. 52.

36. Cooper, D. (1974). *The lesson of the scaffold: The public execution controversy in Victorian England*. Athens: Ohio University Press.

37. The Death Penalty Information Center (www.deathpenaltyinfo.org) was invaluable in documenting the history of capital punishment.

38. Randa, L. (1997). *Society's final solution: A history and discussion of the death penalty*. Lanham, MD.: University Press of America, p. 95.

39. Thompson, E. (1976). *Whigs and hunters: The origin of the black act*. New York: Pantheon Books.

40. Gatrell, V. (1994). *The hanging tree: Execution and the English people 1770–1868*. Oxford: Oxford University Press, p. 10

41. Randa, L. (1997). *Society's final solution : A history and discussion of the death penalty*. Lanham, MD: University Press of America, p. 22.

42. Newman, G. (1978). *The punishment response*. Philadelphia: Lippincott, p. 145.

43. Vila, B. & Morris, C. (1997). *Capital punishment in the United States: A documentary history*. Westport, CT: Greenwood Press, p. 17.

44. Mackey, P. (1976). *Voices against death: American opposition to capital punishment, 1787–1975*. New York: Burt Franklin & Co., Inc, p. xvi-xvii.

45. Hay, D. (1975). *Albion's fatal tree: Crime and society in eighteenth-century England*. New York: Pantheon Book, p. 114; Newman, G. (1978). *The punishment response*. Philadelphia: Lippincott, p. 125–130.

46. Gatrell, V. (1994). *The hanging tree: Execution and the English people 1770–1868*. Oxford: Oxford University Press, p. 7.

47. Foucault, M. (1995). *Discipline and punish, the birth of a prison* (2nd ed., Alan Sheridan, trans). New York: Vintage Books, p. 3–5.

48. Mackey, P. (1976). *Voices against death: American opposition to capital punishment, 1787–1975*. New York: Burt Franklin & Co., Inc., p. xix-xxv.

49. Baird, R & Rosenbaum, S. (Eds.). (1995). *Punishment and the death penalty: The current debate*. Amherst, NY: Prometheus Book, p. 110.

50. Gatrell, V. (1994). *The hanging tree: Execution and the English people 1770–1868*. Oxford: Oxford University Press, p. 590.

51. Mackey, P. (1976). *Voices against death: American opposition to capital punishment, 1787–1975*. New York: Burt Franklin & Co., Inc., p. xvii-xviii.

52. Ibid, p. xxx-xxxi.

53. Ibid, p. 15.

54. Marquart, J., Ekland-Olson , S. & Sorensen, J. (1994). *The rope, the chair and the needle: Capital punishment in Texas, 1923–1990*. Austin: University of Texas Press, p. 13.

55. Vila ,B. & Morris, C. (1997). *Capital punishment in the United States: A documentary history*. Westport, CT: Greenwood Press.

56. Mackey, P. (1976). *Voices against death: American opposition to capital punishment, 1787–1975.* New York: Burt Franklin & Co., Inc., p. xxxii

57. Johnson, R. (1998). *Death work: A study of the modern execution process* (2nd ed.). Belmont, CA: West/Wadsworth, p. 46.

58. Schabas, W. (1997). *The abolition of the death penalty in international law* (2nd ed.). Cambridge, UK: Cambridge University Press.

59. Vila, B. & Morris, C. (1997). *Capital punishment in the United States: A documentary history.* Westport, CT: Greenwood Press, p. 89.

60. Mackey, P. (1976). *Voices against death: American opposition to capital punishment, 1787–1975.* New York: Burt Franklin & Co., Inc., p. xxxii-xxxiv.

61. Schwed, R. (1983). *Abolition and capital punishment; the United States' judicial, political, and moral barometer.* New York: AMS Press, p. 95.

62. Vila, B. & Morris, C. (1997). *Capital punishment in the United States: A documentary history.* Westport, CT: Greenwood Press, p. 110.

63. Bedau, H. (1982). *The death penalty in America* (3rd ed.). New York: Oxford University Press, p. 82.

64. Ibid, p. 17.

65. Kaminer, W. (2002, July 7). The way we live now. *The New York Times,* p. F7.

66. Alter, J. (2000, June 12). The death penalty on trial. *Newsweek,* p. 27.

67. Vila, B. & Morris, C. (1997). *Capital punishment in the United States: A documentary history.* Westport, CT: Greenwood Press, p. 309.

68. Keve, P. (1991). *Prisons and the American conscience: a history of U.S. federal corrections.* Carbondale : Southern Illinois University Press, p. 9.

69. Johnson, R. (1998). *Death work: A study of the modern execution process* (2nd ed.). Belmont, CA : West/Wadsworth, p. 6.

70. Messerschmidt, J. (1997). *Crime as structured action: Gender, race, class, and crime in the making.* Thousand Oaks, CA: Sage Publications.

71. 81.7 percent as of April 15, 2006, Death Penalty Information Center.

72. Von Drehle, D. (1995). *Among the lowest of the dead: The culture of death row.* New York: Times Books.

73. Zedner, L. (1991). *Women, crime and custody in Victorian England.* Oxford: Clarendon Press, p. 8.

74. Baird, R & Rosenbaum, S. (Eds.). (1995). *Punishment and the death penalty: The current debate.* Amherst, NY: Prometheus Book, p. 8.

75. O'Shea, K. (1999). *Women and the death penalty in the United States, 1900–1998.* Westport, CT: Praeger, p. xvii.

76. Death Penalty Information Center, as of April 14, 2006.

77. Death Penalty Information Center, 2006.

78. Gatrell, V. (1994). *The hanging tree: Execution and the English people 1770–1868.* Oxford: Oxford University Press.

79. Johnson, R. (1998). *Death work: A study of the modern execution process* (2nd ed.). Belmont, CA : West/Wadsworth.

80. Much of the material regarding Leopold and Loeb was taken from: Geis, G. & Bienen, L. (1998). *Crimes Of The Century: From Leopold and Loeb to O.J. Simpson.* Boston: Northeastern University Press; Douglas Linder's website Famous Trials (Leopold and Loeb) http://www.law.umkc.edu/faculty/projects/ftrials/leoploeb/leopold.htm.

81. Vila, B. & Morris, C. (1997). *Capital punishment in the United States: A documentary history.* Westport, CT: Greenwood Press, p. 89.

82. Douglas Linder's website Famous Trials (Leopold and Loeb). http://www.law.umkc.edu/faculty/projects/ftrials/leoploeb/leopold.htm.

83. Ibid.

84. Vila, B. & Morris, C. (1997). *Capital punishment in the United States: A documentary history.* Westport, CT: Greenwood Press, p. 89.

85. I relied heavily on Montgomery, R. (1960). *Sacco-Vanzetti: The murder and the myth.* New York: The Devin-Adair Company; Ehrmann, H. (1969). *The case that will not die: commonwealth vs. Sacco and Vanzetti.* Boston: Little, Brown and Company; and Joughin, G. & Morgan, E. (1948). *The legacy of Sacco and Vanzetti.* New York: Harcourt, Brace and Company for my information on the Sacco and Vanzetti case.

86. Montgomery, R. (1960). *Sacco-Vanzetti: The murder and the myth.* New York: The Devin-Adair Company.

87. Ahlgren, G. & Monier, S. (1993). *Crime of the century: The Lindbergh kidnapping hoax.* Boston, MA: Branden Books.

88. I relied on Carter, D. (1979). *Scottsboro: A tragedy of the American South.* Baton Rouge: Louisiana State University Press; and Goodman, J. (1994). *Stories of Scottsboro.* New York: Pantheon Books for my research on the Scottsboro case.

89. Schuetz, J. (1994). *The logic of women on trial: Case studies of popular American trials.* Carbondale: Southern Illinois University Press, p. 120–121.

90. I relied on Parker, F. (1975). *Caryl Chessman: The red light bandit.* Chicago: Nelson-Hall; and Hamm, T. (2001). *Rebel and a cause: Caryl Chessman and the politics of the death penalty in postwar California, 1948–1974.* Berkeley: University of California Press for information on the Chessman case.

91. Jenkins, P. (1994). *Using murder: The social construction of serial homicide.* New York: Alaine de Gruyter, pp. 51–54.

92. Lindsey, R. (1984, January 21). Officials cite a rise in killers who roam U.S. for victims. *The New York Times*, p. A1.

93. Jenkins, P. (1994). *Using murder: The social construction of serial homicide.* New York: Alaine de Gruyter.

94. Ibid, pp. 22, 69.

95. Ibid, pp. 51–52.

96. Serial killer movies. (1994, August). *USA Today Magazine*, Aug 94, p. 7.

97. Interview with David Von Drehle, reporter, *The Washington Post* on March 28, 2002.

98. Scott, J. & Dart, J. (1989, January 30). Bundy's tape fuels dispute on porn, antisocial behavior. *Los Angeles Times*, p. A1.

99. Jones, T. (1989, January 25). Bundy confession may end family's 14 years of agony. *The Los Angeles Times*, p. 1.

100. Nordheimer, J. (1978, December 10). All-american boy on trial. *The New York Times Sunday Magazine*, p. 46.

101. Man held in killing escapes 2nd time. (1978, January 1). *Los Angeles Times*, p. A1; Ex-student held in death flees week before trial. (1978, January 2). *The New York Times*, p. A11.

102. Mass murder suspect on F.B.I. fugitive list. (1978, February 11). *The New York Times*, p. A8.

103. Bundy trial judge allows jury to see slaying photos. (1979, July 12). *The New York Times*, p. A16.

104. Nordheimer, J. (1978, March 12). Florida inmate a suspect in killings of 36 women, but police lack decisive evidence. *The New York Times*, p. A1.

105. King, W. (1979, July 25). Bundy guilty of murders of two florida women. *The New York Times*, p. A1.

106. Bearak, B. (1989, January 25). Bundy is electrocuted as crowd of 500 cheers. *Los Angeles Times*, p. A1.

107. King, L. (1987, December 18). Bundy was competent. *St. Petersburg Times*, p. A1.

108. Morgan, L., Nickens, T., Lavin, C. & Dahl, D. (1989, January 24). Bundy is set to die at 7 A.M. *St. Petersburg Times*, p. 1A.

109. Bundy trial judge allows jury to see slaying photos. (1979, July 12). *The New York Times*, p. A16.

110. Bundy trial judge allows jury to see slaying photos. (1979, July 12). *The New York Times*, p. A16.

111. Morgan, L. & Nickens, T. (1989, January 25). Bundy goes quietly to death. *St. Petersburg Times*, p. A1.

112. Supreme court refuses to block Bundy death. (1989, January 24). *The New York Times*, p. A14.

113. Morgan, L. & Nickens, T. (1989, January 25). Bundy goes quietly to death. *St. Petersburg Times*, p. A1.

114. Interview with Lucy Morgan, reporter, *St. Petersburg Times* on June 22, 2001.

115. Morgan, L. & Nickens, T. (1989, January 25). Bundy goes quietly to death. *St. Petersburg Times*, p. A1.

116. Interview with Tim Nickens, news editor,*St. Petersburg Times* on June 23, 2001.

117. Hein, R. (1994, May 8). John Gacy's last hours. *Chicago Sun-Times*, p. A18.

118. Mount, C. & Kozol, R. (1978, December 23). Bodies of 4 boys found. *Chicago Tribune*, p. A1.

119. Sheppard, N. (1980, March 13). Gacy is found guilty in killing 33, record for us mass murder. *The New York Times*, p. A1.

120. Mount, C. & Kozol, R. (1978, December 23). Bodies of 4 boys found. *Chicago Tribune*, p. A1.

121. Kozol, R. & Sneed, M. (1978, December 30). 6 bodies put toll at 28. *Chicago Tribune*, p. A1.

122. *Los Angeles Times*, (1980, February 22) & *Los Angeles Times*, (1980, March 16).

123. Ibid.

124. Rich, F. (1982, January 30) Theater: indictment of all-American family. *The New York Times*, p. A11.

125. Baker, B. (1985, August 27). "Doesn't meet any profile" pattern. *Los Angeles Times*, p. A1.

126. Shulruff, L. (1991, April 12). Mass killer puts focus on federal appeal policy. *The New York Times*, p. B16.

127. Buamann, E. & O'Brien, J. (1990, June 1). Hell's Belle living with the widow Gunness was murder. *Chicago Tribune*, p. A1.

128. Drogin, B. & Gerstenzang, J. (1988, October 10). Dukakis deplores flyer as "political garbage." *Los Angeles Times*, p. A27.

129. Fornek, S. (1994, April 18). Death penalty debate grows. *Chicago Sun-Times*, p. A1.

130. Feder, R. (1994, May 5). Gacy's execution pulls media circus. *Chicago Sun-Times*, p. A47 & Byrne, D. (1994, May 5). Talk of death becomes lively topic. *Chicago Sun-Times*, p. A37.

131. Drell, A. & Long, R. (1994, May 9). Gacy's hours dwindle. *Chicago Sun-Times*, p. A1.

132. Braun, S. (1994, May 9). Few obstacles remain to gacy's execution. *Los Angeles Times*, p. A14.

133. Fornek, S. (1994, April 18). Death penalty debate grows. *Chicago Sun-Times*, p. A1. & Cotliar

134. Kifner, J. (1994, May 10). Man who killed 33 is executed in Illinois. *The New York Times*, p. A12.

135. Interview with Stephen Braun, reporter, *Los Angeles Times* on January 25, 2002.

136. Vogt, A. (1994, May 17). Is it right to kill the killers? *Chicago Tribune*, p. A1.

137. Kuczka, S. & Karwath, R. (1994, May 11). No tears, no cheers for Gacy's death. *Chicago Tribune*, p. A1.

138. Freed, D. (1985, September 5). Night Stalker Suspect Tied To '84 Killing. *Los Angeles Times*, p. A1.

139. Feldman, P. (1986, March 11). Night stalker victim identifies ramirez. *Los Angeles Times*, p. 1.

140. Chen, E. (1989, February 7). Witness says ramirez was at murder scene. *Los Angeles Times*, p. B3.

141. Harris, S. (1985, October 10). LAPD wants to tie in to print computer. *Los Angeles Times*, p. B4.

142. *Los Angeles Times*, (1985, August 28).

143. Baker, B. (1985, August 29). Psychological profile: Probing killer's mind. *Los Angeles Times,* p. B1.

144. Avery, S. (1985, August 31). Night of stalker has a thousand eyes. *Los Angles Times,* p. B1.

145. Sahagun, L. (1989, September 21). Scene of capture unaltered by touch of fame.*Los Angeles Times*, p. A27.

146. Belcher, J. & Skeleton, N. (1985, September 1). Neighbors gang up. *Los Angeles Times,* p. A1.

147. Lindsey, R. (1985, September 1) Man held in coast deaths after capture by citizens. *The New York Times,* p. A20.

148. Chen, E. & Timnick, L. (1989, September 25). What drove Ramirez? *Los Angeles Times,* p. B1.

149. Bearing the cost of prosecution. (1987, November 12). *Los Angeles Times,* p. B2.

150. Hicks, J. (1988, September 30). Items from Kraft home brought to court. *Los Angeles Times,* p. B5.

151. Balzar, J. (1989, May 26). Victims, officials kick off initiative to speed up trials. *Los Angeles Times,* p. B3.

152. Camera ban at Ramirez hearing to face challenge. (1985, December 13). *Los Angeles Times*, p. B3.

153. Night stalker suspect yells at press. (1989, May 8). *Los Angeles Times,* p. A1.

154. Chen, E. (1989, September 21). "Night Stalker" guilty. *Los Angeles Times,* p. A1.

155. Chen, E. & Timnick, L. (1989, September 25). What drove Ramirez? *Los Angeles Times,* p. B1.

156. Lavin, C., White, V. & Ross, J. (1991, June 2). Suspect in serial killings has long, troubled past. *St. Petersburg Times,* p. B1.

157. Bearing the cost of prosecution. (1987, November 12). *Los Angeles Times,* p. B2.

158. Ross, J. (June 2, 1991). Deadly trek threads through Citrus lives. *St. Petersburg Times,* p. 1.

159. Hawthorne, M. (1991, January 18). Suspect in serial killings arrested in Volusia bar. *Daytona News-Journal,* p. 1.

160. Camera ban at Ramirez hearing to face challenge. (1985, December 13). *Los Angeles Times*, p. B3.

161. Balzar, J. (1989, May 26). Victims, officials kick off initiative to speed up trials. *Los Angeles Times,*p. B3.

162. Ibid.

163. Hawthorne, M. (1991, January 18) Suspect in serial killings arrested in Volusia bar. *Daytona News-Journal,* p. 1.

164. Lavin, C., White, V. & Ross, J. (1991, June 2). Suspect in serial killings has long, troubled past. *St. Petersburg Times,* p. B1; Lavin, C. (1991, August 4). The storm within. *St. Petersburg Times,* p. D1; & Ross, J. (1994, October 7). Court upholds Wuornos' convictions. *St. Petersburg Times,* p. A1.

165. News in brief. (1991, November 16). *St. Petersburg Times,* p. B3.

166. Potential jurors are quizzed in highway killings. (1992, January 14). *St. Petersburg Times,* p. B1.

167. Ex-lover testifies in serial killer case. (1992, January 17). *Los Angeles Times,* p. A4.

168. Woman guilty in first of seven road slayings. (1992). *St. Petersburg Times,* p. A1.

169. Death sentence in serial murder case. (1992, February 1). *Los Angeles Times,* p. A25.

170. Prostitute waives trial in 3 killings. (1992, April 2). *St. Petersburg Times,* p. A10.

171. Jury recommends death for Wuornos. (1992, May 8). *St. Petersburg Times,* p. A1.

172. Ross, J. (1992, May 16). Killer condemned, not contained. *St. Petersburg Times,* p. 1B.

173. Froelich, J. (1992, August 4). A kinder, gentler murderer. *St. Petersburg Times,* p. 1D.

174. With a nip and a tuck, T.V. imitates life. (1992, November 17). *The New York Times,* p. C15.

175. Gershman, R. (1993, February, 7). Wuornos gets 6th death penalty. *St. Petersburg Times,* p. A1.

176. Ross, J. (1994, October 7). Court upholds Wuornos' convictions. *St. Petersburg Times,* p.A1.

177. Killer closer to goal: her own death. (2001, July 21). *St. Petersburg Times,* p. A1.

178. Squires, C. (2002, October 10). Cryptic words, and then she dies. *St. Petersburg Times,* p.B1.

179. Jury recommends death for Wuornos. (1992, May 8). *St. Petersburg Times,* p. A1.

180. Interview with David Von Drehle, reporter, *The Washington Post* on March 28, 2002.

181. Interview with Lucy Morgan, reporter, *St. Petersburg Times* on June 22, 2001

182. Ibid.

183. Nordheimer, J. (1978, December 10). All-American boy on trial. *The New York Times Sunday Magazine,* p. 46.

184. Nordheimer, J. (1978, March 12). Florida inmate a suspect in killings of 36 women, but police lack decisive evidence. *The New York Times,* p. A1.

185. Interview with Mark I. Pinsky, reporter, *Los Angeles Times*on January 6, 2002.

186. Ibid.

187. Slaying suspect in restraints. (1978, December, 29). *Los Angeles Times,* p. A5.

188. Freed, D. (1985, September 5). Night stalker suspect tied to '84 killing. *Los Angeles Times,* p. A1.

189. Kifner, J. (1994, May 10). Man who killed 33 is executed in Illinois. *The New York Times,* p. A12.

190. Interview with Edwin Chen, reporter, *Los Angeles Times* on January 25, 2002.

191. Interview with Paul Feldman, reporter, *Los Angeles Times* on February 25, 2002.

192. Feldman, P. (1986, March 24). Chilling stalker testimony turns up few firm links. *Los Angeles Times,* p. B1.

193. Holley, D. (1985, September 8). Recalling Ramirez: Even friends didn't trust him. *Los Angeles Times,* p. 1.

194. del Olmo, F. (1985, September 12). Gratitude and a band of "heroes." *Los Angeles Times,* p. B5.

195. Chen, E. (1989, September 21). "Night Stalker" guilty. *Los Angeles Times,* p. A1.

196. Freed, D. & McGraw, C. (1985, September 1). Citizens capture stalker fugitive. *Los Angeles Times,* p. A1.

197. Satanic symbolism reported in homes of "stalker" victims. (1985, September 2). *Los Angeles Times,* p. A26.

198. Chen, E. (1988, July 17). Ramirez trial may take two years. *Los Angeles Times,* p. A1.

199. Stalker juror ousted for dozing. (1989, August 11). *Los Angeles Times,* p. A1.

200. Chen, E. & Malnic, E. (1989, August 15). Night stalker juror fatally shot at home. *Los Angeles Times,* p. A1.

201. Lavin, C. (1991, January 18). First woman serial killer. *St. Petersburg Times,* p. A1.

202. Death sentence in serial murder case. (1992, January 31). *St. Petersburg Times,* p. A25.

203. Ibid.

204. Lavin, C & Ross, J. (1992, April 20). Murders, movies and a plea to die. *St. Petersburg Times,* p. B1.

205. Glidwell, J. (1998, March 24). Murderous "hobby" buys little fame. *St. Petersburg Times,* p. A1.

206. del Olmo, F. (1985, September 12). "Gratitude and a band of "heroes." *Los Angeles Times,* p. B5.

207. Interview with Jan Glidwell, reporter, *St. Petersburg Times* on June 5, 2002.

208. Ibid.

209. Interview with David Von Drehle, reporter, *The Washington Post* on March 28, 2002.

210. Rust, C. (1992, June 14). Amazing grace; Array of supporters believe Karla Tucker shouldn't die. *Houston Chronicle*, p. A1.

211. Jury recommends death for Wuornos. (1992, May 8). *St. Petersburg Times*, p. A1.

212. Ibid.

213. Ibid.

214. Interview with Jan Glidwell, reporter, *St. Petersburg Times* on June 5, 2002.

215. A crime that shocked America. (1998, January 30) BBC News Online. http://news.bbc.co.uk/1.hi/special_report/1998//karla_faye_tucker/48796

216. Milling, T. (1998, February 1). Karla Faye's last chance. *Houston Chronicle*, p. A15.

217. Nordheimer, J (1978, December 10). All-American boy on trial. *The New York Times Sunday Magazine*, p. 46.

218. Drennan, C. (1986, March 28). On death row; pickax murderer finds a "new life." *Houston Chronicle*, p. A1; & Drennan, C. (1986, March 28). The embodiment of evil? *Houston Chronicle*, p. A20.

219. Drennan, C. (1986, March 28). On death row; pickax murderer finds a "new life." *Houston Chronicle*, p. A1.

220. Drennan, C. (1986, March 28). The embodiment of evil? *Houston Chronicle*, p. A20.

221. Rust, C. (1992, June 23). Court grants Tucker stay of execution. *Houston Chronicle*, p. A1; & Texas set to execute first woman since 1863. (1992, June 21). *The New York Times*, p. 17.

222. Katz, J. (1998, January 9). Should Karla Faye Tucker be executed? *Los Angeles Times*, p. A1.

223. Rust, C. (1992, June 14). Amazing grace; Array of supporters believe Karla Tucker shouldn't die. *Houston Chronicle*, p. A1.

224. Marks, E. (1992, June 23). No sympathy for this born-again murderess. *Houston Chronicle*, p. A15.

225. McDaniel, M. (1992, September 3). Tonight on TV. *Houston Chronicle*, p. A6; & Fair, K. & Rust, C. (1993, June 16). Death row inmate dies of natural causes. *Houston Chronicle*, p. A21.

226. Walt, K. & Asin, S. (1997, December 9). Path clear for woman's execution. *Houston Chronicle*, p. A1.

227. Rosenburg, H. (1998, January 21). Her court of opinion would be closed here. *Los Angeles Times*, p. F1.

228. Butterfield, F. (1998, January 25). The Nation: Ambivalence? Incompetence? Fairness? Behind the death row bottleneck. *The New York Times*, p. D1.

229. Herbert, B. (1998, January, 4). In America; Death penalty dilemma. *The New York Times,* p. D11.

230. Verhovek, S. (1998, January 1). As woman's execution nears, Texas squirms. *The New York Times,* p. A1.

231. Walt, K. (1998, February 1). Should Tucker be executed? *The Houston Chronicle,* p. A1.

232. The execution of Karla Faye Tucker. (1998, February 4). *The Houston Chronicle,* p. A11.

233. Katz, J. (1998, February 4). Texas executes born-again woman after appeal fails. *Los Angeles Times,* p. A1.

234. Verhovek, S. (1998, February 4). Execution in Texas: The overview. *The New York Times,* p. A1.

235. Ayers, B. (1998, March 23). Political briefing; Death penalty support declines after execution. *The New York Times,* p. A12.

236. Johnson, T. & Hobbs, M. (1981, December 10). One who raised his voice. *The Philadelphia Inquirer,* p. A1.

237. Terry, R. & Hobbs, M. (1981, December 10). Policeman shot to death: radio newsman charged. *The Philadelphia Inquirer,* p. A1.

238. Johnson, T. & Hobbs, M. (1981, December 10). One who raised his voice. *The Philadelphia Inquirer,* p. A1.

239. Ibid.

240. Assefa, H. & Wahrhaftig, P. (1998). *The MOVE crisis in Philadelphia.* Pittsburgh: University of Pittsburgh Press.

241. Gemperlein, J. (1982, March 19). Abu-Jamal is denied information on witnesses. *The Philadelphia Inquirer,* p. A1.

242. Kaufman, M. (1982, June 10). Abu-Jamal selection of jurors halted. *The Philadelphia Inquirer,* p. A1.

243. Kaufman, M. (1982, June 17). Jury selection completed for Abu-Jamal's murder trial. *The Philadelphia Inquirer,* p. A1.

244. Kaufman, M. (1982, June 18). Abu-Jamal cannot defend self. *The Philadelphia Inquirer,* p. A1.

245. Kaufman, M. (1982, July 3). Abu-Jamal found guilty of murder. *The Philadelphia Inquirer,* p. A1.

246. Kaufman, M. (1983, May 26). Abu-Jamal, sentenced to die, threatens the judge. *The Philadelphia Inquirer* p. A1.

247. Interview with Marc Kaufman, reporter, *The Philadelphia Inquirer* (1980–1998) on November 19, 2002.

248. Copeland, L. (1990, July 15). Abu-Jamal stirs foes of execution. *The Philadelphia Inquirer,* p. A1.

249. Interview with Marc Kaufman, reporter, *The Philadelphia Inquirer* (1980–1998) on November 19, 2002.

250. Eshleman Jr., R. (1994, April 13). Death warrant at issue for Casey. *The Philadelphia Inquirer,* p. A1.

251. Kaufman, M. & Cass, J. (1994, June 4). Death warrant reprises clash over police killing Abu-Jamal is seen as killer and victim. *The Philadelphia Inquirer*, p. A1.

252. Policeman's death stirs race tension. (1981, December 13). *The New York Times*, p. A35.

253. Kolber, E. (1994, May 17). Public radio won't use commentary by inmate. *The New York Times*, p. A12.

254. Snow, S. (1994, May 17). Morning report: Radio. *Los Angeles Times*, p. F2.

255. Kaufman, M., Cass, J. & Morello, C. (1995, August 13). Abu-Jamal's long climb to a world stage from death-row cell to global cause celebre. *The Philadelphia Inquirer*, p. A1.

256. Cass, J. (1995, June 12). FBI file tracks Abu-Jamal through his teenage years. *The Philadelphia Inquirer*, p. A1.

257. Jones, R. & Marder, D. (1995, August 13). Abu-Jamal rally draws a peaceful, diverse contingent thousands came to city all. *The Philadelphia Inquirer*, p. A1.

258. Kaufman, M., Cass, J. & Morello, C. (1995, August 13). Abu-Jamal's long climb to a world stage from death-row cell to global cause celebre. *The Philadelphia Inquirer*, p. A1.

259. Kaufman, M., Cass, J. & Morello, C. (1995, August 13). Abu-Jamal's long climb to a world stage from death-row cell to global cause celebre. *The Philadelphia Inquirer*, p. A1.

260. Abu-Jamal lawyers: Killing was mob hit. (2001, May 5). *The Philadelphia Inquirer*, p. A1.

261. Interview with David Von Drehle, reporter, *The Washington Post* on March 28, 2002.

262. Interview with Carol Rust, reporter, *Houston Chronicle* on June 5, 2002.

263. Spelman, E. (1988). *Inessential woman: Problems of exclusion in feminist thought*. Boston: Beacon Press, p. 53.

264. Goodman, E. (1998, February 15). Karla Tucker gave death row a human face. *The Houston Chronicle*, p. A6.

265. Verhovek, S. (1998, February 4). Execution in Texas: The overview. *The New York Times*, p. A1.

266. Hewitt, B., Maier, A. & Stewart, B. (1998, February 2). Reborn too late. *People Magazine*, p. 109.

267. Katz, J. (1998, January 9). Should Karla Faye Tucker be executed? *Los Angeles Times*, p. A1.

268. Death Penalty Information Center, as of 8/15/06.

269. Katz, J. (1998, January 9). Should Karla Faye Tucker be executed? *Los Angeles Times*, p. A1.

270. Verhovek, S. (1998, February 4). Execution in Texas: The overview. *The New York Times*, p. A1.

271. Ibid.

272. Hewitt, B., Maier, A. & Stewart, B. (1998, February 2). Reborn too late. *People Magazine*, p. 109.

273. Walt, K. (1997, December 15). Execution may haunt Texas. *Houston Chronicle,* p. A1.

274. Katz, Jesse. (1998, February 12). Texas takes another life, minus crowds, crusaders and cameras. *Los Angeles Times,* p. A5.

275. Boylan, T. (1998, March 23) Florida to execute woman amid no outcry, celebrities. *USA Today,* p. A1.

276. Rhode, D. (1995). Media Images, Feminist Issues. *Signs. 20: 3,* p. 696.

277. Lowry, B. (1992). *Crossed over: A murder/a memoir.* New York: Alfred A. Knopf, p. 13.

278. Boylan, T. (1998, March 23). Florida to execute woman amid no outcry, celebrities. *USA Today,* p. A1.

279. Niebuhr, G. (1998, February 4). Execution in Texas: Religious debate. *The New York Times,* p. A20.

280. Verhovek, S. (1998, February 3). Texas, in first time in 135 tears, is set to execute woman. *The New York Times,* p. A1.

281. Verhovek, S. (1998, February 5). Karla Tucker is now gone, but several debates linger. *The New York Times,* p. A12.

282. Goodman, E. (1998, February 15). Karla Tucker gave death row a human face. *Houston Chronicle,* p. A6.

283. Katz, J. (1998, January 9). Should Karla Faye Tucker be executed? *Los Angeles Times,* p. A1.

284. Pearson, P. (1998, January 13). Sex discrimination on death row. *The New York Times,* p. A19.

285. Verhovek, S. (1998, January 1). As woman's execution nears, Texas squirms. *The New York Times,* p. A1; Katz, J. (1998, January 9). Should Karla Faye Tucker be executed? *Los Angeles Times,* p. A1; & Rosenburg, H. (1998, January 21). Her court of opinion would be closed here. *Los Angeles Times,* p. F1.

286. Niebuhr, G. (1998, February 4). Execution in Texas: Religious debate. *The New York Times,* p. A20.

287. Katz, Jesse. (1998, February 12). Texas takes another life, minus crowds, crusaders and cameras. *Los Angeles Times,* p. A5.

288. Verhovek, S. (1998, February 5). Karla Tucker is now gone, but several debates linger. *The New York Times,* p. A12; Katz, J. (1998, January 9). "Should Karla Faye Tucker be executed? *Los Angeles Times,* p. A1; & Verhovek, S. (1998, January 1). As woman's execution nears, Texas squirms. *The New York Times,* p. A1.

289. Verhovek, S. (1998, February 5). Karla Tucker is now gone, but several debates linger. *The New York Times,* p. A12.

290. Ayers, B. (1998, March 23). Political briefing; Death penalty support declines after execution. *The New York Times,* p. A12.

291. Goodman, E. (1998, February 15). Karla Tucker gave death row a human face. *Houston Chronicle*p. A6.

292. Interview with Carol Rust, reporter, *Houston Chronicle* on June 5, 2002.

293. Terry, D. (1995, August 8). Black journalist granted stay of execution by the judge who sentenced him. *The New York Times,* p. A10.

294. Terry, D. (1995, July 30). A fight for life is waged in an angry courtroom. *The New York Times,* p. A24.

295. Fulwood, S. (1995, August 7). Activists galvanized by death row inmate's case. *Los Angeles Times,* p. A1.

296. Terry, D. (1995, August 8). Black journalist granted stay of execution by the judge who sentenced him. *The New York Times,* p. A10.

297. Clines, F. (1995, August 13). The case that brought back radical chic. *The New York Times,* p. D1.

298. Ibid.

299. Abraham, L. (1995, August 13). Mumia Abu-Jamal, celebrity cop killer. *The New York Times,* p. A22.

300. Mulshine, P. (1995, August 20). Rallying round the wrong cause. *Los Angeles Times,* p. M5; & Kraft, S. (1995, September 6). ".S. inmate has a hold on Europe's power elite. *Los Angeles Times,* p. A1.

301. Boxall, B. (1995, September 12). A widow fights back. *Los Angeles Times,* p. B1; & Zoroya, G. (1995, September 13). Journalist's death sentence has people judging the judge. *Los Angeles Times,* p. E4.

302. Cass, J. (1995, June 12). FBI file tracks Abu-Jamal through his teenage years. *The Philadelphia Inquirer,* p. A1.

303. Fish, L., Goldman, H. & Lelyveld, N. (1999, April 22). Vast network devoted to Abu-Jamal rally. *The Philadelphia Inquirer,* p. A1.

304. McCoy, C. (1999, April 23). Why Abu-Jamal's cause stirs up supporters and detractors alike. *The Philadelphia Inquirer,* p. A1.

305. Not millions, but a peaceful march. (1999, April 25). *The Philadelphia Inquirer,* p. A1.

306. Interview with Marc Kaufman, reporter, *The Philadelphia Inquirer* on November 19, 2002.

307. Interview with David Von Drehle, reporter, *The Washington Post* on March 28, 2002.

308. Ibid.

309. Federal death penalty cases: Recommendations concerning the cost and quality of defense representation. (1998, May). prepared by: Subcommittee on Federal Death Penalty Cases Committee on Defender Services Judicial Conference of the United States.

310. Death Penalty Information Center, 2003

311. Dao, J. (1994, December 23). The subway firebomb: Reaction. *The New York Times,* p. B2.

312. Sullivan, J. (1993, July 29). Florio signs death penalty aimed at terrorist murders. *The New York Times,* p. B4.

313. Reuters, 2001.

314. Kohut, A. (2001, May 10). The declining support for executions. *The New York Times,* p. A33.

315. Ibid.

316. Serrano, R. (1997, September 30). Jury selection for bomb trial begins. *Los Angeles Times,* p. A3.

317. Baldwin, D. & Clay, N. (1995, December 11). FBI keeps photos bomb defendant took at waco. *The Oklahoman,* p. A1.

318. Serrano, R. (1997, November 14). Nichols wanted out, witness says. *Los Angeles Times,* p. A3.

319. Puzzle pieces don't always fit perfectly. (1995, May 1). *The Oklahoman,* p. A10.

320. Johnston, D. (1995, April 22). Terror in Oklahoma: The investigation. *The New York Times,* A11.

321. Terry, D. (1995, April 22). Terror in Oklahoma: Junction city. *The New York Times,* p. A9.

322. Kifner, J. (1995, April 22). Terror in Oklahoma: The suspect; authorities hold a man of "extreme right-wing views." *The New York Times,* p. A9.

323. Ellis, R. (1995, April 23). Neighbor describes men's use of homemade bombs. *The Oklahoman,* p. A1.

324. Serrano, R. (1995, November 21). Death penalty opposed in bombing case. *Los Angeles Times,* p. A19.

325. Parker, J. (1996, May 2). Bomb prosecutors push for capital punishment. *The Oklahoman,* p. A1.

326. Kifner, J. (1995, April 25). Terror in Oklahoma: Mistaken identity. *The New York Times,* p. A18; & Casteel, C. (1995, April 30). Militias see government as threat. *The Oklahoman,* p. A1.

327. Casteel, C. (1995, June 16). Militias defend anti-government role to senators. *The Oklahoman,* p. A1.

328. Sanger, L. & Thornton, A. (1996, February 21). Two Oklahoma cities accept trial's Denver setting. *The Oklahoman,* p. A1; & Boczkiewicz, R. (1996, February 24). Court rules ban cameras. *The Oklahoman,* p. A1.

329. For McVeigh, a penalty as severe as his crime. (1997, June 12). *Los Angeles Times,* p. B8.

330. Thomas, J. (1997, May 30). McVeigh Described as Terrorist And as Victim of Circumstance. *The New York Times,* p. A1.

331. Rosenburg, H. (1997, June 4). Looking at bomb verdict coverage through a filter. *Los Angeles Times,* p. F1.

332. King, P. (1997, June 15). McVeigh: Killing a killer. *Los Angles Times,* p. A3.

333. Surette, Ray. (1998). *Media, crime and criminal justice: Images and realities* (2nd ed.). Belmont, CA: West Wadsworth.

334. The top stories of 1998. (1998, December 27). *Houston Chronicle,* p. A24; & Serrano, R. (1999, December 30). Stories that shaped the century. *Los Angeles Times,* p. B6.

335. Interview with Penny Owen, reporter, *The Oklahoman* on May 27, 2003.

336. Clay, N. (2001, February 11). McVeigh suggests televised execution. *The Oklahoman,* p. A1.

337. Witnesses to an execution. (2001, April 13). *The New York Times,* p. A16.

338. Media "city" predicted at execution—1,300 plan to cover McVeigh's last day. (2001, March 5). *The Oklahoman,* p. A1.

339. Bragg, R. (2001, June 12). The McVeigh execution: The overview. *The New York Times,* p. A1.

340. Belluck, P. (2001, June 12). The McVeigh execution: The scene. *The New York Times,* p. A27.

341. Interview with Penny Owen, reporter, *The Oklahoman* on May 27, 2003.

342. Belluck, P. (2001, June 12). The McVeigh execution: The scene. *The New York Times,* p. A27.

343. Bragg, R. (2001, June 12). The McVeigh execution: The overview. *The New York Times,* p. A1.

344. Bragg, R. (2001, June 10). On eve of his execution, McVeigh's legacy remains death and pain. *The New York Times,* p. A26.

345. Interview with Penny Owen, reporter, *The Oklahoman* on May 27, 2003.

346. Ibid.

347. On December 13, 2006, Angel Nieves Diaz was executed in Florida. The lethal injection was not properly administered and he had to be administered a second round of the lethal drugs. The whole process took about 34 minutes, and Diaz was reportedly moving and mouthing words after the first set of drugs— deathpenaltyinfo.org.

348. Brown, D. (1990, July2). Retarded Va. inmate seeking rehearing of murder vase. *The Washington Post,* p. A1.

349. Masters, B. (2000, October 3). DNA clears inmate in 1982 slaying; Gilmore pardon doesn't ensure Va. man's freedom. *The Washington Post,* p. A1.

350. Masters, B. (2000, December 1). Missteps on road to injustice; In Va., innocent man was nearly executed. *The Washington Post,* p. A1.

351. Ibid.

352. Ibid.

353. Pardoned ex-inmate files civil lawsuit; Va. action targets police, prosecutors. (2002, October 1).*The Washington Post,* p. B7.

354. Masters, B. (2000, December 1). Missteps on road to injustice; In Va., innocent man was nearly executed. *The Washington Post,* p. A1.

355. Timberg, C. (2000, December 2). DNA spurs change in Va.; crime panel debates evidence, new trials. *The Washington Post,* p. B1.

356. Miller, B. (1993, December 31). Wilder undecided on plea for DNA-based pardon. *The Washington Post,* p. D1.

357. Raspberry, W. (1994, January 5). Full pardon for Earl Washington Jr. *The Washington Post,* p. A19.

358. Ibid.

359. Baker, P. (1994, January 15). Death-row inmate gets clemency; agreement ends day of suspense. *The Washington Post*, p. A1.

360. Masters, B. (2000, June 2). Gilmore orders DNA testing for man imprisoned since '83. *The Washington Post*, p. A1.

361. Masters, B. (2000, October 3). DNA clears inmate in 1982 slaying; Gilmore pardon doesn't ensure Va. man's freedom. *The Washington Post*, p. A1.

362. Masters, B. (2000, October 4). Va. Inmate to get back "good time"; man pardoned in killing could be released soon. *The Washington Post*, p. B1.

363. Masters, B. (2000, October 5). Pardoned inmate to wait for a chance at freedom; Va. parole board to decide in about six weeks. *The Washington Post*, p. A7.

364. Masters, B. (2001, February 8). Ex-death row prisoner told to stay in Va. after release; Planned capitol hill trip barred by state officials. *The Washington Post*, p. B1.

365. Pardoned ex-inmate files civil lawsuit; Va. action targets police, prosecutors. (2002, October 1). *The Washington Post*, p. B7.

366. Markon, J. (2006, May 6). Wrongfully jailed man wins suit; Va. officer falsified confession, jury rules. *The Washington Post*, p. B1.

367. A Prosecution in Virginia; After two decades and one giant miscarriage of justice, Virginia prosecutors start over. (2006, August 27). *The Washington Post*, p. B6.

368. *The Chicago Tribune*. (1982, August 16).

369. *The Chicago Tribune*. (1982, August 17).

370. *The Chicago Tribune*. (1982, August 18).

371. Nicodemus, C. (1999, February 14). How Porter case went awry. *Chicago Sun-Times*, p. 8.

372. Much of the information on Anthony Porter was obtained through Northwestern University Law school and their website: http://www.law.northwestern.edu/depts/clinic/wrongful/exonerations/porter.htm.

373. Nicodemus, C. (1999, February 14). How Porter case went awry. *Chicago Sun-Times*, p. 8.

374. Drell, A. & McKinney, D. (1999, February, 7). Pressure building to halt executions; Porter case raises concern. *Chicago Sun-Times*, p.1.

375. Graber, D. (1980). *Crime news and the public*. New York: Praeger, p. 45.

376. Houlihan-Skilton, M. (1998, September 17). Claim of low IQ used to fight execution for S. Side murders. *Chicago Sun-Times*, p. 16.

377. McKinney, D. (1998, September, 22). Court delays execution of man who shot 2 at pool. *Chicago Sun-Times*, p. 17.

378. Lifton, R. & Mitchell, G. (2000). *Who owns death? Capital punishment, the American conscience, and the end of executions*. New York: Harper Collins, p. xi.

379. Belluck, P. (1999, February, 5). Class of sleuths to rescue on death row. *The New York Times*, p. A 16.

380. Johnson, D. (2000, February 1). Illinois, citing faulty verdicts, bars executions. *The New York Times*, p. A1.

381. Ex-death row inmate Porter sues city, cops. (2000, March 10). *Chicago Sun-Times,* p. 20.

382. Main, F. & Patterson, S. (2005, November 17). Jurors explain why they backed city over ex-Death Row inmate. *Chicago Sun-Times*, p. 11.

383. Belluck, P. (1999, February 5). Class of sleuths to rescue on death row. *The New York Times*. p. A16; & Jeter, J. (1999, February 6). Students' probe ends 16 years on death row for Illinois man." *The Washington Post*, p. A3.

384. Armstrong, K. & Mills, S. (1999, November 4) Death Row justice derailed bias, errors and incompetence in capital cases have turned Illinois' harshest punishment into its least credible series: Tribune investigative report. the failure of the death penalty in Illinois. First of a five-part series. *The Chicago Tribune*, p. 1.

385. A timeout on the death penalty. (2000, February 1). *The New York Times*, p. A1.

386. James, B. (2003, January 14) Clearing of Illinois death row is greeted by cheers overseas. *The New York Times*, p. A10.

387. Greenhouse, L. (2002, June 21) The Supreme Court: the death penalty; citing "national consensus," justices bar death penalty for retarded defendants. *The New York Times*, p. 1.

388. The Death Penalty Information Center provided much of the information about death penalty law across the country.

389. The information on Daryl Atkins was put together through a number of articles in the *Richmond Times-Dispatch* including: Green, F. (2002, February 17) High court to tackle execution case. *Richmond Times-Dispatch*, p. A1; Hardin, P. (2002, February 21). Court gets retarded-killer case. *Richmond Times-Dispatch*, p. B1; Green, F. (2001, May 12). Shielding retarded from death penalty? Supreme Court decision could affect Va. cases. *Richmond Times-Dispatch*, p. A1.

390. Man arrested in airman's death. (1996, August 22). *Richmond Times-Dispatch*, p. B4.

391. Green, F. (2001, May 12). Shielding retarded from death penalty? Supreme Court decision could affect Va. cases. *Richmond Times-Dispatch*, p. A1.

392. Ibid.

393. Green, F. (2002, February 17) High court to tackle execution case. *Richmond Times-Dispatch*, p. A1.

394. Cooper, A. (1999, January 10). Judges upheld in limiting of evidence court of appeals rebuked in 2 cases. *Richmond Times-Dispatch*, p. B4.

395. Green, F. (2002, February 17). High court to tackle execution case. *Richmond Times-Dispatch*, p. A1.

396. Man arrested in airman's death. (1996, August 22). *Richmond Times-Dispatch*, p. B4; second man is arrested in Langley airman's death. (1996, August 23). *Richmond Times-Dispatch*, p. B4; & Jury recommends death in slaying of airman (1998, February 16). *Richmond Times-Dispatch*, p. B4.

397. Greenhouse, L. (2002, February 21). Top court hears argument on execution of retarded. *The New York Times*, p. A21.

398. Greenhouse, L. (2002, June 21). The Supreme Court: The death penalty; citing "national consensus," justices bar death penalty for retarded defendants. *The New York Times*, p. A1.

399. Atkins v. Virginia, No. 00–8452. Argued February 20, 2002—Decided June 20, 2002.

400. Ibid.

401. Death Penalty Information Center, Mental Retardation and the Death Penalty.

402. Campbell, T. (2006, June 9). New trial ordered in Atkins case: Jury must determine again if death-row inmate is retarded. *Richmond Times-Dispatch*, p. B3.

403. Death Penalty Information Center, Juveniles and the Death Penalty.

404. Simmons did not argue these facts during the trial (*Simmons v. State of Missouri*).

405. State of Missouri v. Christopher Simmons *944 S.W.2d 165 (Mo. banc 1997)*.

406. Malone, R. (1993, September 11). Teens killed woman, got $6, police say. *The St. Louis Post-Dispatch*, p. 3B.

407. Bell, K. (1993, September 12). Woman thrown into river alive; teen-agers bound her, police say. *The St. Louis Post-Dispatch*, p. 1D.

408. Malone, R. (1993, September 11). Teens killed woman, got $6, police say. *The St. Louis Post-Dispatch*, p. 3B.

409. Bell, K. (1993, September 12). Woman thrown into river alive; teen-agers bound her, police say. *The St. Louis Post-Dispatch*, p. 1D.

410. Malone, R. (1993, October 7). Woman's accused killer ordered to stand trial. *St. Louis Post-Dispatch*, p. 1; & Malone, R. (1993, October 28). Death penalty sought in case of woman tossed into river. *The St. Louis Post-Dispatch*, p. 3.

411. Youth, 16, charged as adult in killing. (1993, November 17). *The St. Louis Post-Dispatch*, p. 4B.

412. Suspect in kidnap-murder case wants trial moved from county. (1994, June 6). *The St. Louis Post-Dispatch*, p. 6.

413. Malone, R. (1994, June 13). Jury moving to Hillsboro for kidnap-murder case. *The St. Louis Post-Dispatch*, p. 1.

414. Fitzmaurice, L. (1994, June 16). Jury will get case of drowning death. *The St. Louis Post-Dispatch*, p. 3C.

415. Fitzmaurice, L. (1994, June 17). Man, 18, is convicted in slaying of woman; she was bound, gagged and pushed off bridge into river. *The St. Louis Post-Dispatch*, p. C1.

416. Fitzmaurice, L. (1994, June 18). Jury votes for death for woman's killer. *The St. Louis Post-Dispatch*, p. B3.

417. High court refuses to hear death row inmates. (2000, April 25). *The St. Louis Post-Dispatch*, p. B3.

418. Kohler, J. (2002, April 25). High court delays execution that was set for may 1; no explanation is given; neither side had sought a postponement. *The St. Louis Post-Dispatch*, p. B1.

419. Rowden, T. (2002, May 29). Man who killed at 17 gets stay of execution; Missouri judges cite case before U.S. Supreme Court on retardation. *The St. Louis Post-Dispatch*, p. A1.

420. Young, V. (2003, August 27). Court halts executions for crimes by juveniles; Missouri judges cite evolving standards for death penalty. *The St. Louis Post-Dispatch*, p. A1.

421. Greenhouse, L. (2003, January 28). Justices deny inmate appeal in execution of juveniles. *The New York Times*, p. 18.

422. Ibid. 78.

423. Ibid. 79.

424. Roper v. Simmons No. 03—633.Argued October 13, 2004—Decided March 1, 2005.

425. Thompson v. Oklahoma No. 86–6169 Argued: November 9, 1987—Decided: June 29, 1988.

426. Stanford v. Kentucky No. 87–5765 Argued: March 27, 1989—Decided: June 26, 1989.

427. Penry v. Lynaugh No. 87–6177 Argued: January 11, 1989—Decided: June 26, 1989.

428. Greenhouse, L. (2005, March 2). Supreme Court, 5–4, forbids execution in juvenile. *The New York Times*, p. 1.

429. Ibid. 85.

430. Roper v. Simmons No. 03—633.Argued October 13, 2004—Decided March 1, 2005.

431. Ibid.

432. Savage, C. (2005, March 2). Executions barred for juvenile killers in 5–4 ruling, justices invoke global standard. *The Boston Globe*, p. A1.

433. Marquart, J., Ekland-Olson , S. & Sorensen, J. (1994). *The rope, the chair and the needle: Capital punishment in Texas, 1923–1990*. Austin: University of Texas Press, p. 190.

434. Jenkins, P. (1994). *Using murder: The social construction of serial homicide*. New York: Alaine de Gruyter.

435. Atkins v. Virginia, No. 00–8452. Argued February 20, 2002—Decided June 20, 2002.

436. Kohut, A. (2001, May 10). The declining support for executions. *The New York Times*, p. A33.

437. Lifton, R. & Mitchell, G. (2000). *Who owns death? Capital punishment, the American conscience, and the end of executions*. New York: Harper Collins.

438. Gans, H. (1979). *Deciding What's News: A study of CBS evening news, NBC nightly news, Newsweek, and Time*. New York: Pantheon Books; Katz, J. (1987). What makes crime "news"? *Media, culture and society*. 9. pp. 47–75; and Ericson,

R., Baranek, P. & Chan, J.(1987). *Visualizing deviance : A study of news organization.* Toronto: University of Toronto Press.

439. Cohen, S. & Young, J. (1973). *The Manufacture of news: Deviance, social problems and the media.* Beverly Hills, CA: Sage Publications, p. 33–34.

440. Chibnall, S. (1977). *Law-and-order news.* London: Tavistock.

441. Jenkins, P. (1994). *Using murder: The social construction of serial homicide.* New York: Alaine de Gruyter.

442. Interview with Stephen W. Hawkins, Director, National Coalition to Abolish the Death Penalty on November 19, 2002.

443. Roberts, J., Stalans, L., Indermaur, D. & Hough, M. (2003) *Penal populism and public opinion.* New York: Oxford University Press.

444. Interview with David Von Drehle, reporter, *The Washington Post* on March 28, 2002.

445. Surette, R. (1998). *Media, crime and criminal justice: Images and realities* (2nd ed.). Belmont, CA: West Wadsworth; Roberts, J., Stalans, L., Indermaur, D. & Hough, M. (2003). *Penal populism and public opinion.* New York: Oxford University Press, p. 85.

446. Garland, D. (2001) *The culture of control: Crime and social order in contemporary society.* Chicago: University of Chicago Press; Beckett, K. (1997). *Making crime pay: Law and order in contemporary American politics.* New York: Oxford University Press.

Index

About the Author

CHRISTOPHER S. KUDLAC is Assistant Professor of Criminal Justice, Westfield State College.